W9-BYT-168

Cultural Transformations

Cultural Transformations

Youth and Pedagogies of Possibility

WITHDRAWN
TOURO COLLEGE LIBRARY
Kings Hwy

Edited by Korina M. Jocson

HARVARD EDUCATION PRESS
CAMBRIDGE, MASSACHUSETTS

KH

Copyright © 2013 by the President and Fellows of Harvard College

All rights reserved. No part of this publication may be reproduced or transmitted in any form or by any means, electronic or mechanical, including photocopy, recording, or any information storage and retrieval systems, without permission in writing from the publisher.

Library of Congress Control Number 2013941190

Paperback ISBN 978-1-61250-614-2
Library Edition ISBN 978-1-61250-615-9

Published by Harvard Education Press,
an imprint of the Harvard Education Publishing Group

Harvard Education Press
8 Story Street
Cambridge, MA 02138

Cover Design: Ciano Design
Cover Image: Danièle Spellman

The typefaces used in this book are Centaur, Helveltica Neue, Minion, Novarese, Serifa, and Verdana.

9/30/15

To the young in this generation
and the next

Contents

Introduction

Cultural Transformations

Korina M. Jocson

THE UNPREDICTABILITY OF culture often gets the best of us. One bright Saturday morning, a teacher sitting next to me at a café peered at my computer screen as I prepared PowerPoint slides for a workshop. She asked, "What are cultural transformations, and what do they have to do with education?" The title I had just typed on top of the slide had come to me quickly, but the rest of the text did not—at least not until moments later. I was hoping to frame the workshop around culture and how dynamic cultural practices are in part shaped by social differences. And there I was, in the midst of a cultural site (a local favorite) practicing café-going culture among patrons from different racial and cultural backgrounds, several of whom were sharing tidbits about their workweek in languages other than English. Other café-goers were quick about their purchase, a pit stop as they made their way to the farmer's market up the street (another cultural site). The thought of culture as lived, local, and fluid forced me to pause and pay attention to what was happening around me.

As I looked out the window, I caught the bidirectional flow of pedestrians on the sidewalk. I began to realize how fortunate I have been to participate in such a vibrant environment where people from different walks of life come together and take advantage of the neighborhood's offerings. The thought of culture in this way was invigorating. The feeling called for reflection, redirecting my attention back to the computer screen. Strangely, though, everything around me stopped. I was stuck at the cursor.

"What is it?" The teacher's voice echoed.

"Huh?" I turned my head to catch her eyes, breaking the fixed stare.

"Your title, 'Cultural Transformations and Education,' what does it mean?" she prompted.

Her curiosity triggered a mutual smile. Suddenly, I could not resist the invitation to articulate a response, except I was still stuck on the title with no bullet points to support it. I wrestled with the idea of just pointing to my muted headphones to avoid further inquiry (a fake practice in public spaces to connote "I just want to be left alone"). But that would have been cowardly and impolite.

"Well, actually, it's a play on words," I said, pointing at the slide while taking off my headphones. "See here, there's an open and closed parenthesis on 'Trans' to suggest two things: cultural formations and cultural transformations, meaning, culture is formed and can also transform itself, people, and cultural products."

It seemed like a simplistic answer. I proceeded to tell her about the work I have done with teachers in urban schools—teachers who have employed poetry in the classroom to invigorate their teaching practice. I explained that they did it to further recognize and place value on the growing spoken word movement that is taking place for youth in many cities. I asked her whether she had ever attended poetry slams or perhaps seen HBO's *Brave New Voices*.

She shook her head—she had recently moved here from a small town— and took delight in my description without admitting her teacher training in conventional methods. I continued to explain how there are myriad opportunities in school and afterschool programs where young people participate in poetry writing, spoken word performances, and media productions; where young people's participation in these literate practices is shaping today's youth culture; and how young people's words—carefully inked, imaged, and sometimes delivered for wide audiences—are elevating youth voices. I shared how young people's individual and collective voices crack open conversations about things that matter in their lives and how young people draw on everyday experiences to raise important social issues in a manner that also forms culture and transforms lives, starting with their own lives and potentially influencing those of others. I went on to summarize my own growth as an educator, from classroom teaching to coaching sports to collaborating with other educators to serve different groups of young people in schools and outside of them.

At the end of what seemed like a long-winded, fluffy answer, we exchanged contact information. She smiled a bigger smile and so did I. She then got up to leave. At first I thought she was concerned about an expired parking meter because I had rambled on about my own learning. Instead, she admitted that her haste was due to swirling ideas in her head prompting her to make an urgent trip to the adjacent bookstore. Before walking away, she said, "I can't wait to try some new things!"

I was left humbled by that fleeting moment, no longer stuck on my slide but, rather, struck by her profound statement. I spent the rest of the day contemplating what is possible when educators try "new things" and the various cultural (trans)formations taking shape in all corners of the world with young people positioned as stewards of twenty-first century education.

I was jolted as I was inspired. Little did I know that a random encounter on a Saturday morning would become an impetus to a volume highlighting artistic and other cultural projects that create transformative opportunities for young people in school and in society. Little did I know that as I responded to the teacher's question, a range of scenarios with youth and adults working together across different contexts, using all sorts of media technologies and other resources, challenging dominant forms of culture and addressing social issues affecting their lives, would occupy my mind to a point that they now fill the pages of this volume. In time, my once off-the-cuff response would be expanded by the experiences of other educators and cultural workers from whom I have learned a great deal. This volume represents a fuller response to the question "What is cultural transformation, and what does it have to do with education?" Since that moment in the café, I have also been thinking about different pedagogies of possibility that bind the artistic and other cultural projects described here. The term *pedagogies of possibility* is explained below. First, let me share the reasons for this book.

SIGNIFICANCE OF THE BOOK

Cultural Transformations is a collection of pioneering scholarship by educators, artists, and other cultural workers in the field of education. Most of the authors are former teachers who continue to work with pre- and in-service teachers through their respective universities. Others are educators in related fields or artists themselves who work with various arts programs and community-based organizations. Together, the authors represent different racial and cultural groups from different geographical locations to address the need for pedagogical action that can impact the lives of youth, particularly youth of color in urban areas. The term *youth* is used to refer to those who primarily fall within the ages of twelve to twenty-four (and beyond in a couple of instances). The term is loosely referenced throughout; it includes racial minorities, immigrants, and transgender youth. When youth are lumped together with no consideration of the social differences among them, it becomes easy to overlook the complexity that young people face every day. The authors in this volume make an effort to unravel some of young people's experiences in contested terrains of schooling, work, and life. The perspectives are significant yet do not lay claim to represent all experiences of youth.

In the last decade, a growing body of interdisciplinary practice and research in education has explored the intersection of youth, culture, and pedagogy. The resultant knowledge from this exploration has been influential to individuals and communities. The authors in this volume draw on various orientations and methodologies to contribute to ongoing discussions in the field of education. Each of the ten chapters describes a pedagogical practice that builds on different forms of culture with implications for teaching and learning. Examples include, but are not limited to, media production, visual art, playwriting, and music. Each chapter differs in approach and illustrates the potential for influencing the lives of youth in very tangible ways. As a whole, the book offers both theoretical and practical insights from educational projects taking place around the United States (i.e., the San Francisco Bay Area, Albuquerque, Madison, Atlanta, Boston, and parts of New York). Also included are international projects based in Cuba and Australia. Careful not to essentialize youth or reduce youth culture to cultural products, the book highlights youth as complex beings who engage in the production of meaning laden with values, beliefs, and ideas. It is important to offer a glimpse into how teachers, former teachers, artists, and other cultural workers capitalize on the strengths and aspirations of young people who have often been pushed to the margins or perceived by society in limited ways. The book comes at a time when standards and accountability remain at the center of policy making, as if test scores were all that matter in education. Today, resources for arts- or community-based programs are the first to go in places where they are needed the most, and more attention is given to building prisons than to developing public parks, restoring libraries, or redesigning school sites. Today, many people see the further militarizing of schools as the only recourse for addressing violence and gun control in society. The lives of young people are on the very front lines of battle against social ills, and sometimes the only explanation offered is the influence of media or the lack of parenting. While finding answers to societal problems continue to be a challenge, it is possible to move in a more positive direction than existing approaches and practices have achieved in education.

In 2009 I put together a seminar series at Washington University in St. Louis to think through important issues in education. I immediately identified academics and artists who have taken bolder approaches in creating opportunities for young people to make meaning of their realities. These professionals have helped young people express themselves in ways that build self-confidence and self-efficacy. Through the unique approaches of these academics and artists, youth have raised questions about schooling processes and how such processes are inextricably linked with their lives outside of school. Many of them have sought to imagine different social and academic pathways in their future, see themselves differently in relation to society, and demand more for themselves and their communities.

Because the list of names was exhaustive, I did not have the capacity (or the resources) to invite everyone to the university campus to participate in a larger conversation about such topics. What I had was a sense of urgency. So I reached out to academics and artists whose cultural projects also reflect a cultural politics that moves particular groups of youth and particular forms of youth culture from the margins to the center of pedagogy. It was a strategic move on my part, not only to narrow down the list but also to focus on an educational agenda around pedagogies of possibility. As I remembered the aforementioned chance encounter with the teacher in the coffee shop, the idea of teaching as trying new things emboldened me.

In essence, this book has been in the making for over five years. Constant reflection paired with old and new conversations have resulted in a two-year seminar series, a journal focus issue, and now this volume. For several reasons, *Cultural Transformations* distinguishes itself from other volumes that discuss youth and education. First, it offers examples across contexts grounded in theory and practice. Second, the approaches presented here are useful to teachers, artists, and youth advocates. Finally, the book's perspectives cut across racial, ethnic, linguistic, class, gender, sexual preference, and geographic lines. The volume lays a common ground for rethinking pedagogy.

ON PEDAGOGY AND POSSIBILITY

To ponder pedagogy is to ponder possibility. It is what educator and philosopher Maxine Greene has long advocated in her dialectic of freedom—to imagine a different world, to seek alternatives for a more humane social order.[1] More than imagination, pondering is a wide-awakening, a becoming, a quest for unrealized possibilities toward new modes of understanding.

In an essay about thought and uncertainty, Greene notes the need to "look through new eyes upon the world around, to listen for new frequencies, to heed shapes and nuances scarcely noticed before."[2]

For educators and youth advocates, this means drawing on pedagogical practices that enable young people to pursue meanings and effect change in their life trajectories. William Ayers, in a tribute to Greene, his former teacher, calls for a pedagogy of possibility that draws on Greene's philosophy as a reminder of intersubjective realities to propel educational projects that can lead toward cultural and social transformation.[3] Similarly, Roger Simon conceives a pedagogy of possibility that involves a "reconstruction of social imagination in the service of human freedom" both in school and across sites of cultural practice.[4] This notion of pedagogy suggests that education should be a moral practice that is collective and democratic. It recognizes that teachers and students can work together to produce meaning and to shape everyday experiences that have political and cultural significance to disrupt uneven relations of power.[5] In their exploration of schooling and popular culture, Henry Giroux and Roger Simon emphasize the role of pedagogy in "creating experiences to organize and disorganize" the different ways we understand the world around us.[6] The phrase *pedagogy of possibility*, as used in this volume, revisits what Giroux and Simon framed twenty-five years ago. Like other critical theorists, Giroux and Simon treat pedagogy as "a deliberate attempt to influence how and what knowledge and identities are produced within and among particular sets of social relations." In other words, pedagogy is more than curricular content, classroom techniques, the use of time and space, or types of evaluation, as many educators may consider it. Pedagogy is what informs those choices; more importantly, pedagogy pays attention to the practices that students and teachers engage in together—practices that allow for dynamic constructions of meaning as well as representations of themselves within their environment.[7] Pedagogy, in this sense, implies a struggle—over different realities, over tensions and modes of expression, and over versions of self. Such forms of struggle with the potential for empowerment become a cultural resource for pedagogies of possibility.[8]

At a minimum, the notion of possibility is about hope. It is what Brazil-ian educator Paulo Freire in his life's work maintained as key to liberation.[9] Those who have suffered forms of oppression have an ontological need to act upon their suffering. A critical hope is necessary. According to Jeffrey Duncan-Andrade, critical hope guards against hopelessness that comes with cycles of failure, suffering, and social misery.[10] He calls for audacious, critical hope to produce long-lasting and transformative practices, particu-larly in urban communities:

> Critical hope is audacious in two ways. First, it boldly stands in solidarity with urban communities, sharing the burden of their undeserved suffer-ing as a manifestation of a humanizing hope in our collective capacity for healing. Second, critical hope audaciously defies the dominant ide-ology of defense, entitlement, and preservation of privileged bodies at the expense of the policing, disposal, and dispossession of marginalized "others." We cannot treat our students as "other people's children"—their pain *is* our pain. False hope would have us believe in individualized notions of success and suffering, but audacious hope demands that we reconnect to the collective by struggling alongside one another, sharing in the victories *and* the pain. This solidarity is the essential ingredient for "radical healing," and healing is an often-overlooked factor for improving achievement in urban schools.[11]

Critical hope is not the only type of hope, but it is an essential con-sideration for those determined to support future generations of young people. Social solidarity, an ingredient for healing, is also the basis for col-lectively imagining possibilities toward improving social conditions in ur-ban schools and communities. Together, hope and solidarity can enable a politics of engagement centered on humanism, agency, and action.[12]

For educators, pedagogy of possibility means regarding art and other forms of self-expression, or reconceiving traditional activities like intern-ships and parent engagement, to allow for self-exploration. The result of such an approach can take many forms. Participants may pursue healthier lives and sustainable communities. Others may enjoy more culturally responsive approaches in teaching and learning and otherwise more supportive educational environments.[13] Such environments provide opportunities for building human capacity or for assisting those in need to better transition into society, and more innovative curricular designs account for complex histories that continue to impact particular groups of students and their families.

For students, pedagogy of possibility means grabbing hold of opportunities that can better shape their academic, career, and life paths. It means accessing available resources inside and outside of school toward self-empowerment and social empowerment. Students can leap from otherwise conventional methods of self-expression and trust those adults who are working directly with them. Pedagogy of possibility insists on positive educational environments that include teachers, parents, and other community members who are also learning alongside them.

In the chapters that follow, we will see some of the ways educators and students, adults and young people, parents and their children, enable pedagogies of possibility. The perspectives in the chapters regard pedagogy of possibility as flexible and dynamic, not as a set of practices with fixed or technical characteristics. After all, pedagogy is a struggle. It remains messy and is often filled with tensions.

At the time of this writing, I am reminded by past and contemporary social struggles for a better world in which young people played an integral part. Political activist and feminist Angela Davis, for instance, in discussing a new documentary about herself and other political prisoners (directed by Shola Lynch and screened at the Toronto International Film Festival 2012), points to young people as the future of social movements as they address principal issues such as the prison industrial complex, capitalism, food, and the environment. Davis keenly acknowledges that young people today have the ability to go farther with their activism than in previous eras because of different sets of social opportunities that were previously not available. I could not agree more. This volume highlights a number of artistic and cultural projects in education that feature young people in this light.

ORGANIZATION OF THE BOOK

The contributors to this volume ponder pedagogy of possibility as a departure point for engaging young people through arts-informed and culturally responsive practices inside and outside of school. They are concerned with how young people are participating in media production and community-based activities that allow for healing and self-expression. For example, in chapter 1, I, with Eli Jacobs-Fantauzzi, discuss youth artists working together through spoken word poetry and filmmaking. The authors highlight a video poem project called "Barely Audible" as a form of remix and as an emerging pedagogical practice in the world of literary and media arts. The multimodal design, production, and distribution of "Barely Audible" signal the potential of purposeful collaboration between youth artists across artistic genres. In chapter 2, Marc Bamuthi Joseph and Brett Cook discuss the role of the arts in transformative education. They share aspects of Life Is Living, an arts festival focused on healing and collaboration to help establish a creative ecosystem in urban communities across the United States. The pedagogy in Life Is Living draws on the talents of artists and community members to specifically involve youth in healthy, sustainable practices. In chapter 3, Maisha Winn offers a unique look at playwriting and performance workshops that serve currently and formerly incarcerated girls. The pedagogy in playmaking suggests a new media for imagining possibilities beyond detainment and incarceration. Winn takes a backstage approach in sharing four stories that illustrate the shaping of different life trajectories as enabled by self-expression. In chapter 4, Michelle Bass and Erica Halverson describe how a digital media seminar, Representing Self Through Media, can create a pedagogical space to explore identity, transition, and the experiences of nondominant students (students from nondominant cultures) in college. The authors demonstrate one African American male student's experience to suggest the importance of multimodal approaches for meaning making.

Other contributors in the volume are concerned with equipping young people with particular forms of knowledge so that they can better navigate work, school, and society. In chapter 5, Lisa Patel and Alexander Gurn, with Melissa Dodd, Sung-Joon Pai, Vanessa Norvilus, Eun Jeong Yang, and Rocío Sanchez Ares, show how different learning may be possible through reimaging the internship, a common school-based requirement, in a professional setting. The authors point out why an internship project designed for critical consciousness rather than assimilation into the world of work is important, particularly for low-income first-generation immigrant youth. The chapter affirms the value of problem-posing pedagogy during critical transitions in these youth's lives. In chapter 6, Na'ilah Nasir, Alea Holman, Maxine McKinney deRoyston, and kihana miraya ross examine the ways that African American male youth experience race in schools. Nasir and colleagues describe two types of race pedagogies, one that is enacted by parents in preparing their black sons to navigate race and racism in schools, and the other enacted by a teacher in an after-school program for black male students. The authors assert how pedagogies of race can provide African American students support for healthy identity development and effective navigation of racism in school and beyond. In chapter 7, Tiffany S. Lee and Nancy López discuss the importance of carving out safe spaces for Native American youth as these young people confront a variety of educational obstacles and hostilities. The pedagogy involves positioning Native American youth to enable their agency and resistance, as well as to strengthen their connections to and knowledge of Native heritage (i.e., language, history, values, and perspectives). In chapter 8, Ed Brockenbrough and Tomás Boatwright portray the experiences of LGBTQ (lesbian, gay, bisexual, transgender, and queer) youth of color at an HIV/AIDS prevention center called the MAC. They examine how two youth participants created a space for themselves by strategically forging transgender-supportive networks inside and outside the center. The chapter illuminates a pedagogy that is more inclusive and attentive to the needs of transgender youth.

The anchoring chapters in the volume provide similar yet different views on pedagogy from an international perspective. In chapter 9, Ezekiel Dixon-Román and Wilfredo Gomez explore the shifting political history of Cuba and its relation to Cuban youth culture. They argue that the growing movement of hip-hop and *reggaetón* in Cuba provide its youth with more democratic modes of expression. To illustrate what they call *pedagogías marginal*, the authors offer a glimpse of En Mi Barrio, a community project founded and directed by Cuban hip-hop artist Lourdes Suarez. In chapter 10, Andy Brader and Allan Luke examine the reengagement of two Australian youth through digital music production. Brader and Luke describe the importance of peer and mentor evaluation of student productions across a flexible education network. The chapter raises questions about the adequacy of conventional measures of educational achievement and engagement with digital media. The pedagogy in this work draws on alternative possibilities toward twenty-first century learning and considers more authentic forms of assessment.

Although these ten chapters represent a specific selection of projects, many other artistic and cultural projects enact the very pedagogies discussed in this volume. In the afterword, Shirley Brice Heath urges us to continue exploring possibilities and expanding our view of education as lifelong learning. While the educational settings discussed here are far from comprehensive, it is not my intent to oversimplify. Instead, I present the various educational projects in this book in an effort to present an array of groundbreaking scholarship. I hope to provoke thinking about twenty-first century education to better support young people as learners and as members of society. Part of my task has been to pull together examples of pedagogies of possibility that might incite other ideas for trying new things to achieve similar goals. The uncertainty in the process requires a reconstruction of social imagination.

1

"Barely Audible"

A Remix of Poetry and Video as Pedagogical Practice

Korina M. Jocson, with Eli Jacobs-Fantauzzi

IT IS NO NEWS that youth collaborate across genre practices such as spoken word poetry, music, and video production. To do so, many youth are using various art-making tools with today's do-it-yourself technologies to create and represent their social worlds in a variety of media platforms. As it has become evident over the years, there is a growing movement among youth who draw on cultural and material remix and who work together toward larger artistic projects. In this chapter, I (Korina) first discuss remix (or the appropriation of existing texts into newer texts) and present an example of a remix project called "Barely Audible." A retrospection by filmmaker Eli Jacobs-Fantauzzi provides a closer look at the making of the video poem. The original poem was written by a high schooler and poet from the San Francisco Bay Area who worked directly with student filmmakers (Eli was one of them) in New York to produce the video poem. In my analysis of the video poem as text, the purposeful collaboration between the writer-poet and filmmaker-producers led to national and international acclaim. The collaboration between these artists—across literary and media arts— was key in reaching a worldwide audience through event screenings, film festivals, personal Web sites, and social media sites. A visual analysis of the video poem also suggests a variety of stylistic choices that render it not only as a product of identity, but also as a form of social critique with possibilities for education. (Note: the reader may access "Barely Audible," by Chinaka Hodge, on YouTube; viewing the video poem beforehand may be helpful to grasp the extent of the analysis). In the end, I share practical implications of remix in literary and media arts to encourage other ideas.

The following treatment of "Barely Audible" is a result of various interactions and interviews with the artists who made the video poem. My discursive entry into literary and media arts was sparked by interactions with local organizations through my earlier research on youth poetry in Northern California.[1] Several youths at the time of my study also participated in community-based organizations such as Youth Speaks and Youth Radio—as writers, producers, interns, or peer mentors; these social spaces allowed for a dynamic interaction among youths with shared interests and adults who supported them. I met Eli long before the making of "Barely Audible" through my professional networks (his late mother was also an educator who advocated for educational equity). It was not a surprise that our common interest in arts-based programs both in school and outside of school allowed for our paths to collide. Today, Eli leads Clenched Fist Productions as an independent filmmaker with a number of documentaries under his belt, including *Inventos: Hip Hop Cubano*; *Homegrown: HipLife in Ghana*; and *Revolucion Sin Muertos: Youth in Medellin, Colombia Using Hip Hop to Grow a Peace Movement*. For the purpose of this chapter, Eli's and my voices come together as part of the discussion to further assert the importance of collaboration in describing the potential of poetry and video production among youth in the digital era. First, a treatment of remix provides a theoretical backdrop for the ensuing discussion.

REMIX IN ART MAKING

The term *remix* is not new. It has been around to trace the development in music, film, literature, and other cultural forms and has been useful to understand language and knowledge construction. By definition, remix means to appropriate, borrow, and blend cultural texts to create new (or newer) texts. Remix can also mean taking something old and making it fresh and therefore making it relevant again. Lawrence Lessig put it this way: "Whether text or beyond, remix is collage; it comes from combining elements of RO [read only] culture; it succeeds by leveraging the meaning created by the reference to build something new."[2] Remix makes sharing products easy and invites the community to participate. In theorizing rhythm science, Paul D. Miller (aka DJ Spooky, That Subliminal Kid) points to the centrality of music sampling to advance a musical genre.[3] The deftness of mixing across sounds and social settings in connection to hip-hop becomes a key component of artistic production. In other words, mixing sounds is in part a manifestation of a larger remix culture that includes graffiti, break dancing, DJ-ing, MC-ing, language, and fashion. Today's remix practices allow for a variety of ways to write, such as fan fiction, manga, photoshopping, and video mash-ups. A recent example of a video mash-up is Kutiman's "Mother of All Funk Chords," which inventively pieces together user-uploaded videos on YouTube to generate a new sound, a polyphonic global session.[4] At the heart of remix is the use of one or more modalities (oral or written language, images, symbols, sounds, gestures, artifacts, etc.) in specific semiotic domains that communicate distinctive types of meaning.[5] Remix, then, is not simply about a change in content (a derivative) but also a change in context (a different meaning). In her study of literacy and media in children's lives, Anne Hass Dyson suggests that children draw on their knowledge of popular cultural texts to make meaning of other texts through processes of recontextualization—that is, "differentiation, appropriation, translation, and the reframing of cultural material across symbolic forms and social practices."[6] The reframing, which in itself is a remix, produces a different meaning, and the process starts again toward the next remix. Central to that meaning are individuals' interactions with others as well as with texts; it does not preclude elements of intertextuality that links the text being designed to one or more series of existing texts.[7]

To further understand remix, it is important to draw on multimodality as a resource for meaning making in media production.[8] Specifically, Gunther Kress and Theo Van Leeuwen offer strata of discourse, design, production, and distribution through which to understand multiple modes of communication.[9] They note that discourse and design relate to the *content* of what is being communicated, while production and distribution relate to *expression*, or the manifestation, of content. In analyzing "Barely Audible" (the video poem), the strata of discourse, design, production, and distribution are important because they account for what is intricately involved in the *articulation* (encoding) and *interpretation* (decoding) of text.

For artists and filmmakers, mode or the particular choice of mode becomes central to production. Mode serves as a resource for representation; mode is also integral to the articulation and interpretation of any text, be it visual, written, or oral-aural. For the artists described in this chapter, the use of multiple modes was key to their collaboration and to the actual production of the video poem. Moreover, social semiotics suggests that encoding reflects the sender's or writer's "grammar," while decoding captures the idiosyncrasy of audience reception.[10] The encoding-decoding binary is without tension, and the idiosyncratic uptake of texts is interpellated, hailed, or marked by discourse and ideology.[11] In other words, any text can be recontextualized or remediated by creators (sender-writer) and by users (audience), depending on where they are in a particular place and time.

The locality of those involved situates any text analysis. Using a multiperspective lens into cultural studies, Douglas Kellner points to the interplay between articulation and interpretation to peel layers of texts with particular meanings.[12] He offers a diagnostic critique using history to read texts, and using texts to read history. Such a dual optic allows insight into the multiple relations between texts and contexts, between media culture and history, and, as I will argue, between the social worlds of a poet-writer and producer-filmmaker. With this in mind, I consider youth's agency and identity positions within media production.[13] I also discuss the politics of rewriting media as a form of social critique embedded in social relations.[14]

Finally, as more digital remix practices develop, the link between media culture, history, and locality provides a way to understand youth who make media based on shared social critique. Critical solidarity is a means by which people acknowledge the social dimensions of their thinking and analyses. According to Robert Ferguson, it requires that people ally themselves with others who share their views toward an "understanding of justice and exploitation and our democratic rights and responsibilities."[15] Noteworthy in the alliance are the interconnections between young people through their social position on media, culture, and respect for fundamental human rights. The notion of critical solidarity draws attention to broader progressive goals of understanding and tolerance among seemingly disparate groups. Building on Len Masterman's critical autonomy, critical solidarity sees individuals and groups (including youth) as having the freedom to judge for themselves the relative merits of alternative possibilities rather than being indoctrinated into a particular worldview.[16] For this chapter, I borrow the term *critical solidarity* to demonstrate the relative autonomy of artists. The term, however, means more than shared interests and social critique. Critical solidarity is reified through a cultural and material remix as a representation of social worlds—that of the artists involved. The production of a larger artistic project between poet-writer and producer-filmmaker, as described on the following pages, reflects a set of critical literacy skills to utilize written, oral, aural, and visual forms of communication (modes) as a means to challenge dominant ideologies and power relationships that underlie them.[17] The making of "Barely Audible" is illustrative.

DATA COLLECTION AND ANALYSIS

To gain some perspective on literary and media arts, I utilized an ethnographic approach that built on existing networks from my earlier study on youth poetry in Northern California. I attended and observed various community media arts events and accessed media texts online or through copies provided by the artists themselves. I was also active in Web sphere search, an approach to studying Web objects and mediated patterns, to follow the dissemination of local youth-made films regionally and nationally from 2005 to 2007.[18] Considering my level of access to media texts and interaction with artists, I focused on two well-circulated video poem projects, "Slip of the Tongue" and "Barely Audible," to understand media production and distribution.[19] Doing so provided a particular lens into youth culture and how youths themselves shaped and were being shaped by remix culture. Data sources include semistructured interviews with poets, artists, and producers; field notes from participant observations; collection of media or related products such as written poems (in draft or published form), audio and video recorded spoken word performances, DVD copies of completed videos; and producer-director commentary.

To organize and understand the collected data, I created a matrix as an analytic tool particularly to understand the complexity of media texts. The matrix took into account the technical, conceptual, and aesthetic elements of production and the various written, visual, and oral-aural modes used to create a media text. As I will discuss in detail, "Barely Audible" blended script, image, and sound according to the idiosyncratic uptakes (i.e., the varied interests and dispositions) of the poet-writer and producer-filmmaker. Special attention to the technical, conceptual, and aesthetic elements of the production demonstrate the locality of their uptakes and stylistic choices rendered in the video poem. A filmmaker's eye and retrospection also provide an in-depth view on the production process; for this reason, Eli offers a firsthand account.

FROM THE BAY TO NYC: THE MAKING OF "BARELY AUDIBLE"

The Poet-Writer and the Poem

Chinaka Hodge, a poet and playwright from Oakland, California, has had her work featured in various nationally recognized magazines and newspapers and on national radio and television shows, including HBO's *Def Poetry*. Her first independently written play, *Mirrors in Every Corner*, was commissioned by San Francisco's Intersection for the Arts and opened in the spring of 2010. She is a graduate of New York University's Gallatin School of the Arts and University of Southern California's School of Cinematic Arts (Writing for Screen and Television); she is an artist in residence at the Headlands Center for the Arts. Chinaka is one of twelve selected writers from around the world to participate in the 2013 Sundance Screenwriters Lab.

Chinaka began to write at an early age. Her father gave her a journal for every birthday and insisted on journal writing as a daily activity. She wrote her first poem at four years old. In the sixth grade, her teacher in the midst of a public school strike asked her and other students to conduct a research project on the history of African Americans. She recalled the following:

> I think my biggest formative year was in the sixth grade. I had to write a two-page report. For a sixth grader, it was okay. I ended up writing my report and was really fascinated by the fact that all the foul stuff happened to black folks that I never heard about even through my very militant family. And then the power that the work had for me and others to kind of bring it to light. I finished it and felt like I was participating in history, something that was important to me.
>
> Then, I also participated in an essay-writing competition, around the time the Cypress Freeway fell down [during the Loma Prieta earthquake in 1989]. They rebuilt the structure, and there was an unveiling, where poems and essays written by West Oakland youth about the future of transportation were featured. My essay won the prize for best essay. And so, that was kind of like seeing that I could write and that there was some tangible reward—I could make a living. I won a computer.

In the ninth grade, Chinaka took an interest in Youth Speaks when a representative conducted a writing workshop in her English class. Chinaka recalled her subsequent involvement in activities both inside and outside school to further develop as a writer. In an interview with me, she noted her literary influences, who included both seasoned and novice writers, some of whom were her mentors and peers at Youth Speaks. Chinaka competed in poetry slams for several years and earned the title grand slam youth poet as a junior in high school. That year, during a national poetry slam, she wrote "Barely Audible." She revealed the following about her writing process:

> I wrote that [poem] about fifteen minutes before leaving the house for the final slam. I had this other poem that I was doing. A poem about my mom or something like that. But it was the first time I had ever written anything that long. Most of my first ones were shorter, and I ended up winning with it. I was basically attaching a sound to a feeling, a sound to an experience, a neighborhood. And so I did that, and it was the first [time] I used sound to convey a point. I remember kind of like piecing it together and not getting to finish it until really right before we walked out the door and being really like, "This is gonna suck but I'm gonna do it anyway." And people back then were like, "What are you gonna do? Don't you have it memorized?" And I was like, "Yeah, I got paper. We'll see what happens." I have grown tremendously as a writer since then. I wrote it when I was seventeen, and so much in my life has changed. I'm a tremendously different person now. But all the issues [in the poem] are still really important and resonate with a lot of people.

The original "Barely Audible" poem from that slam competition has since been revised multiple times for different purposes. The following poem, reprinted with permission, is the version represented in the video.

> *it's 3:30*
> *I'm watching potential martyrs from my window*
> *got my nose pressed against the glass*
> *the sidewalk is drab, grey, dull, cracked*
> *the junior high kids walk down the middle of the street*
> *because the sidewalks got chasms in it*
> *and they can't afford to slip*
> *they step nimbly*
> *over Doritos nacho cheese, syringes and condoms*

they're burdened, carry caskets on their backs
no one's told them that they're still living expected to fail
this is their world

This is Darius' world
he moves feebly
decrepit in the candy apple glow
of Muhammed's Millennium Market

Darius
clutches brown paper bag
all his hopes and dreams, packaged at liquor store
his eyes are red

I tell myself it's because he don't sleep at night
he's up counting stars
he knows how many are in his sky
he can hear the ocean lapping at the edge of the world
he can tell you how many times it hits the shore
but folks don't ask him shit like that
so instead he counts dubs, counts 8ths
drinks fifths and forties
on 18th and Myrtle

Darius
he's dying
his lover knows it
she might stop to mourn,
but then again she might not

This is Trina's world
she walks above it all
ghetto brown gel

slicks cosmos back in her hair easily
she walks quickly
no time to talk
shoots insults over her shoulder
ya mama

She's living for her lover's memory
and he's not even dead yet

this is the sound . . .

pickles and red kool aid
sticking to her lips like
blue now and laters
spiced apple cider
sunflower seeds, chitterlings and
abject poverty

she is 14
womanly
big bosomed
bigger bottomed
everybody wants to hold her thigh
hold her breast
hold her back
no one wants to hold her hand

everyone thinks she's sexy
but really she's divine
and confused
piecing together family
she's pregnant for the second time

and I'm watching this from my window

I'm watching potential buyers
square shoes
spiky hair
authentic bags from faraway places
pressed khakis
aviator glasses
SUVz with plates that read
CONQUISTADORES

they explored the mission
but the dot com's went bust
they can't afford the city so they scope West Oakland
stare right through the ghosts of little children
and see a fixer upper
they're gonna build their homes here
on the graveyard cause
no one's living here anyway

and Trina's staring at them with those big brown eyes
and she's saying
Help Me, Help Me
and I'm banging on the Window, Help Her, Help Her
and if you listen closely you can hear Junior
in the Background
his diaper is pissy
but Trina's piss poor
she's gotta make 10 pampers stretch through the week

She's a potential savior
but she's living herself to death

doing backstrokes to make ends meet
this is atlantic reminiscent
she echoes the hymns of bowels of slave ships
like uh ahh, uh uh uh ahhh
This is the sound

pickles and red kool aid
sticking to her lips
like blue now and laters
spiced apple cider
sunflower seeds, chitterlings
and abject poverty

she's 14, nobody wants to hold her hand
and everybody wants to hold her back
this is the sound

West Oakland becomes auction blocked
ba-bam bam! sold ba-bam bam sold!
sold! sold! sold!
a fine young negress
with much potential
her lover just died so she should be supple
bend her but bam! bam! sold!
sold! sold! sold! sold! sold!

West Oakland becomes auction blocked
and nobody wants to hold her hand

this is the sound
pickles and red kool aid
sticking to her lips

like blue now and laters
spiced apple cider

and it's 3:30, 18th and myrtle,
and it's time to care

The Filmmaker-Producer: Eli's Retrospection

When I (Eli) met Chinaka Hodge, she was a junior at Berkeley High School. We met at CAS (Communication Arts & Sciences), a small school at Berkeley High with a focus on social justice. Our connection would grow as we shared a love for hip-hop, crossing paths at La Peña's open mic, hip-hop in the park jams, and CAS retreats. We both found out around the same time that we were accepted to New York University; she would be going as an undergraduate at the Gallatin, and I would be attending graduate school at the Tisch School of the Arts.

As an educator, I have always told my students not to do their projects just for a grade or for their teachers. They should create something they are proud of and that they can use to show the world what they are capable of. So during my first semester at Tisch, when given the assignment to create a short video, I decided to go beyond what was asked of us (my project team) and make a video that could showcase our skills and have a strong social message. Immediately, I remembered Chinaka's poem "Barely Audible," which she had just performed at the Bowery Poetry Club. While listening to the vivid poem, I was already mentally creating how this could be represented cinematically. I asked the members of the group if they would be interested in creating a visual interpretation of her poem. We all agreed and had Chinaka come record the poem in the school's recording booth. The next step was sitting down and creating a storyboard. We listened to the poem over and over, and wrote down the images that came to mind.

Our goal was to not simply show what Chinaka described in her poem. We wanted to create parallel stories connected to larger issues. We decided to use imagery and sounds that would help place the viewers in the lives of the characters as well as feel some of their anxiety and despera-tion. Chinaka places herself in the poem, watching the kids down below from her window. So we decided to use that as the opening shot, starting more literally and getting more abstract as the poem goes on. At first, we saw it as a dilemma that we were in Brooklyn and not in Oakland, Cali-fornia, where the story in the original poem takes place. After some time, we agreed that the issues of poverty, gentrification, and violence were af-fecting youth all over the country and we could show that these problems were bigger than Oakland.

To shoot the video, we put together a community of artists and friends. We recruited Nyoka Acevedo, an educator and activist, to take the lead role as Trina. Divine (aka Don Divino), who worked closely with Dead Prez, played the role of Darius. We counted on our friends, our students, and their parents to all come and play different roles for our video. When the video was finally completed, it had a great reception by the class as well as the professor. Everyone in our group went on to screen the video for as many people as possible. It screened in film festivals, universities, class-rooms, and afterschool programs—anywhere we could. Eventually we were given the opportunity to broadcast the video nationally on PBS. At the same time that the video was gaining recognition, Chinaka was perform-ing the poem at poetry slams and other events, making a name for herself across the country. She finally went on to perform "Barely Audible" for HBO's *Def Poetry*.

To this day, Chinaka and I work closely together. We are great friends. Our latest collaboration was on a project called Life Is Living—an arts festival centered on sustainability in urban communities. Chinaka helped create the festival in collaborative vision with Marc Bamuthi Joseph and others (see chapter 2). Coincidentally, she wrote the poem "Barely Audible" on Eighteenth Street and Myrtle, just a few blocks from Lil' Bobby Hutton Park (also known as DeFremery Park), where we decided to have the Life Is Living festival. As a community effort, the festival was created to address many of the issues presented in the poem. Our methods, our projects, and our visions as artists may have changed, but our commitment to justice stays constant. When we meet other literary and media artists around the country, whether they are students, teachers, or peers, with the same mission, we form an alliance, and that is how we have created this movement. It is important to us to ally with others, blending our artistic work, whatever it may be, with community work.

From Oakland to Brooklyn: Uptakes in the Video

Visual analysis of the video suggests the idiosyncratic uptakes by producer-filmmaker Eli and his team. For example, it is evident how the social worlds detailed in Chinaka's poem transcend one location and are recontextualized in another. Eli and his team used visual modes to augment meanings embedded in the poem. This is important because it demonstrates a process of meaning making (decoding) that helped to shape the creation (encoding) of another text. Upon reflection, isn't that what we ask of our students in the classroom through reading and writing instruction? The intertextual nature of "Barely Audible," from the written poem to the video poem, is apparent. Locations in "Barely Audible" include sidewalks, street signs, buildings, and a liquor store. Wide-angle shots were common to capture the physical environment. To emphasize particular signs, Eli and his team used close-ups of street names, actors' bodies and faces, and related objects. The articulation of localized meanings set the overall tone and shaped the logic of the video. "Barely Audible" took on a different yet similar narrative, assembling and reassembling particularized meanings conveyed in the original poem. Depictions of Darius and Trina in the context of Oakland (in the poem) and Brooklyn (in the video) revealed the connections between two communities that are experiencing similar social issues. The discourse widens from the local in Oakland—"18th and myrtle"—to the translocal in Brooklyn—"it's time to care" (the last two lines in the poem).

In addition to particularized meanings, Eli pointed out in a director's commentary the significance of cinematic influences in the video. Key figures such as New York–based filmmaker Spike Lee were prominent in choosing camera angles and composition. Lee is known for his use of dolly-tracking shots and filming in the streets of Brooklyn as a setting. Such stylistic choices are traceable and purposeful in "Barely Audible"—borrowed and appropriated, blurring the line between amateur and professional videography. Eli's interpretation of Lee's style has been rearticulated in the design and production. With its multimodal composition and opportunities for cultural and material remix, "Barely Audible" was entered in film festivals and circulated in a variety of media outlets.

Since its release, the video poem has reached various audiences across the globe. Screening in over a dozen local and international festivals further legitimized the work of these upcoming literary and media artists. The distribution of "Barely Audible" online via Eli's YouTube channel named ClenchedFistPro, which currently has about 2.8 million views, and other social media sites, has expanded the possibilities of articulation (and rearticulation) and interpretation (and reinterpretation) in different contexts. Only time will tell how critical solidarity will again take shape between consumers and artists-producers to create the next remix. What other critiques and analyses will propel young people to use media production as a form of social action?

NOW WHAT? FUTURE INTERSECTIONS IN LITERARY AND MEDIA ARTS

The success of "Barely Audible" suggests the untapped potential in literary and media arts. The video's *content* (discourse and design) and *expression* (production and distribution) partly shaped the artists' ability to reach a large audience. In practical terms, the video is now being used in writing, video production, and related workshops where discussions about remix, collaboration, and the power of storytelling create opportunities for envisioning other artistic and cultural projects toward social transformation. The pedagogy of possibility goes beyond what artists like Chinaka and Eli did with "Barely Audible," but rather supposes alternative practices for blending genres as a form of cultural politics—wherever the creator or producer might be. In this particular case, the multiple modes employed in the making of "Barely Audible" are worth noting because they illustrate the various resources for meaning making. First, there is the level of the *script*, the poem written by Chinaka. Second is the level of *image*, shot and sequenced by Eli (and his team). Finally, there is the level of *sound*, the majority of which is provided by Chinaka's recorded voice and performance. Additional sound effects were included during editing. Of interest here is remix—the appropriation, assembling, and reassembling of an already-existing text (the original poem) and how the written and performed poem was designed and redesigned with particular tools to create a video or visual poem. The video illuminates similarities and differences in Chinaka's and Eli's experiences as individuals and as artists committed to social justice—similarities and differences that merged into one text. Chinaka detailed in words what she witnessed in Oakland; Eli captured in image what he saw in Brooklyn. Each creator drew on literal and figurative language. To convey issues of poverty, gentrification, and violence, both artists made subtle and explicit references to race, ethnicity, gender, history, time, and place to suggest the locality of uptakes that represented their respective social worlds. Such uptakes (interests and dispositions) shaped the larger video, where new meanings were constructed while Chinaka's adapted poem in its entirely still rang in the background.

If we as educators take the example of "Barely Audible" both in school and outside it, we might envision pedagogical possibilities that enable human capacities through media production. The purposeful collaboration between youth artists demonstrates how media production is tied to teaching and learning. First, media production reaffirms the participation of young people in the growing movement in literary and media arts. Chinaka and Eli are currently spearheading projects with other artists to augment what they have done in "Barely Audible." They continue to lift up voices of dissent through their respective work, encourage young people (particularly young people of color) to make sense of lived realities, and challenge social inequities that affect poor and marginalized populations around the globe. Second, media production like "Barely Audible" pushes us to rethink the teaching and learning paradigm, at the very least questioning who is an expert and who is a novice in the digital age. Often in classrooms, teachers take on a role as authoritative figures, and students are treated as passive receptors. What if teachers became learners, and students became more active as facilitators of learning? What stones might finally be turned with new conversations and altered interactions in the classroom? It is a hopeful endeavor as many young people are at the forefront of experimenting with innovations in media technology. The potential of remix in education challenges educators to consider ways that the different young people can facilitate learning by:

- Building on each other's talents, skills, and experiences
- Working together as critical consumers and producers to create new(er) multimodal texts
- Disrupting dominant notions regarding the way things should be
- Pushing the field of youth media arts as tech-savvy amateurs/ professionals
- Distributing high quality multimedia products to reach larger audiences in shaping media culture, history, and society

Finally, media production reinforces the importance of arts education through the building of strong ties between students, teachers, community members, and artists as partners in education. Literary and media arts as part of youth culture can offer a place from where to draw a range of ideas relevant to literacy, teaching, and learning.[20] As I (Korina) have increasingly observed in high school classrooms, the mixing and remixing of poetry as one form of media production can open up doors for understanding literature and for expanding instructional approaches to composition. Indeed, young people will continue to adapt existing texts, whether the material is produced by peers or extracted from textbooks and supplementary sources. Young people will continue to appropriate, design, and produce other texts on their own or with others.

The concept of remix is certainly not new. However, with today's media technologies, remix further invigorates what is happening and what is possible in classrooms. If interpretation (reading) and articulation (writing and producing)—through the strata of design, discourse, production, and distribution—are key in the multimodal process, then how might media production in an English language arts classroom be further conceived?[21] How can high schools create projects where literary arts classes work together with media arts classes? What might the collaboration look like if it were between high school and college students? In what ways might emerging practices lead to larger artistic projects toward an understanding of social justice, participatory democracy, and human rights?

The opportunity for material and cultural remix offers a creative exercise for students to play out various possible meanings. The use of different modes and media platforms also influences students' idiosyncratic uptakes of the text—uptakes that are replicable across contexts. The type of remix described in this chapter coincides with new directions in digital media and connected learning, where young people, their interests, and their skills are at the center of dialogue. With advances in technology, remix in literary and media arts will remain a fruitful pedagogical practice to be explored.

ACKNOWLEDGMENTS

The authors are grateful to Chinaka Hodge for her willingness to have her work discussed and reproduced in various formats. Special thanks to filmmakers Vivian Wen Li and Katherine Copeland for their production of "Barely Audible." And to Analicia Rangel-Garcia for her careful eye in the final editing stages.

2

Life Is Living

An Arts Festival Focused on Healing, Community Collaboration, and the Creative Ecosystem

Marc Bamuthi Joseph and Brett Cook

WHAT IS THE RELATIONSHIP between the arts, healing, and social change? For several years now, Life Is Living, an artistic and cultural project focused on sustainability in urban communities, has involved community members, local organizations, and social services agencies to harness the power of collaboration and vision for a creative ecosystem. Life Is Living has reached thousands of youth, particularly youth of color ages thirteen to twenty-one in several major U.S. cities. In this chapter, we discuss Life Is Living and our roles in the project and beyond. As artists and educators committed to change, we have helped to effect change in the communities where we work and visit, and to expand the impact that Life Is Living can have on people's lives. So, what is Life Is Living? How did it start? And why should Life Is Living matter to today's students? We offer an exchange to demonstrate the potential of the arts toward sustainability and transformative education.

BRETT: When I first attended Life Is Living at DeFremery Park in Oakland, California, in 2008, it was called something else. The organizers named it "red black and GREEN" to reflect Marcus Garvey's vision of a Pan-African unity and an African American repatriation from the United States and the Caribbean to Liberia. Presumably, the word *GREEN* was in all caps to emphasize the double entendre of a cohesive, post-Garvey vision of African America and the nomenclature of effective environmental thought and practice. I can't say all these things were readily apparent at the event itself, but what *was* clear was the intersection of art, sports, the activation of the park, and hip-hop. Beyond Garvey, can you talk about other points of genesis for the work?

MARC: Once upon a time, amid a once-in-a-generation sweep of civil and human rights activity in America, an act of Congress initiated the founding of the National Endowment for the Arts (NEA). The first class of NEA grantees included the market grants—the Martha Graham Dance Company; a pilot program in New York City, Detroit, and Pittsburgh titled Poets to the Schools; and the renowned dancer-choreographers Merce Cunningham, José Limón, and Paul Taylor. While arguing on the floor on behalf of the NEA, Senator Claiborne Pell said, "I believe that this cause and its implementation has a worldwide application, for as our cultural life is enhanced and strengthened, so does it project itself unto the world beyond our shores. Let us apply renewed energies to the very concept we seek to advance a true renaissance—the reawakening, the quickening, and above all, the unstunted growth of our cultural vitality."[1]

In the same debate, Senator Hubert Humphrey argued, "This is at its best a modest acknowledgement . . . the arts have a significant place in our lives. And I can think of no better time to place some primary emphasis on it than in this day and age when most people live in constant fear of the weapons of destruction which cloud man's mind and spirit and really pose an atmosphere of hopelessness for millions and millions of people . . . The arts seldom make the headlines. We are always talking about a bigger bomb . . . I wonder if we would be willing to put as much money in the arts and the preservation of what has made mankind and civilization as we are in . . . the lack of civilization, namely war."[2]

Financial support for the economies of art and ideas was a matter of national priority in the late 1970s. In 1978, the NEA's annual budget was $124 million, or about $400 million dollars in today's economy. And then something happened: Morning in America (or as the critics of Ronald Reagan's political campaign called it, Mourning in America). In the midst of deficits and high unemployment, Reagan sought to impel Congress to completely phase out funding for the NEA over a three-year period. Though he was unsuccessful, Reagan's signal served as a harbinger of future attacks on cultural funding that have played out since then; primary villains of federal cultural funding have included Donald Wildmon of the American Family Association, Senator Jesse Helms, Newt Gingrich, Pat Robertson, and Pat Buchanan. Against the backdrop of cultural war and xenophobia, private cultural philanthropy has served as tool of resistance and sustainability for the arts sector in America.

This context is important to understand because part of the frame of the Life Is Living enterprise is this intersection of cultural arts and practice, private and public philanthropy, and sustainability models.

BRETT: Yes, I remember sitting in a meeting with you and a program officer at the East Bay Community Foundation, and that's precisely the argument that you were making. You were trying to articulate that the same funds being used in the environmental portfolio should be used to support the Life Is Living festival, which the officer was saying belonged strictly in the performing-arts portfolio. Can you talk more about this crossover between art, social ecology, and physical ecology?

MARC: A hero of mine, Ken Foster, is the executive director of Yerba Buena Center for the Arts in San Francisco. In his book, *Performing Arts Presenting: From Theory to Practice*, Foster discusses the contraction of the NEA, its procedural and infrastructural impact on the business of making and presenting art, the correlation between the conservative rhetoric and the culture war, and the conservative tendency to shy away from risk taking by arts presenters in America. He dubs the latest era of adaptation an "age of collaboration," an ecological way that many of us now view the arts. In framing cultural production in this environmental way, he talks about the performance experience as an equilateral relationship between the artist, the art, and the audience, and further articulates that inside this relationship, there is a "collective responsibility," if you will, to the greater good of the arts matrix. I use these ideas to embrace the philanthropists' role in relationship to the sustainability of creativity in America, and I draw on my personal experience as an artist to answer a number of questions about the philanthropists' responsibility in desperate times.

So these are the big questions: what is the twenty-first-century response to Pell's notion of "unstunted growth of our cultural vitality"? What does collaboration inside the arts ecology look like? What is the artist's role and, very specifically, the theater company's function in the twenty-first-century arts matrix? How does a theater company function in the twenty-first century? In general, I have this thing about the velocity of change. You can't keep up with it; you can't outrun it. But you can anticipate its direction; in a future-thinking way, get out in front of it before it leaves you behind altogether.

BRETT: So how did you move from a codified art practice with social reverberations to a social practice with artistic inflection?

MARC: Let me give an example. My theater company is a fairly ordinary theater company in the Bay Area called the Living Word Project. Though our methodology and mission statement fall out of familiar norms for American theater companies, our modalities and presentations do not. We do things like *Word Becomes Flesh*, which is a transitional work moving from solo performance to ensemble presentation to canonical text. The work, supported by the National Performance Network, is performed by alumni of the Brave New Voices network of Youth Speaks and is currently touring throughout the United States and Europe. We do Left Coast Leaning, which is a curatorial exercise meant to codify an aesthetic, to enhance audience understanding and appreciation of regional synergies, and to increase the visibility of local and regional artists. We present the idea that aesthetic tastes reach beyond immediate aesthetic manifestations. And of course, Reflections of Healing, which is your project, Brett. Using a theatrical methodology very similar to Anna Deavere Smith's, we place different murals throughout Oakland's public library system and beyond. The result is changing the iconography of the local environment.

There are also *The Breaks* and *red, black & GREEN: a blues*, two works produced in the last three years and scheduled to tour for more than a hundred performances in more than fifteen cities. In partnership with Intersection for the Arts in San Francisco, we develop and produce new works by emerging playwrights—for example, *Mirrors in Every Corner* and *Tree City Legends*. The plays enjoy runs of five weeks or more in a local theater. We have a hybrid program of artists and residents in public educational residency programs and maintain a family of frequently updated social networks to promote the work.

So in summary, we do repertory work that pulls from a pipeline of artists in our young-artist affiliate. We have a robust curatorial practice. We have a visual arts ethnography and iconography study. We have a national touring schedule. We have local development and production slates. We have a pedagogical framework with internal and exported manifestations, and a visible and shifting online life. But with all this activity, we had to ask ourselves, Is this enough? Is this too much?

BRETT: It seems like a dynamic way of pulling talents together—where young people exercise their right to participate in something bigger than themselves. It is a collaboration of ideas into performance and action.

MARC: Exactly. We began to distill the approach of one of our principal collaborators, Theaster Gates, and used a more expansive view of both ourselves and our community accountability to widen our self-definition. First, we began with adopting the emergent theory that intentional community design is arts practice. Second, we adopted a strategy similar to that of a commercial developer. That is, by developing and encouraging several youth arts programs that are geographically or philosophically close, we made the most of our resources when the various programs synergistically built off of one another. We melded these two philosophies into a theory of change, and in an essay commissioned by the Doris Duke Charitable Foundation, Jeff Chang described the theory under the idea of "the creative ecosystem." The theory is lived by our theater company and more than one hundred partner organizations across the country, all working together in a performance structure, a civic engine resource called Life Is Living.

To get the full picture, let me explain critical adjacency. The retail model looks something like this: Let's say a developer builds a Safeway on the corner of Fifty-First and Broadway in Oakland. The Safeway is at a great location and serves four neighborhoods, with an aggregate of fifty thousand residents. However, the Safeway becomes an even more attractive destination when the same or another developer puts a Payless shoe store next to it. And then adds a Wells Fargo next to that. And a Starbucks. And a Long's Drugs, and so on. In this way, an artificial community is created on the basis of diverse consumption and proximity. Among these entities, the shared value is the amassment of profit, though they have different methods of building wealth.

Life Is Living applies a similar logic, but instead of real estate, community is constructed on an art- and pedagogy-based cornerstone, and instead of financial profit at the center of these partnerships or adjacencies, the partners, led by the Living Word Project, place one critical issue at the center—life. In this model, the foundational partners are a philanthropic organization, an artist, an academic institution, an arts presenter, and an environmental agency. Each is called to convene a group of constituents in an open, shared setting built around a singular question: what sustains life in your community? The answers are sometimes rooted in environmental sustainability, but often veer toward the colloquial and the absurd: "Frenchy's chicken shack sustains life in Houston, just as Beyoncé does" or "City Slicker Farms sustains life in Oakland, just like Urban ReLeaf does." The composite responses that these partners and constituents elicit become the foundation for Life Is Living's single-day, eco-themed festival in an under-resourced public space. Like the retail model, Life Is Living involves a shared value and a plurality of methodologies. What we create, however, is a model built on relationships. And that's where we are today.

BRETT: You know, I think I've always been struck by a particular moment at the first Life Is Living festival, in 2008. There was all this activity going on and there were thousands of people, but I think for many, the most exciting part of the festival was the Hood Games, which was an exposition of black skateboarders and bike riders hosted by organizer Keith "K Dub" Williams. The then-new Town Park (skate park) was at the edge of DeFremery Park in West Oakland, and they had their own DJs, MCs, and sound system to accompany all the action. I loved what was happening there because of all the activity in the park. It was clear that this was the most integral. In other words, most of the stages and murals and exhibits were going to go away after the festival was over, but the skate and bike ramps were going to stay, and in fact were going to be used more because it was something the community really wanted. The moment for me, though, was when Mos Def was on the stage at the other end of the park and I decided to visit the skate park to see if it was still happening. Even though this celebrity MC was onstage doing this free concert, the skateboard kids couldn't have cared less. For them, they themselves—not Mos Def—were at the center, and their investment in the day was in the community they were building through activity and self-made culture. While the effort to be more ecologically responsible or musically hip was emphasized in the promotion, those social conventions were really parts of a system creating opportunities for folks to reintroduce themselves to their community through self-curated cultural investment.

MARC: When we first produced this festival five years ago, the event itself was our focus, and we adopted the available language to describe our intentions. We called it a GREEN festival, which was code for "If we call it green, maybe participants will respond in an environmentally responsible way to the sight of Mos Def performing for free at a local park." Interestingly, after we were scolded by folks doing critical environmental work about our use of their terminology, we conceded that we were excellent at drawing crowds and producing art, but it was disingenuous to claim to be an eco-agency, when that so clearly wasn't our area of expertise. Instead we fell back on the two pillars of our mission statement. One, we create a safe space, and two, we perform interdisciplinary collaboration. And so we shifted from placing the event at the center to placing the varied relationships we have created at the center of our work. We concentrated on the event as an extension of our mission to make a safe space, and engaged in sustained conversations with a plurality of groups, asking them each to consider the question of life.

As Freirean pedagogues, that is, as educators who believe in the importance of a person's culture and personal experience to transformative learning, we consider the idea of inviting multiple constituents to develop language and participatory responses to one question consistent with our ultimate desire to impel radical change within our communities. Very simply, in addition to local and touring repertory work, visual arts projects, educational programming, and online life, our theater company's most successful modality is its function as the hub of a localized interdisciplinary network. The network meets monthly, shares ideas, builds community, and produces shared space in which to make collective ideas manifest. The Life Is Living tree connects artists, philanthropists, academic institutions, community, the environment, and health. This model presents a learning opportunity for both art makers and grant makers. For our theater company, in relationship to the question of enough, our primary lesson is that it is *not* enough to place art in community without community context.

In a mercurial way, there is an obvious truth to our efforts from an audience development perspective. On the one hand, we've built up a cache in our local community by hosting a free, popular public event every year. Not so coincidentally, we hosted 2011's Life Is Living on Saturday, October 8, and premiered a new work ten miles, or three BART (Bay Area Rapid Transit) stops away on Wednesday, October 13. No amount of Facebook posts or flyer distribution can substitute for genuine public proximity and investment. In addition, by partnering with thirty organizations over several months, we've welcomed grassroots momentum into what Michael Kaiser of the Kennedy Center calls our "family," broadening our own constituent circle by organizing safe space for other organizations to share resources, intellectual property, and audience exposure. Life Is Living is a laboratory of crossover experiences wherein hip-hop-generation audiences are exposed to multiple platforms for relationships. Presumably, this means the young man who came to the festival just to produce bicycle-powered energy for the dance stage will fall in love with Talib Kweli and will join us in the theater space because of an experiential trust, not just an aesthetic curiosity.

Most importantly, this model reflects Theaster's suggestion that art happens everywhere and can happen for anyone, which partly means that more than exporting art into traditional performance spaces, we can import performance aesthetics into nontraditional public spaces. The ultimate thesis for this particular model is that art is not *object* or *outcome* only, but is a *process* and an *opportunity* for community as well. Correspondingly, grant making in the arts can't solely be about objects and outcomes. Innovative grant making also anticipates process and encourages collective opportunities.

BRETT: The wide-lens view of philanthropy seems to make sense to me in that it affirms a more interdependent means of activism and cultural output. Given that, why do you think you've had difficulty convincing foundations to rethink their approach?

MARC: In the arts community, we have difficulty tracking how the arts economy affects the civic community, because we tend to focus on objects like plays, paintings, CDs, and the corresponding sales figures. It is also difficult to track the true thrust in the environmental economy, because we focus on discrete specifics like solar panels or polar bears or the Amazon. But the actual overall stimulus provided by the arts includes everything, such as clothes bought for a night out at the ballet. Similarly, the true effect of cultural stimulus cannot be measured just by the aggregate of dance works, compositions, and sculptures that are supported by the public or private sector. The hidden metric of cultural stimulus in America is the scale and health of partnerships within creative ecosystems, the degree to which all organizations or artists benefit from the success of others, and the degree to which organizations or artists can tie their successes to the growth of others.

We can change the disproportionate emphasis on object and focus on interdependence, supplanting the idea of "ego system" with the radical notion of ecosystem. That is a macro-environmental, economical, and cultural-stimulus view of Life Is Living. And that's where you and other collaborators come in. The work has grown exponentially since. It is about relationships.

BRETT: When I was younger, I used to think collaboration meant that I have an idea, you can help me do it, and we'll call it collaboration. At this point, I think of collaboration as a practice that participants, including myself, contribute to in reciprocal ways in both the conceptual process and the product. In a skillful collaboration, we all have expertise that we share in the manifestation of that collective action. So in groups, I will often teach collaboration by asking, "Let's take three breaths together." Breathing is something we all have to do, we all want to do it, and we each do it in our own ways. Some people take longer inhalations, some people use more of their diaphragm, some people puff out their belly, but it's something that we all can do together. Part of a good collaboration is finding out what our different expertise is and, with this awareness, sharing the making of something together with that expertise.

Thich Nhat Hanh teaches regularly about the practice of breathing as a way to cultivate our awareness about the interconnectedness of all things. Breathing for him is a meditation, which includes reflection and action. When we meditate, we don't necessarily walk on water and go to nirvana—we are reflecting on consciousness and acting on our own subconscious. It's about reflection and action.

MARC: I have heard you describe art making as a combination of reflection and action. When we are creating, we are deeply listening to ourselves, and while deeply listening, we see the manifestation of our actions, our subconscious, into form. How does reflection and action relate to teaching or ecosystem building?

BRETT: Reflection and action in my teaching and learning practice borrows, as you mentioned earlier, from Paulo Freire's work. In the late 1960s to early 1970s in Brazil, Freire transformed contemporary education and is well known for his book *Pedagogy of the Oppressed*, in which he talks about dialogue as reflection and action. That is, if you have reflection without action, that's not really dialogue, which is a stereotypical criticism of academe. Or conversely, if you have action without reflection, it can be dangerous or even harmful.

MARC: The famous Freirean praxis of reflection and action is fundamental to the life of the creative ecosystem. The act of inviting multiple constituents to develop language and participatory responses to a question is a form of liberation pedagogy in which all the participants take turns being teachers and students. From early on in our relationship, I have recognized your work as a vehicle you drive to simultaneously teach and learn. There is liberation pedagogy inside of your teaching and in the public projects you cocreate. Where did your interest in education and your multifaceted understanding of teaching strategies come from?

BRETT: My parents were educators, and I grew up in a multiethnic family as a product of the civil rights movement, and the benefits of that societal transformation are evident in my life. For example, my birthday parties growing up foreshadowed more than a lifetime of my cohosting fun parties; my birthdays foreshadowed a life not segregated. In terms of class and culture, my birthday parties were very dynamic. Diversity is subsequently part of my being, a polycultural literacy I have lived my entire lifetime. Being the child of teachers also meant that I had access to educational and learning resources at a young age, including books on many topics and lots of paper for drawing.

I went to college to study zoology, but I was always drawing and clandestinely spray-painting walls in the middle of the night. When I finally proposed to my parents that I would change my college major to the practice of art they said, "You know what? We always said you can be whatever you want to be—but you can't be an artist." So my parents encouraged me to be an educator as a way to support myself, and during college, they got me summer jobs where I would teach. I started out working at an elementary school, then junior high schools, and then high school. Eventually I ended up at Satellite Academy, in the Lower East Side of Manhattan.

Satellite Academy is an alternative public high school, a "last chance" school founded in 1979 to help young people who have not been successful in traditional New York City public high schools or who are returning to study after a long absence. The school works with students from all five boroughs. Of the two hundred students, approximately 60 percent of them are African American and 40 percent Latino; 80 percent of the kids are eligible for free lunch. The school had active partnerships with the Drawing Center, Art in General, Threadwaxing Space, Artist's Space, and Lower Manhattan Cultural Council for extraordinary arts exposure, resources, and programming. My role was to work with these partners to integrate contemporary arts culture into a multidisciplinary curriculum throughout the entire school. And while graduate students of Bankstreet Graduate School of Education were coming to study the craft of teaching with the staff at Satellite, I was learning pedagogy from everyone and how to work together. Support from the Soros Foundation and the Empire State Partnership Program forced me to learn how to do assessment that generated more curriculum—which in my case included an exhibition developed, curated, and produced by the students using blue-chip art from the Bohen Foundation Collection and, subsequently, Artist's Space slide registry.

MARC: It sounds like a rich learning and teaching experience. What a way to extend one's pedagogy! Can you say more about that?

BRETT: Let me share a piece from the student-curated exhibit. The piece is about one of the students from Satellite: Erica—Erica "Puff Mommy Combs." This piece was made when Sean "Puff Daddy" Combs had just hit the music scene. Erica had a crush so intense that she believed she was going to marry Puff Daddy—to the extent that she signed *all* of her papers "Erica Puff Mommy Combs." As a part of the exhibition, I and each of my students created a piece in which they contributed ten things that represented themselves. Among other things, Erica's list included a picture of Puff Daddy, her favorite pair of jeans, her nails from getting her nails done, her razor that she used to shave her eyebrows, and her contact lens case. Subsequently, a viewer can get an idea of Erica from her painted image, and a viewer can get another idea of Erica from her materials. Combined, the piece shows a representation that we created collaboratively in a process that included reflection and action. This intentionally reflective process of portraiture recognizes the *verb* in art making; the Western history emphasis on portraiture as a *noun* frequently overlooks this aspect of art. Conceptually, the collaboration is also very different from the history of portraiture, which is usually about wealthy people and disproportionally about men.

And so what does it mean to collaboratively create and publicly display images of people who are not from the traditional archetype? What does it mean to see young people in the creation of a collective cultural narrative? And especially, when are young people of color represented in society, much less in galleries and museums? Such an iconoclastic representation of young black women in America, in a personal, self-determined, and participatory way, in a repository for precious objects is very rare.

I saw this as transformative, so I started to create projects with people all over: in Harlem where I was living, in private schools, in public schools, with nonprofit organizations, in people's homes in North Philadelphia, at women's health clinics, in universities like the Harvard School of Education, and internationally. And in all of these processes, we were developing rubrics, generating dialogues, having collaborative conversations, and making learning visible. My artistic process continued to evolve through my ongoing learning and teaching practice that was always broadening and being refined at the same time. I like to say that art is a kind of debris of someone in radical transformation, radical exploratory growth. And I think of it as a documentation of that growth.

MARC: Life Is Living as an event has also evolved through transformation and growth. What started as a onetime park jam with an emphasis on the event itself has changed into an ongoing nurturing of relationships between stakeholders, and this process culminates annually in an urban festival. The growth of the yearly Life Is Living event exemplifies the debris of the creative ecosystem.

BRETT: Which brings us to DeFremery Park and the part I played in the creative ecosystem that is evolving there. DeFremery Park has a lot of history, but is best known for the Black Panthers. DeFremery was where they would hold public presentations, feed people lunches, talk about their ten-point program, and host different activities. In thinking about this legacy, when I was invited to be part of the ecosystem, I worked not only with you but also with other Life Is Living organizers to identify eight people in Oakland whose work or legacy is about healing. I asked these people, who served as role models but also artistic models, to generate a question about healing, and I worked this question into the script from which to conduct their interviews. So unlike a more traditional researcher, who would approach the inquiry with a hypothesis and research it, I had the subjects themselves dictate the dialogue. We called this interactive project Reflections of Healing.

The models of Reflections of Healing talk about healing in very divergent ways. There is, for instance, an artist, a musician, a meditation teacher, a martial arts *sifu*, an urban peace activist, and a chef, like Bryant Terry. Bryant went to school for history, was getting his master's degree, and then ended up going to the culinary arts school in New York. Now, using food and culture, he is engaged in a myriad of social justice initiatives and has written a vegan soul-food cookbook that's in its seventh printing. And Bryant's question, "How can we replace prevailing notions of aging with new ideas and images that imagine people becoming more whole and healthy as they get older?" is just one example of the range of how we are talking about healing.

So, with that in mind for Life Is Living, I invited the eight models to give me pictures of themselves when they were adolescents. From their childhood photographs, I made drawings to scaffold the next opportunity highlighting interconnection through community creation. I invited all the participants and their friends to trace images of themselves projected eight feet tall. It was another opportunity for the participants to come together and collectively create.

MARC: The relationships are like a feedback loop that includes social relevance and localized solutions. Reflections of Healing celebrates community healers who reflect the immediate location of the work's installation while providing public, noncommercial venues showcasing a variety of participatory activities. The selection of prominent Oakland role models pictured as adolescents emphasizes the collective potential of youth in the creation of a loving community.

BRETT: And like a Tibetan sand mandala, in which monastics use grains of sand to make incredibly detailed pieces about transformation, it is okay to let go of the object, to sweep up the beautiful result of days of labor, and throw it in the ocean. As you said, it's not that Life Is Living is the most important thing as an outcome, but the transformation of those involved is bound up in the process of making it as well. Part of my practice is sharing a creative process with people, where we become the monastics and create these objects as a part of our transformation.

In 2010, for example, we had Red, Bike, and Green, an Oakland biking group for African-descended people who promote health and community interaction by leading rides in West and East Oakland, organize the ways that people can ride their bikes to the event. And we generated the electricity for the stages with Rock the Bike, a setup in which people pedaled bikes to power the dance stage, which included many types of contemporary dance. We also had a solar truck that generated the energy for the main stage where the Glide Memorial Church Choir performed before youth poets. Then there was Estria's Graffiti Battle, where artists from across the country painted together and repositioned where art takes place, what the experiences are, who art is for, and who the viable audiences are. Reflections of Healing was there, too, so people were able to color and add to each of the eight portraits of local heroes. The resulting festival acted as a unique kind of rubric for what art is, because it is specifically made by and for that space. And there was the skate park, where three hundred kids are doing grinds, flying, all day. And the aquaponic system growing tilapia, using reclaimed water and creating a garden in an urban landscape. And a petting zoo in this inner-city park in West Oakland. Because individuals, the neighborhood, and other organizations made contributions, all the participants nurture their relationship and their shared investment in the ecosystem.

MARC: At this time of unparalleled global connection among humanity, there is a growing discussion in academic circles about broader cultural and social political considerations that involve collaborative practices. These social practices are being acknowledged as methods to develop cross-cultural dialogue without sacrificing the unique identities of individual speakers. *Social practice* is now a popular term in Western art circles, but working together to make things in a symbiotic way is not really new and certainly not limited to the Western art worlds.

BRETT: In the Congo, there are objects called *nkisi nkonde*. When people in a community need some help about some idea, they'll sometimes visit a divinator. This person will make a container and insert some magic stuff, the juju part, into it and put a mirror on it to show that the flash of the spirit is contained within. And then sometimes the members of the community come and add nails, fabric, or other ritual materials to the object as a part of their own intention and commitment to the project. Part of what I am doing as an artist and an educator in Life Is Living, and in general, is inspired by the role of the divinator, who is making these containers for people to physically create artifacts of transformation.

And so, after people colored the portraits at the 2010 festival, I took them back to my studio and painted them according to how they were colored while also bringing out the spirit of each person. When they were finished, the models, community members and I had an exhibition of the paintings with other participatory elements: pamphlets about the process and people involved; a map where people could add their own reflections of healing in their community; healing encyclopedias; a video of the interviews made by Eli Jacobs-Fantauzzi; a place to make healing monuments out of clay; spaces to color healing quotes written in Arabic, Spanish, Korean, Chinese, English, and Amharic; local choreographer Amara Tabor Smith shared her signature recession stew; and music. Then for the whole summer, we installed in various Oakland public libraries all the pieces that thousands of people had made. We supplied maps that showed the installation locations and biographies of each of the models and their work. The project has become the method to build containers where people are developing relationships, not just as consumers, but also as participants. What started as this tiny part of the Life Is Living ecosystem has ended up growing like rhizomes to new manifestations because the work is about relationships and the ongoing evolution of things that the participants in those relationships want.

MARC: The relationships then become a main part of what is crafted in collaboration. The means by which people learn, practice, and sustain being together is the conceptual scaffold that the creative ecosystem represents. Can you talk about how the site is a part of that framework, or how the location of Life Is Living is part of what is considered in the nurturing of relationships?

BRETT: On April 6, 1968, not far from DeFremery Park, eight Black Panther Party members, including Bobby Hutton, Eldridge Cleaver, and David Hilliard, were traveling in two cars ambushed by the Oakland Police. Cleaver and Hutton ran for cover and found themselves in a basement surrounded by officers. The building was fired upon for over an hour. When a tear-gas canister was thrown into the basement, the two men inside decided to surrender. Cleaver was wounded in the leg, and so Hutton said he would go first. When Hutton left the building with his hands in the air, now watched by a crowd of community residents, he was shot twelve times by the police and was killed. The murder of Bobby Hutton was a major event in the Black Panther Party's history, and DeFremery Park in Oakland has been unofficially named in his honor.

So one of the Reflections of Healing images started in 2010 is of Bobby Hutton, along with the seven other portraits of living champions of healing. In 2011, we installed all the portraits again in Lil' Bobby Hutton Park, where Life Is Living takes place. We laid out several things: the map where healing was again happening in Oakland, mounds of clay so that people could create healing monuments, and rolls of paper with printed questions about healing for coloring. And we started another Bobby Hutton portrait that people colored. It's a cyclical practice of awareness through building these containers of reflections and action. The *Little Bobby Hutton Power Figure* was then installed in the Oakland Museum of California as a part of the annual 2012 Día De Los Muertos Exhibition. The portraits of the eleven living Reflections of Healing models are about to be permanently installed throughout Oakland. The results are original images of young people who are healers, talking about healing with their own voice.

MARC: And while the works document the unique array of healers who live and work locally, the project transforms the local consumer-driven landscape through events and artworks that model production as well as wholeness, encouraging a new community aesthetic. The inclusive research and production process of the project provides a method for Oakland residents to participate in the creation of their environment in a meaningful way with tangible outcomes. In showcasing ecological pathways for a new population of younger and widely diverse inhabitants, community projects like Life Is Living and Reflections of Healing shift the current archetype of the environmental movement ecosystem to promote inclusive participation in life-affirming, healing practices to change the world.

BRETT: And the change is self-actualized by the widely diverse inhabitants who populate the community in which Life Is Living takes place. It is like the difference between treatment and healing that Andrew Weil speaks about. Treatment originates outside, and healing comes from within— the word *healing* means "making whole," that is, restoring integrity and balance. So why, despite a very well-known and relatively recent history about Oakland and Bobby Hutton, has the city of Oakland never previously acknowledged his death? And what does it mean to then make something that honors him and have it read by thousands of people of different classes, ages, and cultural backgrounds?

MARC: It is the nurturing of a positive vision of Oakland, through the genuine invitation to a myriad of voices, that makes the event successful. A tangible outcome is that this public place, which also has a reputation for being impersonal and dangerous, is shown to be intimate and safe. The intangibles include a sense of caring and fellowship that acknowledges the past and creates the future by our collective existence in the present. This is part of the vision. We see this taking place in various cities. What we have experienced in Oakland can happen elsewhere.

BRETT: Social collaboration transcends individual privileges, where separate expectations are replaced with equality and collective self-interest. By creating experiences of dynamic demographics, with exercises that everyone can create in, there is a collective unification, a support of new community that is inclusive in its being. At the center of these exercises for positive shared experience is an artistic representation of diverse partnership and healing. Life Is Living—and its Reflections of Healing offshoot—illuminates the experience and history of the people of Oakland.[3] It is a reminder that we are changed as individuals in making our world together.

3

"I Am That Character"

Playmaking and Listening to the Voices of Formerly Incarcerated Youth

Maisha T. Winn

IN THE NOVEL *The Language of Flowers*, readers meet a young woman, Victoria Jones, who spent her entire life being shuffled from one foster home or group home to another. She was held back twice in kindergarten and twice in second grade, yet somehow managed to find solace in using flowers as a way to communicate when words, language, and dialogue did not seem easily accessible or possible.[1] In one of the many compelling scenes in this novel, Victoria's foster mother, Elizabeth, marvels over Victoria's translations for rosemary ("remembrance"), columbine ("desertion"), holly ("foresight"), and lavender ("mistrust"). Elizabeth's surprise at Victoria's knowledge is informed by the report Victoria's social worker, Meredith, provided. "Why did Meredith tell me you couldn't learn?" asked Elizabeth. As Victoria pondered Elizabeth's reaction, the young woman thought to herself, "I wasn't faking inability; I'd just never been asked."

It took one foster mother to see Victoria in her full humanity and to provide a space where she could find her language in the language of flowers. In this chapter, I attempt to use a humanizing research methodology that focuses on themes of resilience in the lives of teenage African American girls from fourteen to seventeen. The girls I have studied have experienced incarceration and have passed through the hands of many foster families, yet have found a way to use theater as a language in a playwriting and performance workshop I have followed since 2006.[2]

By focusing on how scholars build networks and other relationships with youth and their communities, a humanizing research methodology complicates the view that the participants, sites, and researcher's position are objective. In many ways, I am doing what my colleagues, Eve Tuck and Wayne Yang, call "refusing research"—that is, I do not wish to solely tell hard-luck stories of youth who have been variously pushed out, locked up, and marginalized.[3] Scholarship, according to Tuck, all too often focuses on "damage-centered" research while omitting key turning points, changes, and other experiences that demonstrate what is possible and how youth and their communities forge a clearing that is not easily detected by people on the outside.[4] For the purpose of this chapter, I move backstage to spotlight the stories of four formerly incarcerated girls who were also in the foster care system during their work with an urban southeastern playwriting and performance program.[5] Taraji, Jill, Jennifer, and Rae (all names are pseudonyms) take their rightful places center stage with their stories, their analysis of the plays in which they were cast, and their plans for possible lives. Like the protagonist Victoria in *The Language of Flowers*, these girls had gifts that often went unseen by adults in their world. However, when given the opportunity to participate in something that inspired participation, Taraji, Jill, Jennifer, and Rae created literate identities through ensemble building and thus learning to trust and be trustworthy, urban playwriting, staging a play, rehearsing, performing for the public and incarcerated youth, and talking with and back to audiences.[6]

Why are these stories so critical at this time? As America continues to earn its reputation as an incarceration nation, its youth are experiencing detainment as well.[7] More specifically, African American, American Indian, and Latino youth are often trapped in a school-prison nexus as a result of schools' zero-tolerance policies that often target youth of color for suspensions and expulsions. In an open letter to Secretary Arne Duncan of the U.S. Department of Education, the Civil Rights Project/Proyecto Derechos Civiles (CRP) commended the State Department for releasing the 2009–2012 Civil Rights Data Collection (CRDC) to the public. Consistent with findings from the American Civil Liberties Union and the NAACP Legal Defense Fund, CRDC revealed the overrepresentation of black, Latino, American Indian, and English learners in school suspensions and expulsions. CRP, however, challenged CRDC to disaggregate data by race and gender and to recognize the potential in early interventions in a child's education:

> A great deal can be accomplished through earlier interventions, support and training for teachers and leaders, and system-wide approaches that are proven effective at promoting positive behavior. Toward these ends, the disciplinary data collected in the CRDC is invaluable to parents, educators, and policymakers who seek to improve both student behavior and achievement using methods that help to keep struggling students in school.[8]

CRP's Gary Orfield (codirector) and Dan Losen (director of Center for Civil Rights Remedies at CRP) pen the letter in particular. Both scholars call for additional data collection, including public reporting of information such as "causes of school-based arrests and referrals" and "comprehensive data on incarcerated youth." I would argue that there needs to be data collected on grassroots organizations serving incarcerated and formerly incarcerated youth and offering opportunities for youth to engage in meaningful and productive activities that lead to more civil engagement and participation. Opportunities and experiences like Girl Time, which I discuss in this chapter, are just one outlet for formerly and currently incarcerated youth. Yet the efforts of such outlets often go unnoticed in spite of their commitment to providing robust educational opportunities for youth who have been entangled in the juvenile justice and foster care systems.

Most recently, I participated on two panels for Harvard Law School's Closing the School-to-Prison Pipeline conference in March 2012. On one panel, the participants were asked to review case studies of youth entangled in the juvenile justice system. It was difficult to read these cases as an educator and not raise questions about what could have been done to disrupt the cycle of the children who were central to the cases being detained. In his backstory of the See Forever School for youth who experienced arrests and detainment, John Forman Jr. recounts his trajectory as a defense attorney in Washington, D.C., and how hard it was to find suitable alternatives to jails and prisons.[9] In the Girl Time summer program, where I met Taraji, Jill, Jennifer, and Rae, teaching artists were committed to providing a space for formerly incarcerated girls to produce the works of the girls' incarcerated peers through a paid internship as professional actors. The program was held at a Department of Juvenile Justice Multi-Service Center, which served court-involved youth and youth who were on probation. Teaching artists refused to believe that the formerly incarcerated girls they worked with were only the sum of their charges and offenses. In this space, the girls were so much more than these narrow labels.

Girls who take center stage in this chapter like to draw, while others love writing. It is important to mention that throughout my work with incarcerated and formerly incarcerated youth under the age of eighteen, I purposefully use the terms *girls* and *boys* to underscore that these are children and not adults. One of the girls has even started writing her autobiography at age sixteen. The girls have various future plans, including college, modeling, and owning businesses. These girls hail from different cities, including Atlanta, the Bronx in New York, Miami, and New Orleans. However, what they do have in common is that they were entangled in both the juvenile justice and foster care systems.

In this article, presented as a series of acts and scenes, I offer dialogue between a powerful community of girls—hereby referred to as student artists—who at once articulated desire and possibility through their narratives and lives as playwrights and actors. Like a narrator, I offer context for the scenes as well as a discussion. However, I purposefully do my best to keep the conversations intact. Writing in a series of acts and scenes is modeled after the playwriting format used as a tool to encourage incarcerated and formerly incarcerated girls to develop and sustain critical literacies. Because each conversation with a student artist was an act of mutual trust, commitment, and respect, I sought to preserve the integrity of the dialogue that ensued from a set of guiding questions. Each act and scene emerges from qualitative interview data; I sat with student artists for thirty- or forty-minute interviews that took place on site during the Girl Time summer program in 2008. There, formerly incarcerated girls prepared to stage eight to ten plays written by their peers in regional youth detention center (RYDC) workshops. Overall, during the Girl Time season, student artists write nearly one hundred plays, which are performed on the second day of a two-day workshop in an RYDC. The audience consists of families, incarcerated boys and girls, and the detention center staff. Because the summer program can only stage between eight and ten plays from the season, it is generally very difficult to decide which plays will be performed.

My study is guided by the following questions: In what ways does playwriting and performing literacy mediate the "betwixt and between" lives of formerly incarcerated girls who are in the foster care system? How do girls view their participation in a theater program, and how does this program help formerly incarcerated girls in foster care build literate identities?

Taraji, Jill, Jennifer, and Rae were unique in the context of the Girl Time summer program. Because they lived together in one foster home, they not only shared the experience of Girl Time, but also shared the different aspects of their foster home, where they were valued and where their skills and gifts were put to work. The four girls lived in a group home that was owned by a church. The pastor, an African American woman, employed the girls in the church's children's center. While the girls certainly had their struggles with each other, they considered themselves sisters and often said they kept each other going in the program.

A HUMANIZING RESEARCH METHODOLOGY

Although I initially believed I was asking the right kinds of questions to student artists in the Girl Time summer program, I realized after the first cohort I worked with in 2006–2007 that student artists were telling me what they thought I wanted to hear. That is, they gave me an incarceration discourse that privileges safe and strategic responses conveying regret and redemption. As I studied transcripts and ethnographic video of interviews, I decided to implement a role-playing question. I would ask the student artists to respond to an administrator or a policy maker who wanted to end the funding for the Girl Time program. It was in this line of questioning that I experienced some of the most passionate responses throughout the qualitative interviewing process. In the series of acts and scenes, you will hear how student artists respond to the naysayers and critics. These responses demonstrate how student artists learn to resist incarceration discourse and, as one student artist, Taraji, noted, demonstrate that "words are powerful and good." Elsewhere I discuss my role as a researcher, a teaching artist in Girl Time, a youth advocate, and a citizen committed to encouraging people to rethink the concept of jails for children. I use Keisha Green's "double dutch" methodology, which considers the dual positioning of researchers as insider and outsider.[10] As I struggled to determine how my insider/outside status best served this community of girls, I learned that the role of narrator best captured my work as an ethnographer learning and doing. I narrate the "findings" presented here while preserving the dialogue. In Act 1, you meet Taraji, who was a leader in the community, both outgoing and spunky, as evidenced by the interview. In Act 2, you will meet Jill, whom all the girls went to for problem solving, as she was a great listener. Jennifer, the protagonist in Act 3, was a girl of few words but always opened up on stage. Much like Jennifer, Rae in Act 4 came alive while performing but also exhibited a great deal of passion in the interview, when I engaged in role playing as a naysayer and an administrator threatening to end the funding for Girl Time. Collectively, these girls have big dreams, ideas, and imaginations that even in this format are difficult to convey in print.

ACT 1, SCENE 1: "Words Are Powerful and Good" —Taraji

Taraji was a featured playwright in the 2008 summer program. Her co-authored play, *Trouble in Castlehood*, was an unexpected blend of fantasy and the urban. The "hood" (purposefully added to "castle"), as well as the development of the character Mafia Dragon, creatively used fantasy to demonstrate how the drug trade, and subsequently drug addiction, could potentially impact youth. Taraji participated in Girl Time's RYDC workshop in a county outside the city limits. Girl Time teaching artists were ecstatic when a playwright was actually able to participate in the summer program and see her play fully realized. Although it was not standard for playwrights to perform in their own work, an exception was made for Taraji, who really wanted to be in *Castlehood*.

> TARAJI: [I wrote] *Trouble in Castlehood* [see appendix]. Basically, the play was about Kevin and Devin and the Mafia Dragon. Kevin was me and Devin was my sister. Basically [my character] was into drugs and stuff like that, weak. I was selling it and I was a thug. And then my brother was trying to take care of me . . . but I never wanted to listen to him.
>
> MAISHA: Where did the story come from? So you're in detention and you get an opportunity to write a play. What was that experience like for you? What kind of story did you want to tell, and why did you want to tell this particular story?
>
> TARAJI: I wanted to tell this story, I guess, because some of it is what I have done. So I just thought that in the writing, I would try to tell people just don't do it if you don't want to end up in jail like I was.
>
> MAISHA: You told the story about something serious that happens for real but you gave it a fairy-tale quality with [characters] such as dragons instead of actual people. Tell me about how you came up with that idea.
>
> TARAJI: The dragons was, you know, tough and just crazy. And I used to always watch *Dragon Tales*. I used to like *Dragon Tales*, so I was like, "Okay, let's just do *Dragon Tales*."
>
> [*Laughter*]

ACT 1, SCENE 2: "Do Something for the Females"

Taraji has many books of poems she penned and enjoys writing. She proudly revealed that anyone who reads her poems and stories thinks her writing must be based on reality. Like many of the student artists and other youth I worked with, Taraji was already engaged in literate practices, but few had ever asked about her writing.

> TARAJI: At first [being in Girl Time] wasn't important to me and I wanted to do something else . . . but when [the teaching artists] told me I would have to make my own play I said okay, 'cause I was going to do something for the females. I never thought I was gonna end up doing my play live in front of people. I just thought I was just doing it. I never thought [my play] was gonna make it [in the summer performance].
>
> MAISHA: And had you been a writer before? Poems? Journals?
>
> TARAJI: Yes, I love doing poems. I have books of poems at home right now. And then I let people read them, and judges like them. They [say], "You have a very good imagination," and they feel like some of the people want to know if it happened for true 'cause it don't seem like your imagination could go that deep. Words are powerful and good when I write them down. I just love them.

ACT 1, SCENE 3: "I Am That Character"

One of the questions I began asking was in what ways playwriting and performance supported learning in other contexts. And while I did not observe student artists in other settings formally, I did record their self-reported data.

> MAISHA: So now that you're in the summer program, what do you think you're learning here that you think will help you with school or work? And what are you learning socially and what are you learning personally by being a part of this ensemble?
>
> TARAJI: Well, I'm learning a lot of patience and confidence. You have to have confidence, and when you want something, you got to work for it. Because here, I never thought I'd memorize all these lines. I forget some, but I'm gonna get it. And I just learned a lot of stuff. I mean it was just great.

Maisha: What do you think you'll take from [the experience] personally?

Taraji: That I can do something on my own.

Maisha: How do you feel about taking your play back to the detention center?

Taraji: Now see, that one. It just took me when they told me that. I was like, "You know you going back to jail to perform it?" I said, "No way." I was like, "Oh my God, they gonna look at me like I'm stupid." But then I was like, "I don't care." I just don't want to go through them doors. It just—that's a lot.

Maisha: What do you think the audience will think about this play?

Taraji: I hope it means a lot to them. I hope it changes their life like it did mine 'cause I don't do drugs no more. The girl who I wrote the play with taught me a lot.

Maisha: What are your plans for the near future?

Taraji: I want to be a choreographer and a model. I wanna be a great role model to people, but first I gotta graduate from high school and then do my college, and I'm gonna get there. I know I am. I might go through some bumps, but I'm gonna get there.

Maisha: If someone who was making decisions about a program like Girl Time—like an administrator—said, "I don't think this program is helping" or "I don't know if I really want this program in here" or "These girls are in trouble anyway" so they don't get to do anything like this, what would your response be to someone who said something like that?

Taraji: I would say no, it's not true, because it did help me and I'm sure it did help a lot of people at [lists all the various detention centers] 'cause it helps a lot of females, 'cause a lot of females really wrote these poems and plays in RYDCs. And I know it helped me because I'm not going through no trouble since I been out of jail. I been there, done that. I got all my life, and I'm tired of changing.

Maisha: So was it that you got to tell your story? I'm trying to figure out what it was about it that helped you change exactly. Like what was it exactly.

Taraji: What was it that changed me?

Maisha: Well, you said that the program has helped you, but there are probably other things that helped you, too.

TARAJI: . . . 'cause the other plays, I mean, I don't know, it's like when I sat there beside other females and teachers doing the plays, I thought back and was like, "Oh my god, I'm that character. I'm that character." I'm like, "Oh my god, I remember doing the stuff that they are saying." And then all the plays have something good at the end, so it's great.

MAISHA: What do you like about the Girl Time teachers?

TARAJI: Y'all are so dramatic . . . not in a bad way . . . everything I do, like [the first day], I didn't want to come there. And then we got in the circle and I said, "Hold on, I remember this clapping thing." Y'all make me laugh, especially when you are so dramatic.

Certainly, teaching artists were dramatic; this ensemble of women actors from theater, film, television, and commercials were unafraid to use their voices and bodies to commit to characters even if it meant being serious, silly, or, in some cases, vulnerable, thus inviting student artists to do the same. Teaching artists were equally inspired by Taraji. Her energy was magnetic. She was determined and exhibited courage when facing many uncertainties. Taraji taught me the power of getting into character; her declaration (and revelation) "I am that character" is an example of how the performances allow girls to try on new costumes while playing them out on a stage for all to see. Getting into character was practice terrain for real-life encounters. Taraji also had a sense of loyalty to do the work for other girls, or other "females," as she would say. She was insightful that her words—words that were written down in poetry, prose, and now in plays—had the potential to support her peers in personal growth and development. Taraji's underscored statement "Words are powerful and good when I write them down. I just love them" was humbling for me to hear. These are all things I believe, yet I was not looking for them in this context. By listening—and I mean really listening—I learned that Taraji came to Girl Time, her foster home, the detention center, and schools with a wealth of knowledge, a love of language, and insight that was simply waiting for a venue. In the next act, you will meet one of Taraji's "sisters," and while they did not share a bloodline, they nevertheless looked out for each other.

ACT 2, SCENE 1: "We Tell Them the Truth" —Jill

Jill had a big-sister stance with Taraji, Jennifer, and Rae, and she carried this stance into the summer 2008 cohort. She moved around the Girl Time spaces with confidence and a sense of belonging. Jill also had that "I'm from New York City" swagger that the other student artists admired. When there were challenges between the other girls, Jill merely observed and only got involved when someone went to her for advice, which was quite a bit. She, too, was a playwright from the RYDC workshops. However, she was more excited about her roles in the plays. In *Sky, Lead the Way*, Jill essentially played God or a higher power who was helping a young woman make healthy decisions about her life. Jill found this role appropriate because she was always the one people came to for help. While Jill revealed very real and difficult aspects of her life, she retained enthusiasm for being able to have a fresh start when she turned eighteen years old.

> **JILL:** [Life] was really hard . . . but I've been in and out of group homes and foster homes, so when my mom wanted me to move with her, I was kind of skeptical, but she had asked me to move down here with her. I talked to the director of the group home, and he said, "You should give your mother a chance." I guess it's been okay, but I'm back inside the system.
>
> It all started because me and my mom had an argument and I kind of broke the window in the house and she called the police. Then I got on probation. Then I violated probation, and then I was committed to the state. This will be finished in August when I go to school . . . and everything will be expunged.
>
> [*Jill and Maisha gave each other high fives.*]
>
> From second to sixth, I was in a gifted instrument orchestra type of school, and sixth through ninth, I was in Choir Academy of Harlem. I only play two [instruments], which was the trumpet and the trombone. The trombone is okay, but you have to use a lot of air and drink a lot of water.

MAISHA: So [the South] is still a new home for you.

JILL: That was my second time because I had came back because I violated probation. The second time, I spent three years because they sent me to Boys and Girls [school] and then I came back 'cause that's when they committed me. I left [the facility] in August and I haven't been back. I've seen officers from there, and they say I did not deserve to be there.

Jill and other student artists taught me how they formed kinship networks with junior correctional officers and probation officers (POs); I often witnessed such relationships during our summer program housed in a Department of Juvenile Justice facility for youth on probation to visit their POs. POs often showed their support of us and were welcoming of any activity that would provide a positive outlet for the youth they served. Jill was initially reluctant to be in the Girl Time summer cohort, and she discusses this in the next scene.

ACT 2, SCENE 2: "Our Sides of the Story"

MAISHA: How was the [Girl Time] experience?

JILL: I didn't want to come, but as we got into it, I started changing my thoughts and behaviors and started focusing on plays. I guess it was because of the friendliness of the teachers and directors. Ms. Kaya [program director], and you, and Zaire [teaching artist]. Because when I'm in a crowd, I like to step in the back and look and see if I want to be a part of it . . . writing it and saying, "Okay are we going to write about love or what we been through?" We wanted to do something comedy . . . so I think that was the best part of it. I didn't get to act it out, because I think that day, I couldn't act it out because something happened to my toe and I had to have surgery.

MAISHA: What did it mean to you at that time? First of all, this city. You're in this city you didn't want to live in.

JILL: It gave us time off the pods and it gave us snacks [laughter] . . . but I guess because we can actually show our sides of the story. Other people think one thing about us, and we tell them the truth about it in a play so they actually see what we've been going through. And maybe it can give them a different perspective on how girls are.

ACT 2, SCENE 3: "Make It into One"

Because Jill was one of the Girl Time playwrights in an RYDC workshop, her insight as a playwright and an actor was invaluable, since she had experienced the process full circle.

> JILL: We wrote *RYDC Love*.[11] And me and Juliet didn't know each other, and then I asked her if she had a brother. Anyway, we based the characters on her brother, and I named the girl after my sister, so it was something that happened to me. Two boys were fighting over me and one boy lied . . . so that's basically the inspiration for the play.
>
> MAISHA: What did you learn from the entire experience? Not just writing the play but [working with others].
>
> JILL: We have different backgrounds. I'm from New York. My coauthor is from Georgia. She has different ethnicity, and so I guess it doesn't matter who you are and what you've been through. You can come together and decide on something that you've all shared and combine it. Like what she's been through, what I've been through, what other girls been through. We can all make it into one. So I think that was good.

ACT 2, SCENE 4: "Sky"

> JILL: I'm in *Sky, Leading the Way*. And Sky is basically like God, and she's basically leading a girl who doesn't know her way, so basically she asks God—well, Sky—to lead her in the right direction. Crystal does some things that she shouldn't do and Sky still helped her.
>
> MAISHA: Do you connect with the play in some ways?
>
> JILL: Me, personally, I connect with the character because a lot of my friends come to me for advice. Like one of my friends said she hates home. I would beg to be home right now, and I'd rather be home with all the drama, all the arguments, and cursing out than be in a group home. I really do connect

with Sky, and my friends come to me and I should lead them in the right direction and tell them where they don't want to go—where I've been.

MAISHA: You and the girls from the group home seem like sisters.

JILL: Like, they are actually another reason I keep coming, because they say we are going to have fun, we are going to have fun.

ACT 2, SCENE 5: "People Are Not Listening"

MAISHA: If someone said they wanted to cut our funding.

JILL: I would say they stupid. But I would really get upset because I think that Girl Time is for girls our age, from eleven [on], because I know there are a lot of girls out there getting in trouble from eleven to eighteen. People are not listening to us. Like they hear one side of the story and they just want to believe it. So Girl Time lets us write out our thoughts and express them in ways that other people wouldn't. So it's like we're doing good for ourselves and we're showing other people that we have been through that stuff and we can move on from it.

MAISHA: Well, you guys are getting ready to take your plays to the detention centers. Tell me about how you're feeling about that and what this experience is going to do for you and the young girls you see.

JILL: I personally hope there's no [girls in the audience] I was in jail with because it would just—it would hurt. Because we all say once we get out, we never going back. And if they do, it's just like, "What happened? What went wrong?" But if they are there, I could show them that they can overcome it. I left about eleven months ago, and I haven't been back. And I've graduated and I'm going to college and I'm going for my major that I want to major in. So it's like you can do it; you just have to put your mind to it.

MAISHA: The play you are in has some interesting messages—

JILL: In *Hi, My Name Is Mariah*, I play the guy buying sex. That play is very deep. I think it's going to touch some girls who have been prostituting and who have lost their babies.

I started to ask Girl Time student artists a provocative question about funding and funders to learn more about their passion, if any, for the experience. Jill took on this challenge wholeheartedly. She had a great deal of wisdom around issues surrounding girls; however, Jill's biggest critique of schools, families, the juvenile justice system, and foster care systems was "People are not listening" to girls in particular. She was solemn when she made this statement; according to Jill, when girls did not have confidantes or sustained relationships with adults and other people who were actually listening, girls sought other opportunities to be seen and heard, and these opportunities could become destructive. Jill believed that people had become too comfortable with stereotypes of girls who had been "in trouble." When these girls were given labels like *bad*, *promiscuous*, and *rebellious*, Jill believed that the girls ceased listening. Jill also confirmed what I had learned from six years of talking to incarcerated and formerly incarcerated girls who were also entangled in the foster care system. Although many of them wanted to move on and have peaceful lives, many people involved with these girls held the girls back through their low or limited expectations.

ACT 3, SCENE 1: "You Feel Like a Star" —Jennifer

Jennifer (or Jen) was easily the shyest student artist in this particular group; once on stage, however, she pushed herself and surrendered to her characters. She was proud to be from Miami, although she had moved between Florida and Georgia several times since she turned ten years old (she was sixteen when we met in 2008). Jen loved mathematics and was taking Algebra I. "I'm writing a book now," she revealed. "It's kind of my life history, but it got extra details." Although Jen really liked the girls she shared a group home with, she just wanted to get back home. In the play *Hi, My Name Is Mariah*, Jen played a social worker and used a stern yet caring voice with the protagonist. In *Meditations of the Heart*, she played an inmate in a women's correctional facility who—with her peers—reflected about how they got there and looked forward to what they wanted to do once they were released.

> **JENNIFER (JEN):** I was really excited to be in a play. I never done nothing like this before.
>
> **MAISHA:** I thought you've been in a play before—

JEN: At church.

MAISHA: But you have the ability! I can see it.

JEN: But I've never done it in front of a whole bunch of people! You feel like a star!

MAISHA: So, you're looking forward to the performance this weekend?

JEN: Yeah.

MAISHA: What do you think you will get from the experience? Why is it important to you?

JEN: I am a very, very shy person, and me doing this in front of [people] shows my confidence. I don't know.

MAISHA: Where do you think the confidence comes from?

JEN: My heart.

MAISHA: So tell me about the plays you're in this summer.

JEN: One of them is *Hi, My Name Is Mariah*. In that one, I'm a social worker trying to help this girl get her life together. So that's pretty good.

MAISHA: What do you think about that play? Do you think it relates to your peers' lives? Is it realistic to you? How does it touch people's lives?

JEN: To me it's realistic because it is people out there who will help people who is doing bad on the streets. And to me, it helps others because they'll know that maybe there is somebody out there who cares. Because some people don't even know why they doing this or that.

ACT 3, SCENE 2: "Prove Them Wrong"

MAISHA: What do you think about returning to the RYDC to perform this play?

JEN: It's going to be crazy because I'd never think I'd be able to go to [the detention center] without having to wear that uniform.

MAISHA: What do you think the girls will get from seeing you?

JEN: They be like, "Wow, she was in here the same place I'm in now. But now she's standing in front of us doing the show." I think the [junior correctional officers] will be happy for me.

MAISHA: Can you relate to *Meditations of the Heart*?

JEN: I can really relate because I play a girl who wanted—well, she didn't want to be there, but she's like not like the other girls talking about they man and stuff. But that's not important to me right now, and that's how it is.

When I was locked up, like, my whole mind was focused on, "When I get out, I'ma do this and do this—I'm going to go back to school." I wasn't focused on no boys. I know can't nobody help me get out of there, so I was focused on what I would do to keep myself out of there.

MAISHA: If an administrator or, like, the boss person over the detention center said, "I don't think we should have this program anymore. We are going to cut funding," what would you say to someone like that?

JEN: I don't know really. But I know I would be mad. I would feel like that person is doubting me or whatever and then I [would] try to prove them wrong and stuff like that.

MAISHA: How? Tell me the things about the program that you could tell this person that would convince him or her that closing it or shutting down the program is a bad idea.

JEN: While we here, we are off the streets from doing wrong. We trying to learn stuff and do good. And then when we at home, we practicing. So we ain't got time to do nothing wrong.

MAISHA: Tell me about the Girl Time teachers. What are the qualities you appreciate in the teachers? What do you like about how the teachers work with you and what the teachers do? What stands out in your mind as being really great about the teachers?

JEN: They give you a lot of support. We could really be doing terrible and they be like, "It's okay, you got it." And that gets you up and keep you hyped. [They] still say, "No, you're doing great."

MAISHA: What does this opportunity mean to you at this point in your life? You've been out of the detention center since January, and you haven't been back. Why is it important to have [Girl Time] in your life right now?

JEN: Because it's keeping me focused and busy. And I'm gonna be able to send a message out to other young females.

Listening to Jen helped me begin to understand how hard girls in the foster care and juvenile justice systems worked to prove to others that they were deserving, worthy, and valuable. I dared to imagine what their lives would look like if they did not have to worry so much about what others thought. Growing, maturing, becoming wiser is difficult enough; however, if you are doing this in the context of always having to seek others' approval or making up time, then the task can seem Herculean. In the midst of all that the girls in the summer program had to consider—when and if they would go home, educational opportunities, housing, families—they found this corner of the world where they could play, pretend, imagine, and experience the satisfaction of producing something that touched other people's lives. In the fourth and final act, you meet Rae, who, like Jill, felt strongly that girls were often seen but not heard. While the act is short, Rae's responses were both thoughtful and compelling.

ACT 4, SCENE 1: "People Don't Listen to Girls" —Rae

In this last act, Rae opens up about her family, her roles in the plays in which she was cast, and how she relates to the characters she plays. Rae's brevity captures her personality; she is always brief and straightforward. Watching her on stage was such a joy; she emerged from this petite frame as her character and filled up the room with her words. School was "boring" for this student artist who preferred to draw (she shared her portfolio with teaching artists and other student artists) and to write her autobiography. Rae also disclosed that the Girl Time summer "interrupted" her writing process, as she had plans to do some writing the week of rehearsal. She brought countless pages of her autobiography to a rehearsal and my nervous researcher self asked her if she wanted help scanning it or making copies so that it was in multiple places, but she declined my offer. I cannot say I blamed her, as she lost so much in moving around, she wanted to literally hold on to these pages.

MAISHA: Where did you begin your autobiography?

RAE: It started when I was younger. I had a house fire. It was my sister's birthday—I forget which one. We was poor, so we was all in the closet and my
   brother had some change so we went to the store and bought a twenty-five-
   cent cake. We had a candle, and we was all singing happy birthday in a little
   bitty closet, and we were gonna give my sister her present. So my sister had

the candle, and she got scared and dropped it on the tire. She dropped it on the bike tire. As [the fire] got bigger, she got scared and pushed me in the fire and ran out and shut me in the closet. And my brother came back to get me.

MAISHA: Wow. So you all go out safely?

RAE: Yeah.

MAISHA: So you start your autobiography with that story. If I'm reading it, I'm immediately going to be into it. I bet it's really going to hold the attention of your readers.

Rae talked a great deal about her family dynamics, which I will not discuss in this chapter. However, what I found compelling is the way she talked about her pastor who owned the group home where she lived and the daycare center where she worked. Rae's pastor was helping her train for a Breast Cancer Walk and supported her in every way possible. Rae was playing the lead character in *Hi, My Name Is Mariah*, and talked about this role.

RAE: [My character] Mariah got put out when she was fourteen, and I got put out when I was thirteen. So I connected with that. She is like a prostitute and had to do whatever she had to do to survive. She was out there, and she wound up pregnant. So she wanted to shape her life for her baby. She tried, and it wasn't working. She ran into a giant—which was the drugs—and she couldn't handle it, so she lost her baby [to the system]. Then a social worker helped her get [her life together].

MAISHA: Why do you think this story is an important story to tell?

RAE: I think it's important for the parents to understand what the kids go through when they put them out. And [it's important] for some people who just don't know.

MAISHA: Why is it important for people who just don't know?

RAE: They won't judge us when they see us out there. They'll try to help. Try to bring us out of something.

A dialogue about judgment ensued and Rae continued to talk more about her family.

ACT 4, SCENE 2: "Letting Go of Their Hurt"

MAISHA: Tell me this, if someone who was in charge of the detention center, like the administrator, said, "You know, this Girl Time program is a waste of time and money. We are gonna cut it back. These girls are in trouble anyway so they don't deserve to have anything like this, so we are just cutting this—"

RAE: I would say they don't understand. It helps them a lot. This is [girls'] way of letting go of their hurt and putting it into something they're proud of. Moving on from whatever they been through because they put the hurt out.

MAISHA: Help them how?

RAE: It helps them move on and grow up and be a different person.

MAISHA: But how? I'm pushing you on purpose here.

RAE: It helps them get over whatever they been through. To let them know that they have a voice and they can be heard.

MAISHA: When you say voice, what do you mean?

RAE: Because to me, people don't listen to girls. And to see that a girl wrote [a play] is giving them the power to speak up and people are actually listening.

MAISHA: Why do you think people don't listen to girls?

RAE: Because they don't take them seriously. And lots of girls doubting themselves. Like confidence is low and girls have a lot of issues and we need to be taken seriously.

MAISHA: What are the qualities [Girl Time teachers] have that you like, and how are the relationships with Girl Time teachers either the same as, or different from, other teachers in your life?

RAE: It's about the same because everybody, mostly adults, are always trying to push me to do my best, and that's important to me. All of them try to make us better than what we are when we first began to do plays. They want us to have the confidence and not to give up. I really like [Girl Time] because I'm gonna put it in my book. I think it could be a whole chapter!

MAISHA: We get a chapter? Wow! That's great.

Rae was able to articulate precisely what it was about playwriting and performing that helped her and some of her peers generate goals and objectives for their very near futures. Because of the nature of our relationship, Rae allowed me to ask several follow-up "how" questions and specifically how participation in Girl Time provided girls with the support they needed and deserved. Rae said it best: "This is girls' way of letting go of their hurt and putting it into something they're proud of."

EPILOGUE

There is something that theater people get. It is something that I wish I had known when I was alone in my classroom and that I now pass on to preservice teachers in schools and educators in out-of-school contexts. Girl Time student artists and teaching artists taught me that ensemble building, playwriting, and performing are humanizing processes for girls who have been moved around in the juvenile justice and child welfare systems. Taraji, Jill, Jen, and Rae teach all of us that girls have the power to speak up in spite of hurt, silencing, and oppression in various forms. They teach us that with a dedicated community of women who make space for them to own their work as artists, the girls can take it from there.

However, they also teach us that many resources and stakeholders must work together on the girls' behalf. It is not enough to have the space for art; nor is it enough to have the space only for education and schooling. It is not a coincidence that girls are writing poems, plays, and autobiographies at the tender age of sixteen; in many cases, their lives are full of experiences that reach beyond the realm of childhood. The fragmentation of services for girls in juvenile and foster care services must cease; many hands of healing, including the girls' hands, are needed in this work. In a new documentary *Sing Your Song*, which details the journey of Harry Belafonte as a singer, a performer, and an activist, the final scenes show Belafonte in juvenile justice facilities or jails for children trying to make sense of how much work was still ahead for the civil rights movement, with so many black and brown youth behind bars. Using his star power, Belafonte hosts a forum to call attention to the juvenile and criminal justice systems. Ruby Dee, an actor and activist, passionately approaches the microphone and asks, "What is my assignment? I come to so many things like this, and I leave without an assignment. What is my assignment?"

Everyone needs an assignment when it comes to disrupting the school-prison nexus for girls in the foster care system and other vulnerable girls. *Everyone* includes teachers, schools, parents, the juvenile justice and foster care systems, and the girls themselves. Jill and Rae teach us that most of the work is listening to girls. Girls will tell us what we need to know about how to best support them. We also learn from Taraji and Jennifer that the experience of writing and seeing this writing performed can be liberating and powerful.

Appendix

Trouble in Castlehood,
by Taraji, Lea, and Maya

CHARACTERS

Kevin and Devin, twin brothers who are dragons

Mafia Dragon

SCENE 1: A Room in the Castle Hood, NYC

Kevin: What's up, bro'?

[*They share a secret claw shake.*]

Devin: Nothing, chillin'. Chillin', ya know, hangin' out in the NYC Castle
Hood. Oh man, my scales are fallin' off.

Kevin: What ya been doin'?

Devin: Man, what ya talkin' about? I told ya, I just been chillin' with my
dragon boys.

Kevin: Then why you flexin'?

Devin: Nobody flexin', I'm just telling you the truth.

[*Devin's phone rings.*]

Devin: Hello? Don't worry about it. I got it. I got it!

[*Devin hangs up the phone.*]

Kevin [*looks at Devin funny*]: Who was that on the scale phone?

Devin: Nobody important.

KEVIN: Why you sweatin'? You know you can tell your brother anything.

DEVIN [*with attitude*]: If I wanted to tell you something, I would tell you.

KEVIN: Why you getting an attitude?

DEVIN: I hate people getting in my business! [*DEVIN walks out.*]

SCENE 2: Devin's Room in the Castle Hood

KEVIN: There's something suspicious about him and that dragon call. I'm
gonna look under his rock and see what I can snoop out and find. [*KEVIN
looks around; searches under his brother's rock and finds something.*]

KEVIN: What is that? [*Pulls out what he has found; looks surprised.*] It's a
rockspence! I can't believe my brother would do something like this!
[*Smoke comes out his nose; fire comes out of his mouth.*]

[*DEVIN enters. He catches KEVIN searching his rock. Both have shocked and
angry looks on their faces.*]

DEVIN [*gasps*]: Huuh!

SCENE 3: Two Days Later, Devin and Kevin on the Street

[*Enter MAFIA DRAGON.*]

MAFIA DRAGON [*to DEVIN*]: You better have my golden pesos in three days or
I'll jump you and skin your scales. I'll take your wings so you won't be able
to fly!

[*DEVIN breaks down.*]

KEVIN: You better get out of this!

DEVIN: I can't! There's only two things I can do: get the mafia dragons their
golden pesos or we can jump them before they jump us.

KEVIN: *We*??? Hold up, lil dragon boy! Since when did I come into this?

DEVIN: I thought we was bros and dragon boys for life.

KEVIN: Whooaa . . . hold on. We are but smugglin' dragonspence and owing
golden pesos to the mafia dragons, the biggest drug dragons in the Castle
Hood? I'm not down with all that.

DEVIN: Well, you won't necessarily be in this situation; you'll just give me the
golden pesos. You'll be helping me out of the situation.

KEVIN: Do I look like the Castle Bank to you?

DEVIN: Well, since you don't want to give me the golden pesos, then I'm just going to have to jump them before they jump me.

KEVIN: Oh no, you not going anywhere by yourself. There's more of them than there is of you. You have a baby dragon to tend to.

DEVIN: Just a minute ago you said you didn't want any part of this, and now you're all in it and all for it. What happened to you? Did a goddess strike you?

KEVIN: I just don't wanna come to your fire-breathing funeral. I love you, lil' dragon bro. We are twins and have been flying by each other for eighteen decades. We are a good dragon team and we're gonna stick together whether it's a negative or a positive goal.

[*Suddenly, we hear a loud banging of thunder; the gate at the drawbridge crashes down!*]

KEVIN and DEVIN [*together*]: Dragon brothers unite! [*They do the secret claw shake again.*] Flames of Fire, activate!

THE END

Play reprinted with permission.

4

Representing Self Through Media

Supporting Transitions to College with Digital Self-Representations

Michelle B. Bass and Erica Rosenfeld Halverson

And also just like the connection that everybody had with each other, I really liked that. I don't know, I thought of it as a family away from family because I couldn't be with my real family, my blood family, so it was kind of like another family.

—CHRIS, INTERVIEW WITH AUTHORS, APRIL 2011

CHRIS WAS A STUDENT in our freshman seminar, Representing Self Through Media: A Personal Journey Through *This American Life*, at University of Wisconsin–Madison. And like many students of color at our predominantly white university, he was required to enroll in a freshman program designed to make the college experience more accessible. But as Chris describes, the class was more than a requirement; it was another family. As Chris's words highlight, the freshman college classroom can be a powerful space to engage underrepresented young people in transformative pedagogical experiences. While these experiences are typically constructed in the context of the K–12 classroom, our work with a First-Year Interest

Group (FIG) program on a large midwestern college campus represents an effort to take the insights of scholars from this volume and from the field at large to the college classroom.[1] Our goal is to understand whether and how the production of digital representations of self, in this case digital radio episodes, improves learning for underrepresented student populations, specifically, students of color and first-generation college goers. Very little research has been done to identify the pedagogical experiences that support productive college transitions for these young people, despite continued inequities in college success and graduation rates for students of color.[2] We hope that this chapter begins to open up the conversation around transformative pedagogical practices in the college classroom.

To that end, we begin by first theorizing the transition to college and its importance for young people in general and for those who may lack support structures for college success in particular. We then describe how attention to digital media production processes creates a pedagogical space to explore the identity, transition, and experiences of nondominant students on campus. Finally, we explore some of the key features of our freshman seminar, focusing on Chris and how he experienced pedagogies of possibility in the college classroom.

COLLEGE AS A SITE FOR PEDAGOGIES OF POSSIBILITY

College is an institution that supports the development and understanding of emerging adulthood, a newer conceptualization of the extended transition between childhood and adulthood that has come to characterize many twenty-first-century societies.[3] College has long been considered a site of "institutionalized moratorium" for young people, a space where identity crises can be explored and resolved.[4] Philip and Barbara Newman stress the importance of choosing the right college, because it is here that youth's identity is shaped or because college at least serves as a safe place for figuring out who you want to be.[5] Indeed, the university setting is an "identity transforming one" where the individuals within it are "not yet likely to have fully established a viable adult identity."[6] Given the role that the college setting plays in identity transformation, we extend the reach of youth development to include college students, emerging adults in transition from childhood, and adolescence to adulthood. Specifically, we define *youth* as inclusive of adolescents through young adults, thirteen to twenty-three, from middle school through institutions of higher education, including universities and community colleges.

THE COLLEGE TRANSITION AND MINORITY STUDENT POPULATIONS

The transition to college is an important developmental milestone for all students; this period is especially important for young people who are more likely to struggle in the college environment. Such youth include students from low-income families, racial and ethnic minority students, and first-generation college goers. These students often experience a disconnect between their college and noncollege lives, making persistence difficult.[7] Specifically, there is a strong correlation between a student's family income and his or her college completion; currently, fewer than half of the African American students who enter college complete their degree within six years.[8] In this chapter, we share how the participation by one black male youth, Chris, in our freshman seminar exemplifies the opportunities for self-expression and reflection created by engaging in a pedagogy of possibility in the transition to college.

Many college communities have responded to the challenges of a student's entering, completing, and succeeding in college with the development of supportive transition programs. In transitional experiences, students explore what it means to be college students and to define who they are. While programs such as these have been around since the 1970s, very little attention has been paid to understanding how the programs help traditionally marginalized student populations.[9] Meanwhile, emerging research has demonstrated that participation in artistic production supports positive identity development for traditionally marginalized groups. Specifically, autobiographical art helps adolescents explore their own identities in the face of their traditionally stigmatized identities.[10] Furthermore, artistic production supports both individual and collective conceptions of identity, opening up the possibility that multiple models for development can be accommodated within the same type of instructional setting, an important feature for learning environments that hope to include students from a variety of home communities and to facilitate positive developmental trajectories.[11]

DIGITAL MEDIA PRODUCTION AND IDENTITY IN THE CLASSROOM

Digital art-making is a fundamentally representational practice—the digital media that youth create should serve as an expanded way to learn about how young people represent their own identity and experiences. Digital media literacy as a social practice enables young people to "embrace multimodal forms, combining, and remixing visual images and video clips, words, sounds and songs, dance and gesture, and costume . . . [and use] their bodies as canvases in communication and self expression."[12] The task for adolescent literacy researchers and practitioners is to create "culturally responsive pedagogy" to "shake things up [in their teaching] in ways that still uphold rigor and excellence."[13] It is up to students and teachers to codesign their own multimodal worlds.

Digital media production has become an essential outlet for many adolescents to think about and represent their changing identity as they progress from adolescence to adulthood. Many young people make this transition in a collegiate environment. While the literature chronicling new college students' participation in digital media literacy and production activities is limited, the literature on out-of-school media production organizations that work with adolescents aged fourteen to twenty shows the value of these opportunities for empowering young people through digital media literacy.[14]

In our work, we used radio as the digital production medium for the Representing Self Through Media course. The use of radio as a digital medium for young people to represent themselves has been studied almost exclusively in out-of-school settings, with a focus on middle school and high school students.[15] In radio production, they are empowered to express ideas that matter to them and to bring these issues to a public audience.[16] Through the process, young people learn valuable literacy skills, most notably the ability to monitor the quality of their own work through critique.[17]

One way to turn an explicit focus toward identity in the college setting is to construct an environment where students can share their personal stories. hooks notes that the telling and sharing of stories of personal experience can provide a meaningful context for students from underrepresented groups to connect to an academic context.[18] However, when stories are represented in a traditional academic text based mode, it may "alienate most folks who are not also academically trained and reinforces the notion that the academic world is separate from real life."[19] Author bell hooks reminds us that we have choices when we represent self: we choose our audience, which voices to share, which voices to silence, and the language and mode of representation. The choices of representation for today's young people, regardless of their status as underrepresented or in the majority culture, are not limited to traditional academic texts. They have available to them an arsenal of new digital media technologies to make artistic meaning and present their identity to any audience they choose.

In analyzing our freshman seminar course, we explore the pedagogy associated with digital art production, with a focus on how these pedagogical practices affect students of color and first-generation college goers. The research on the use of digital art production in college settings is sparse. We hope that a focus on the course as it directly relates to the identity development and artistic self-expression of underrepresented students demonstrates the value of digital media production in institutions of higher education.

THE COURSE AND THE PARTICIPANTS

Our freshman seminar was part of the First-Year Interest Group program at the University of Wisconsin–Madison. FIGs are "learning communities of about 20 students who are enrolled in a cluster of three classes that are linked by a common theme."[20] Throughout the ten-year existence of the FIG program at this large midwestern university, students who have participated in the program have demonstrated higher GPAs and higher student satisfaction than their non-FIG peers.[21] The university is predominantly white, and the FIG program targets underrepresented student populations to enroll in its courses; however, FIG courses are open to all incoming first-year students at the university. Students select from among forty unique FIG course sequences during their summer orientation session. Many students—including Chris and several others in our seminar—are required to enroll in a FIG experience because of their participation in a summer bridge or student support program. As a result, students of color and first-generation college students are overrepresented in FIG courses, though their academic accomplishments are comparable to the broader student population.

All of our students were traditional college freshmen at the time of the study and were eighteen years old when the course started in September 2010. Of the nineteen participants, five identified as first-generation college students. The breakdown of students' self-identification of ethnicity was as follows: two black, one Hispanic or Latino, five "other" (e.g., multiracial or multiple ethnic identifications), and eleven white. Ethnic minorities comprised 37 percent of the class and constituted a much larger percentage than the overall 11 percent at the university.

REPRESENTING SELF THROUGH MEDIA

The learning goals of the course were defined in terms of both theory and practice. The course covered three topics: identity, literacy, and representation. For identity, we explored both sociological and psychological constructs. We took a new literacies approach to the study of literacy, focusing on both a paradigmatic and an operational shift from traditional conceptions of literacy.[22] Holistically, we considered literacy a situated practice within the contexts in which ideas are produced, where meanings are not fixed but rather constructed through interactions between people and tools. Operationally, we discussed literacy as moving beyond the ability to read and write text, but rather as inclusive of all available media forms that convey images and hold meaning.

Finally, we used representation as a bridging concept between identity and literacy, focusing on the role of external representations in the development of meaning, specifically how different tools for representation afford communication of meaning. The practice-based component of the course involved the creation of a representational identity piece as a radio show in the style of National Public Radio's *This American Life*. Each episode of *This American Life* airs stories grouped around a theme; the producers describe the format as a "movies for radio" approach rather than a news or talk show format.[23] Students participated in a complementary small seminar course focused on radio production, which afforded them the opportunity to focus on the technical skills necessary for their piece's creation.

Chris as a Case Study

Chris's experiences are nested in a larger research study that explored how the Representing Self Through Media seminar affected the students' transition to college.[24] In this chapter, we take an intrinsic case study approach, focusing on Chris's experiences in the seminar and the radio piece that he produced.[25] Using observational data, interviews, and a multimodal analysis of Chris's radio piece, we aim to paint a picture of Chris's engagement with issues of personal identity in the freshman college classroom.[26] Our goal here is not to use Chris as representative of the experience in our class; nor is it to speak to the experience of African American male students on our campus. Rather, we aim to highlight how the course engaged Chris in conversations about race and class on the college campus, how these issues are connected to his emerging sense of self, and how digital media production afforded exploration and representation.

Chris is from a large urban metropolis outside Wisconsin. He is also a first-generation college student and the son of immigrants from Jamaica. Chris initially reported his ethnic identity as black, but then changed his self-report to Jamaican American at the end of the semester. Perhaps connected to this change, the radio piece Chris produced for the class placed a heavy focus on his Jamaican identity and how his parents' journey to America has allowed him to become the strong, independent man he is today. Growing up in a predominantly black urban neighborhood, Chris was a member of the majority population. It was not until he began high school at a private school that his ethnic identity as a black man became a significant marker. Similarly, at the university, Chris's ethnic identity placed him distinctly in the minority of the student population. These changing identity markers were the subject of in-class discussions, his radio piece, and interviews conducted with Chris outside the classroom.

THE IMPORTANCE OF CLASSROOM CONVERSATIONS

Since the course had both theoretical and practical goals, most of the classroom discussions addressed the relationship between theories presented in the course readings and the creation of multimodal representations of self. One conversation in particular stood out for its power to engage students in the relationship between race, class, and personal and social identity. Late in the semester, we engaged in a class session titled "What's so bad about stereotype?" To prepare for the discussion, the class read Nicole Fleetwood's "Authenticating Practices: Producing Realness, Performing Youth," which explores the challenges of representing real youth voice in the context of guided media production.[27] One of us (Erica) began class by explaining why she had chosen the reading and by providing guiding questions:

> I think Fleetwood raises a lot of interesting issues about representation and what makes a representation real . . . If you're making a piece of art that is supposed to be about personal experience, what makes that experience real? How do you understand the realness of that experience?[28]

The main thrust of the initial conversation involved describing normative and non-normative populations, and whether highlighting minority groups as "non-normative" exacerbates their isolation or helps shed light on existing inequities. Bryan, a young man who identified as Mexican

American, described a situation on campus where an invitation to represent the campus in photos was sent to a campus group composed predominantly of students of color:

> They wanted to take a picture of this group at school . . . a very diverse group. The e-mail said, "Come to these three points at these three times. We want to take a picture representing the university," and that does not represent the university at all. In that situation, their obligation is to tell the people who are receiving this picture, this is not what campus is like . . . The e-mail never said a representation of the group; it said a representation of campus.

Stephanie, a multiracial young woman, commented that the e-mail made her angry: "They are just trying to show, 'Hey, we have people of color!'" Maggie, a white middle-class student, shared a similar situation. Her Catholic high school tried to make sure a certain number of students of color were in photos in the school's brochure.

Seeing that the class seemed to be agreeing on the impropriety of the photo, Erica presented a counterargument:

> To be fair, part of the argument is, if we just take a random picture of white people on campus, that doesn't capture the scope of the experience, because there are lots of different kids of color on this campus. This room is relatively multicolored compared to the broad array of color on campus. I have also walked into rooms of a whole lot of white people. Which is the truer representation of folks on campus? Are we just keeping up with the dichotomy? . . . Are we just perpetuating it?

At this point Chris, the only black male in the class, said that he supported the idea of a photo that targets minority students:

> They are just trying to attract more students of different backgrounds. Not anything wrong with that personally. If you are just taking pictures, they see pictures of white people all the time, but when they see a group of people of minorities, they think there are minorities here. If you want

to find out the statistic, you can go online. If you see diverse people, it will draw or attract more diversity. By them taking that picture, it appeals to someone who is searching for school.

Chris also argued that the university needed to place a caption under the picture, which led the discussion back to the idea of representation and how different media affords varied tools for representation. Another white male student pushed back, asking if it was honest to try to attract minority groups by using a picture of minority students. Chris reiterated the importance of the words or the statement the university put under the picture: "If they are saying that this is what the university represents, that is not true. But if they put it with a group of other pictures, they are being true, saying that there is more than one race at this school—that there is a big group of minority students."

Chris's strong position on the importance of including a picture with minority students as part of the representation of the student body at the university may have stemmed from his transition from primary to secondary school, where he went from being in a school that was "all black with just one or two white people in the whole school" to a high school where there were multiple races and "twenty percent of the high school was black."[29] While Chris was no longer in the majority at his high school, "it was enough. There were enough black people there where I didn't feel like I was an outcast or just like I was alone. I just felt like there were other people there that I could communicate to."[30]

Erica continued the class discussion by talking about truth statements, particularly the idea that "kids of color on this campus prefer experiences with other kids of color because it makes them feel more at home." Noting that this observation is not true for all students of color (though it holds for many), Erica asked the class, "When we are talking about reality, what do we do with a statement like this?" The students of color in the class represented these differing perspectives. Sarah, a young African American woman, remarked that she did not want "to be on black-people island for all four years," while Stephanie, who is multiracial, represented the other side. She said that the group being represented in the picture is "a place for minority students" who see it as their "home." All three of these young people—Sarah, Stephanie, and Chris—describe the relationship between their personal racial identity and the representation of students of color on campus. Informed by their varied backgrounds with other young people of color—Chris grew up in a predominantly black neighborhood, Stephanie and Sarah did not—conversations such as these afforded opportunities for a mixed classroom to openly discuss how minority students are represented on a predominantly white campus and how students can challenge these representations in their own work. These nuanced understandings of the relationship between race or ethnicity and representation made their way into many students' final pieces and into the students' reflections on the pieces.

THE PRODUCTION PROCESS AS A SPACE FOR EXPLORING IDENTITY

Against a backdrop of readings by Fleetwood and by Vivian Chávez and Elisabeth Soep, conversations such as the one recounted above, and opportunities to reflect on these ideas in written responses, students were asked to create radio pieces in the style of *This American Life*. The task was to explore and represent their personal identities in the productions. While the theme for the pieces was left open, many students chose to engage in explorations of their race, ethnicity, social class, or sexuality as influenced by their course readings and in-class discussions about identity. Chris's story about his parents was featured in an episode titled "The American Dream"; he focused on how his parents' immigration from Jamaica to the United States shaped the lives of their children, especially, Chris.

To unpack Chris's representational choices, we analyze his use of the medium's modal features, which for radio include dialogue, soundtrack, tone, and timbre. Producers need to choose not only the individual features but also how these features interact with one another and what is created as a result of their interaction.[31] Andrew Burn and David Parker make this interaction concrete, calling it the *kineikonic mode*, "literally, the mode of the moving image."[32] While in radio there is no moving image on a screen, the ways the modes, or features, of the radio piece interact can, and should, create a visual story for the listener. The kineikonic mode best describes how meaning is made when elements are combined in specific and deliberate ways.[33]

Chris's production experience exemplifies the role of multimodal production in exploring and representing issues of identity. He used the kineikonic mode, in particular the interaction between dialogue and song lyrics, to represent his parents' Jamaican identity and his own Jamaican American identity. Using the lyrics of Bob Marley, Jamaica's musical bard, Chris wove a connective thread throughout his piece as complements to his spoken-word poetry messages of thanks, interviews with his parents discussing Marley lyrics and their importance in their lives, and informal sing-alongs. The interaction between the dialogue and lyrics created for the listener Chris's desire to represent himself as a young man with utmost respect for his parents' American dream and how their dream has allowed him to live his own American dream.

Chris knew which part of his identity he wanted to discuss in his radio piece from the first assignment, the initial story idea. He posted on the learning management system (LMS) site a post titled "My Parents' Success Story":

> I look to up to my parents as my heroes, as do a lot of kids, but not just because of everything that they have done for me in my life and the things that they have given me but for the many things they had to overcome in order for me to be where I am at today. My parents are immigrants from Jamaica. They both are from a family of 10. The way that they were raised they had to do things on there [sic] own since they were little kids. They did not really have any role models to help them. All they had were there [sic] brothers and sisters. They did not have as many opportunities as I did growing up. They came here to America just so that me, my brother,

and sisters do not have to go through the same problems that they had to go through. I would like to tell there [sic] story and how I was raised, leading up to me being who I am today.

Chris met with his peers as the group-episode decision progressed, but he maintained the message of thanks and understanding that he wanted to express to his Jamaican parents in his story throughout. In an editing session leading up to his group's final episode presentation, Chris and one of us (Michelle) discussed some of his representational choices:

The reason why I put the thank you at the beginning is because mine is more on how my parents influence me. Like the whole central theme is the American dream. Mine more is how my parents influenced me, what they've gone through to make my American dream. Like, I'm not going to say directly what my American dream is. But it's like how my parents had an American dream when they came here and how they influenced me to just become the person who I am.[34]

Chris does indeed open and close his story with a thank you to his parents for giving him the ability to make his own American dream, with a special focus on his connection to his Jamaican identity. However, it is not just Chris who tells the story. He is aided by the lyrics of Bob Marley.

[*The song "Buffalo Soldier," performed by Bob Marley and the Wailers, plays, and* Chris *starts humming along.*]

Chris: *Dreadlock Rasta* . . . I remember as a kid, we'd be driving in the car, and you guys would play this song so much and sing along off-key. At first I didn't want to, but then I joined in to sing with you guys. I never really understood, though, why you played this song so much back then. I always remember having a good time mumbling the words and trying to sing along. But then I matured a little more, I then realized you guys both wanted me to be sure that I never forget that I was a Jamaican. And the Jamaican roots that are inside of me will help to make me a stronger person mentally, and they have made me the person who I am today, and who I will one day become. Thank you.

[*Chris's father sings along to "Three Little Birds," as Chris and his dad share laughs.*]

"Buffalo Soldier," with its familiar, but slightly incongruous, mixture of cheerful Jamaican syncopation and sorrowful lyrics about African slaves being brought to the Americas, continues to play in the background as Chris speaks.

While it is technically well-balanced and does not interfere with the listener's understanding of Chris's dialogue, Bob Marley's music and lyrics help the listener appreciate how influential Jamaica, his parent's journey to America, and Marley's music itself, have been to Chris's identity as a Jamaican living in America. His parents have worked hard to provide a good life for their children since their arrival in the United States, and it is this hard work that Chris wants to acknowledge and thank them for in his piece.

In between his monologues at the beginning and end of his piece, we hear selections of interviews Chris had with his parents. They share stories about growing up in Jamaica, their decision to move to America, and how they tried to raise Chris and his siblings so that their children could have an easier life than they had. The conversation is always interspersed with Marley's music, with Chris using lyrics to emphasize a point from their stories or to share his revelation about the songs' message.

In the opening interview segment, Chris's mom and dad tell him Marley's songs "always have a message." Chris asks his parents if Marley's songs have touched them in some way. His mother replies, "Yes, especially the song about emancipate yourself from mental slavery. If you listen to his song closely, there is always some type of message, one love, you know. Or no woman no cry." In the most familiar version of "No Woman, No Cry" the song starts with the audience and Marley singing together the opening words "No woman, no cry."

Chris's mom and dad share memories of their childhood and playing outside in the hot Jamaican climate. His mom recalls:

> We were poor, but we were proud. If we didn't have, we'd do without. We wouldn't go begging to other people, but we'd work to achieve whatever we have and they [her parents] always stressed the importance of education to better ourselves.

The emphasis on education and emancipating the self from mental slavery is reiterated in "Redemption Song," which plays after this interview segment.

Chris then includes his parents' discussion of why they came to America. His dad speaks about the financial influence:

> Some people I know, they leave to come to America; they said it's a great country. You can work hard and make some more money than working in Jamaica and make the money. So that's why I really come to America. And I understand that a lot of people come to this country because it's a better country and to work, [make] money.

Chris's dad was sponsored to become a U.S. resident following an apprenticeship in the jewelry business. Because his parents were married, Chris's mother was "part of the package." They had two children in America, and then his mother went back to school, she explains, "'cause I figure with education you can go as far—the sky was the limit. And you can achieve anything you put your mind to." Chris explicitly asks his parents about their American dreams, to which his dad responds, "Money." His mom says it's to work hard to make a better life for herself, her children, and her relatives in Jamaica. Chris asks if their dreams are still the same after living in this country for more than half their lives. His dad responds that he has worked hard "trying to make you guys [his family, specifically his children] happy, send you to school and whatever it is. Try to make some money to make life easier, and that's about it, really." His mother's dream is very similar to her original one, though she is now more focused on her children's happiness and success:

> Mom: My American dream now is to see—hope—that I have planned or set the foundation for my children so that they can achieve anything they want in life and they'll have a better life than I did. Money isn't the total driver here. I just want you guys to be happy.
>
> Dad: Right.
>
> Mom: In whatever you do.

His parents go on to talk about their American dreams when they came to the United States as young people: Chris's father's dream was economically focused, and his mother's was centered on giving her children a chance at a better life than what she had. Chris closes his piece with a statement of gratitude and love for the opportunity to live out his own American dream as a result of theirs from so many years ago:

> Mom and Dad, you know what? I love you. I know this might be stupid, but it's something that I never say. You always say how strong Jamaican men are, so I don't want to come off as weak by saying this, but you always want the best for me. As a child, I never realized how much you guys sacrificed and how stressful life really was for us, because you worked so hard to make sure we didn't notice. You were living a stressful life just for us, just for me. I never realized that Bob Marley's words are not just words, but it's about the blood flowing through our veins, helping me to survive, and live life with the traits, morals, and values that you have instilled within me. I no longer mumble these words to the songs that helped you get over tribulations and the homesickness. Because they now help me get over the difficult times that I am having in my life. I know that you don't approve everything that I do in life, Mom and Dad. But I want you to know that I will not let you down. With my American dream of being successful and having a happy life, derived from your American dream of your children having an easier life than you had, I am now the Buffalo Soldier with the Emancipated Soul living life Jammin'.

The opening chords of "Jammin'" then lead us out of Chris's piece. While his piece was focused by the episode's theme of the American dream, Chris's story had the added thread of thanks and understanding of how his parent's American dreams allow him to be living his. He uses the words of Bob Marley to show the listener that songs can be more than just melodies; they can hold the messages that support dreams generations over. Chris's use of monologue, interviews, and song lyrics in combination is just one example of how the kineikonic mode was used to create meaning through purposeful interactions between modes for representation in students' radio pieces in the Representing Self Through Media course.

THE COLLEGE CLASSROOM, TRANSITION, AND PEDAGOGIES OF POSSIBILITY

Course experiences like Representing Self Through Media are part of the emerging movement to design for pedagogies of possibility. By working at the intersection of identity, literacy, and representation, the class focused on why making autobiographical art matters and the theories behind the creation and sharing of digital representations of self. Through this focus, we asked students to embrace "an inherent creativity in the ways in which people use and do literacy, which, rather than being decried as a loss of standards, can be embraced as the achievements of people making meaning for themselves and others in their lives."[35] We were especially interested in how embracing multimodal forms of communication and destabilizing the relationship between codified knowledge and students' experiences could support students who may feel marginalized by the university academic context. Many students, Chris included, felt that we accomplished this goal.

Many scholars have demonstrated that schools are not organized for the broad-scale adoption of digital media-rich pedagogical practices. School environments have not yet changed to accommodate "the evolution of new technologies, geographies, and communicative modes" that young people use in their out-of-school lives.[36] Furthermore, most school-based production practices continue to focus on single-mode communication and top-down structures for teaching and learning rather than embracing "a world replete with multimodal text, remixing and mashing, and fluid novice–expert relations."[37] Most research on the experiences of minority students in university settings focuses on students' acceptance and retention rates. However, very little research examines the black box between the first day of college and graduation day. Differences between high school and college for all students include dramatic changes in the relationship between students and teachers, in expectations for work, and in intellectual development. Moreover, most young people are experiencing their first significant separation from family and, importantly, from the role of child; it should be no wonder, therefore, that the transition from high school to college is a difficult one.[38] As a result it is crucial to provide opportunities in the freshman year to explicitly attend to transition and identity development, especially for underrepresented students, who often lack positive experiences with respect to their minority status at this transition time.[39]

While support for the positive identity development of these students needs to be addressed at all levels of the education system, our particular interest is the college classroom, specifically in courses targeted toward freshman students. Our focus on the creation of digital representations of self in a course using autobiographical digital art-making demonstrates that it is important to embrace a pedagogy of possibility in the college classroom through an explicit focus on the relationship between identity and narrative in the digital context.

5

Imaging and Reimaging Internships

Immigrant Youth, Community-Based Research, and Cultural Transformation

Lisa (Leigh) Patel and Alexander Gurn, with Melissa Dodd, Sung-Joon Pai, Vanessa Norvilus, Eun Jeong Yang, and Rocío Sanchez Ares

IN THIS ERA OF high-stakes testing, learning objectives, grade-level standards, and interventions are all tightly prescribed from the state down, with little room for mobilization of on-the-ground knowledge. In this chapter, we discuss how learning may be possible through imaging and reimaging the common school-based requirement of an internship in a professional setting. We provide glimpses into an internship project designed for critical consciousness and cultural transformation rather than assimilation. Our findings address how existing structures can be modified to manifest opportunities for cultural transformation.

We are meeting with a group of about thirteen high school seniors, all newcomer immigrant youth with fewer than four years in the United States, to discuss their second internship day. At one small table in the corner of the room, Pedro is talking with Emilio (both pseudonyms); both students are from the Dominican Republic.

"You have to show up on time," Pedro says. "No more getting lost. Por que le parece flojo y la doctora dice que no se puede continuar con eso." Pedro is admonishing Emilio for getting lost and showing up late to his first day of work at an internship with a local youth development organization. As Pedro exits the room, he nods to me, as if to say, *Don't worry, I got this. He's gonna be on time tomorrow.* "Hasta mañana, Dr. Patel. Gracias por todo."

If you had met Pedro in one of his classes in the all-immigrant high school, you would have found it incredulous that this seventeen-year-old would be the peer mentor in this situation, acting much like a big brother, reining in the practice of his peer, warning him not to fulfill the stereotype of a lazy kid, and invoking group responsibility. In school, Pedro rarely showed enthusiasm for his own work, let alone the performance of anyone else. He was frequently sullen in class and regularly disrespectful to teachers, particularly female teachers. He tended to only talk and hang out with other young men from Santo Domingo and often made fun of his peers. School leaders had tried to discern how much of Pedro's oppositional behavior in school was connected to his home life and relationship with his mother, whom he had been living with since having been separated from the rest of his family.

In essence, in school and at home, Pedro's behavior reflected the Western-based educational psychology literature that depicts adolescents as rebellious and experimental.[1] But in the internship meetings, he was a leader: respectful to himself and others, a regular contributor to the group. Pedro had, in essence, found a space where he didn't have to be just a student, just an English language learner, just an adolescent, and just rebellious. And not insignificantly, one of us (Leigh) did not have to be just a female whose authority was in question. When Leigh asked Pedro to take on additional responsibility and look after another male in the group, his chest almost literally swelled. He, in essence, rose to the challenge. Or seen from another perspective, the internship project rose to the challenge of providing a way for Pedro to be something other than a male student in need of remediation and discipline.

It was a shift similar to ones Gloria Ladson-Billings described in her classic book *The Dreamkeepers*, where she describes how providing an opportunity for students to be something other than rebellious often quickly changes the dynamics of how they interact.[2] However, in today's market-driven, high-stakes assessment arena, where essential life experiences like the arts and physical activity are casualties to the reign of simplistically assessed skills, creating spaces for young people to be anything other than students is increasingly a figment of imagination. More specifically, newcomer immigrant youth are often seen through a lens of educational policy, research, and practice or solely as English language learners, ones in need of intensive English-only and remediated instruction to pass the high-stakes assessments.[3] The cumulative effect of this educational arena is a bleak one for young people and teachers and rarely reflects the actual situation in professional workplaces.

In this chapter, we report on our efforts to reimage—not just imagine, but deliberately reimage and design—spaces where dynamic, multiply located, and differentially experienced transformation of self and collective can occur. We try to wedge a space in schooling where youth are seen as already skilled, where adults learn about youth other than their student skills, and where young people critically engage with race, capital, and status in society.[4] We describe key features of the design of the project, snapshots of transformation that occurred through the project, and implications for reimaging how educators can conceptualize transformative pedagogical spaces. To conduct this work, we reimaged a common practice of secondary and tertiary institutions: the internship. The contributors to this chapter include a university-based researcher, two graduate students, a volunteer mentor, a professional partner, a high school program leader, and a young immigrant. All of the contributors were intimately involved in the particular moments used in the chapter to illuminate some aspects of this internship project.

TOURO COLLEGE LIBRARY

BACKGROUND: INTERNSHIP PROJECTS, ADOLESCENTS, AND TRANSFORMATION

Internships are understood to be opportunities for high school and college students to increase their understanding of professional contexts, to build and extend social networks, and to investigate the attraction of particular career trajectories.[5] They are sometimes procured and coordinated by high school counselors, through formal programs supported by school and district offices, and even through private companies. One private company in the metropolitan area of Boston, for example, charges as much as $5,000 to place high school and college students in internships in high-status companies and organizations. According to its home Web page, the company offers "a competitive edge when applying to colleges and jobs, letters of recommendation, and a unique opportunity to 'try on' a career."[6]

In less affluent school contexts, the purpose of high school internships may well mimic the goals quoted above, but it typically centers on providing young people with exposure to the cultural and social capital found in contexts outside their school environments. Internships are meant to offer on-the-job training of professional skills, but sometimes have been criticized as yet another institution that tracks racial minority, low-income youth into service-based labor.[7] As one private-public jobs readiness partnership states in its mission statements, "early work experience is a critical factor in determining future success. Students who gain work experience during high school enjoy higher employment rates and earnings later in life. Additionally, these students stay in school, graduate high school, and enroll in college at higher rates than their peers. These benefits compound over a lifetime."[8]

Whether for profit or in the interest of exposing public school students to the cultural capital found in mainstream cultures, dominant cultures often have an intended purpose of assimilation. Members of nondominant cultures are meant to learn the practices, values, and attitudes of the dominant culture.

The goals of this project were to provide a set of experiences in professional settings where immigrant youth could better understand how they are positioned in society and speak back to that positioning. These goals are in active opposition to the research literature on immigrant youth and their social locations within mainstream schooling contexts, which generally falls under the language and conceptual framework of assimilation. Assimilation differs from acculturation, as the latter is defined as the exchange between, and acclimation of, two cultures. Assimilation also differs from transculturation, in which "members of subordinated or marginal groups select and invent from materials transmitted by a dominant or metropolitan culture," a concept first published by sociologist Fernando Ortiz in 1940.[9]

Although the research literature on migrants and societal attainment draws on the nomenclature of acculturation, the content of research scholarship about immigrants' acculturation tends to be teleological and assimilation-driven. This body of research tends to determine the level of immigrants' acculturation *to* the host culture without due attention to the acculturation that may be occurring *within* the host culture.[10] From this framing, the potential and actual impacts on the host culture are obscured, which renders invisible many possible and likely cultural transformations. Put another way, in this framing, only one of the populations in the contact zone between U.S.-born residents and immigrants is subject to measurements of assimilation, and there is little ability to even notice the acculturation occurring within, alongside, and in opposition to these assumptions of assimilation.

With this unidirectional outlook, the extant research literature on immigration is justifiably concerned with the factors most readily associated with societal stability and safety, so factors such as persistence, motivation, and the use of heritage languages are measured and discussed. Little attention is paid to how immigrants, particularly young immigrants, have unique skills developed through and because of their experiences.

This oversight of immigrants' skills and abilities is reflected not just in research literature but also in the daily realities of immigration that is defined heavily by hegemonic economic and political structures in the division of labor and power.[11] The recent waves of immigration from the global south to the north, which is reflected in the narratives of every youth involved in this project, have largely entrenched what geographer and environmental psychologist Cindi Katz refers to as the fractured, globalized capitalist market.[12] Katz contrasts this concept with the ubiquitous yet nebulous nomenclature of globalization. She explains that a fractured, globalized capitalist market readily connects those with high amounts of economic capital (corporation owners and shareholders), enabling expansion of their interests across nation-state borders. These connections facilitate the interests of corporations, and dredges along with those interests, the low-wage workers necessary to put pints of strawberries on gleaming shelves at purchase prices well below what living wages would reflect. From this perspective of global human capital, and the reductive spaces for young people in schools, short of an explicit and intentional reimaging of pedagogical spaces, immigrant youth are likely to follow in the neat trajectories of preexisting contact zones.

Mary Louise Pratt, in her 1991 address to the Modern Language Association, defined *contact zones* as "the social spaces where cultures meet, clash, and grapple with each other, often in contexts of highly asymmetrical relations of power, such as colonialism, slavery, or their aftermaths as they are lived out in many parts of the world today."[13] In this sense, we are all living in figurative and material contact zones, ones that have been indelibly touched by the histories and trajectories of more privileged cultures preserving domination by keeping less privileged cultures in those places. In the United States, Pratt's work has been most comprehensively taken up in the area of participatory action research. Maria Elena Torre, a scholar in this area, has extended Pratt's theories to frame research projects where very differently positioned youth and adults are able to experience and analyze power inequities, together.[14] In reimaging an internship experience for immigrant youth, the most pressing insight of Pratt's conceptual model of contact zones was not in the observation that these zones exist but that they all too often exist along neat lines of colonizer and colonized, of oppressor and oppressed. Minimally, we sought to agitate those contact zones for transformative purposes.

THE CRITICAL TRANSITIONS PROJECT: REIMAGING FOR TRANSFORMATION

In contrast to designing educational and learning experiences for immigrant youth for purposes of acculturation, our goals and practices worked actively to create spaces for the transformation of individuals, adult and young, and of groups. The internship project ran for three years in an urban center of the United States and involved roughly one hundred young people. The project was, at its most basic iteration, an extracurricular opportunity for immigrant youth to both participate in a professional internship and to have peer- and mentor-driven conversations about race, various forms of capital, and status in society.

During the internship project, high school seniors would report to a professional worksite one day a week instead of going to school, for approximately six weeks. Placements for the internships varied from for-profit businesses like real estate companies and Internet sales companies to government and nonprofit community-based organizations. After spending the morning at their internship sites, the students would rejoin as a group (about ten students at a time) in a nonschool space, such as a library, and we would engage in critical conversations about work, status, and privilege in society. In these breakdown afternoon meetings, we would share observations and stories from the internship sites and the adult mentors would use the cognitive and linguistic tools of critical pedagogy and critical race theory to interrogate individualistic explanations of how people attain status and what counts as success and intelligence.[15]

Different from mainstream internship projects, where the beginning, middle, and end responsibilities are only defined by mastery of professional workplace practices, the immigrant youth in the critical internship project also learned about the cultural, social, and economic capital mix that led to different career trajectories.[16] In parallel fashion, students interviewed and, in some cohorts, surveyed members of their families and communities about career pathways, status, success, capital across migrations, and, sometimes, specific social issues. For most of the authors in this chapter, the research inquiry focused on police interactions and policing in communities. This topic arose as one of many that were brainstormed about the problems and other issues experienced by immigrant youth. The facilitators and the rest of the group chose police interactions as the one topic that would be collectively investigated. To that end, the youth constructed questions and interviewed community members and police officers about law enforcement (see figures 5.1 and 5.2 for examples). This research component, in both its focus and its structure, marked the project as substantively different from mainstream internship projects, where the goal—an interaction with professional culture—is neither analyzed nor, consequently, considered a problem. In other words, our internship project was part of the base curriculum for our stance that involved critical problem posing and inquiry.

FIGURE 5.1

Brainstorm of possible interview questions for law enforcement officers and members of the general community

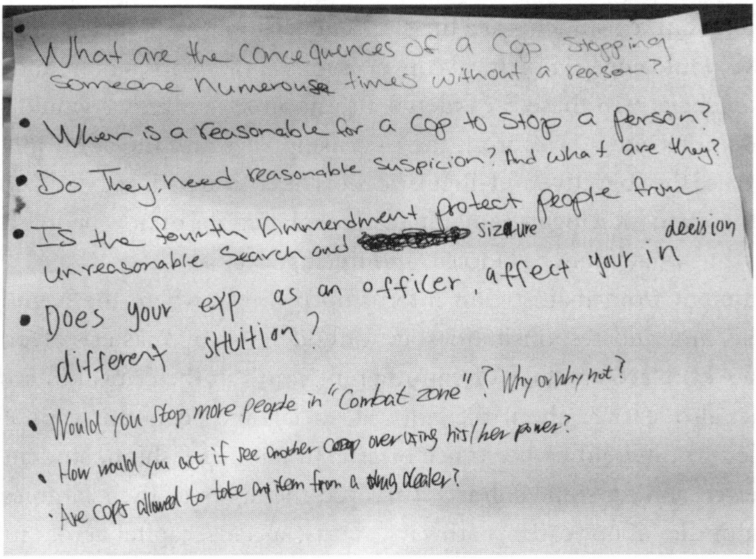

FIGURE 5.2

Brainstorm of possible interview questions for law enforcement officers and members of the general community

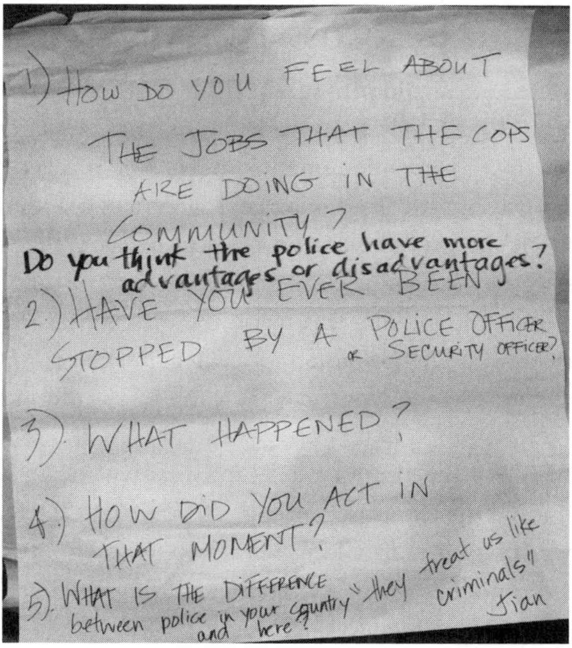

However, the internship project was not just about creating space for young immigrants to be exposed to dominant professional culture in the United States, but also for working adults in those cultures to come into contact with recently immigrated youth. From the onset, we wanted to provide working professional, largely U.S.-born and monolingual adults with an up-close experience with immigrant youth, in the hopes of improving interactions between people in different positions in society. In this way, the combined aspects of the internship, the breakdown afternoon sessions, and the necessary inclusion of partners beyond the school were our building blocks for creating a different kind of contact zone than just colonization. In the following section, we turn to experiences of the internship program through three perspectives, a young immigrant, her workplace mentor, and her high school administrator.

DYNAMIC LEARNING ACROSS PARTICIPANTS

Vanessa is a seventeen-year-old immigrant from Haiti. She has legal documentation to be in the United States—a situation that gives her a relative advantage over many of her undocumented peers. She was generally quiet in her classes and was not involved in any extracurricular activities. At the time of the project, she was a senior enrolled in a comprehensive public school and was seen by her counselors and teachers to be a good but not necessarily standout student. She was recommended to participate in the program by her counselor, who wanted to see her "pushed out of her comfort zone."[17] In Vanessa's own words, she is "kind of shy, don't like to talk too much."

At our first day-long meeting in a local university, Vanessa had significant difficulty finding the campus building where we had started the day's activities. She was texting and talking with one of us (graduate student Rocío), frustrated at not being able to find the building. Rocío remembered her discomfort upon her arrival to the college:

> She was wearing a hood and was waiting by the police station. She got frustrated because she could not find our building. I also remember how confident she felt later in the building when leading most of our discussion on racism and developing questions for the group to ask in their community and internship sites. On our last meeting, I talked to Vanessa, and asked her, "Remember the time we met at BC? I cannot believe you wanted to leave! You were mad at me even, remember?" She replied to me that she got a little frustrated because she's shy, but she said that she would have never left.

Vanessa went on to become a highly engaged member of the group, staying after the end of breakdown sessions to continue talking with adult mentors. She was eventually hired by one of us (Melissa), who had been her mentor where Vanessa had interned, and Vanessa continued working in Melissa's office. This office, part of the central administration of an urban school district, was responsible for envisioning and providing technological infrastructure and support to the district's educators. Melissa was the director of the office. From her perspective, Vanessa and other young interns provided a much-needed infusion of youth experience and insight:

> For me, having Vanessa as an intern has been a powerful reminder and reinforcer of why I do the work that I do. I told Vanessa early on that one of the reasons I got into my field and wanted to work in central educational administration is because I believe in education and I want to help people. Through the internship, I feel like I'm able to have a direct, positive impact on someone, which isn't necessarily how I feel about my daily work. It's a very fulfilling experience for me.
>
> I think for my staff, they have an opportunity to engage with a student—to understand why we do the work that we do and what type of impact it can make on students. I also think it is a great leadership and mentoring opportunity for staff. They are often focused on the day-to-day emergencies and requests that come up from schools or departments. Working with a student gives them the opportunity to share what they know.

Vanessa was matched with Melissa through the work of one of us (Alex). He researched, solicited, and vetted internship sites for the vast majority of the youth who have participated in the project over the past three years. Alex and Melissa are life partners and parents, and in the ebb and flow of daily life, they were able to talk daily about Vanessa and the group's research inquiry into law enforcement. Informed by these ongoing, informal "kitchen" talks, Melissa reached out to a number of central office individuals whom Vanessa could ask about their perspectives on school safety and policing efforts and anything else that she wanted to ask. Through Melissa's efforts to communicate and coordinate these exchanges, Vanessa conducted informal, informational interviews on policing with two school officials. She spoke with the assistant chief operating officer (COO), who is partly charged with overseeing the school police. Vanessa also participated in a student forum (held in the school board room, organized with youth from another high school) with the COO and other district leaders. There, she publicly asked about the need for, or value of, police searches in schools with dogs and guns. This, from a young woman who was reticent to speak beyond a few syllables in the first meetings of our internship groups and who is known by her teachers as the "silent, cooperative type."[18]

On the day she interviewed the COO, Vanessa talked about the exchange in the group's meeting. She recapped some of her conversation and focused on questions she posed about police searches in school:

> I also asked about searches . . . like when I was in a different school, I saw police walking around with a dog, and he talked about it. He said that it happened once in a while that some kids bring guns and drugs to the school and the school didn't have a metal detector so they had to do that to see if any kid had gun or drugs . . . I asked him if that prevented anything from happening because that scared students . . . He said they have to do that because of suspicion for guns or drugs.

From this brief recanting of what she shared in the internship experience, we can see many higher-order thinking and interactive skills, ones that exceed the comparatively flat language objectives typically outlined for English language learners. Vanessa had the confidence not only to speak to a clear authority figure, but also to respectively challenge the claims of the authority figure and then retell the narrative of this exchange to her peers and mentors.

During her internship, all of the people Vanessa worked with at her internship, her workplace, and her high school saw her veritably blossom in her confidence and willingness to engage with others. Without a doubt, there were many dynamic and impermanent factors that supported Vanessa's learning and more extroverted performance of her identity, but one we were able to solidly pinpoint was the bond she created with Melissa. Melissa spoke about developing this relationship:

> I shared personal thoughts and insecurities with Vanessa, to help her feel comfortable enough to open up . . . I began to learn about Vanessa, particularly about what she struggled about herself—for example, her shyness—and how I could help support her with that. I decided to extend the internship opportunity not because Vanessa is interested in technology, but because I knew that having a real-world work opportunity, giving her an opportunity to interact and engage with others, would help her come out of her shell and could potentially help her think about what she wanted to do after she graduated.

Also key was the presence of a cohesive peer group that met regularly to discuss their experiences, provide support to each other, and collaborate on larger projects, in this case about law enforcement. At our final internship breakdown session, Vanessa commented, "This changed me a lot. Now every time I come here, I feel like I am with my little family. Everything I want to say, I say it here. It's because you guys let me say whatever I want to say. And I don't usually have much chance to talk to people and have conversations."

Through the internship, we strove to enact a structure that would productively impact young immigrants' confidence to ultimately disrupt colonizing patterns of interactions, where immigrants most often experience cultural isolation and withdraw from asserting themselves and their knowledge. We were informed by our own relative experiences as insiders and outsiders in various cultural spaces. One of us (internship mentor Yang) is an immigrant from Korea and related to her own experiences what she saw happening with the young people's confidence:

> During my first year in America, I did not know what would be proper to say or how to say certain things in groups and classes. All of a sudden, this unknown atmosphere made me a quiet person. To my surprise, my

lack of English communication skills also affected my personality. The hardest part of my first year in the States was feeling like I suddenly became a nobody here, when I was a somebody in my home country. I was one of the most active people in my old school, and now I was one of the most passive students. I had changed from being one who had vivid voice to one whose voice was unheard, from mainstream to outsider, from a salient person to an invisible person in the group. My lack of English led me to become an isolated person who only had contact with people who spoke the same language and shared the same culture as myself. Creating a space where newly immigrated people can have their own voices and learn from each other would have had a tremendous impact on me, and I know it has a tremendous impact on these students. As the students started talking and being heard in our sessions, they were acting with more and more confidence.

Our last internship breakdown session was a connective, culminating, and somewhat emotional meeting, in which all of us, young people and mentors alike, expressed what a unique and special experience the internship and research project had been. Put against the backdrop of high-stakes assessment, levels and stages of language development, and national standards, our project had created a dynamic learning space certainly for young immigrants, but also for professional partners and adult mentors.

WHAT DOES IT TAKE?

Part of the reason that there was differential learning across educational and professional sectors was that this project was a collaborative venture premised on the buy-in and commitment from involved partners. Put more simply, altering contact zones doesn't happen through just one partner. Granted, not all projects would experience the same kind of thick productivity that grew in this project, for many reasons. Outcomes are always in dynamic relationship to contexts, participants, and priorities. For example, because two of the project partners were also life partners, this instantiation of the internship project carried much more conversation about the work across the contexts of home, school, and work.

The first step in conceptualizing and manifesting the project was to find and work with a high school whose staff was interested in this kind of out-of-school location for learning. At first blush, the prospect of students not going to school one day a week and instead attending an internship could feel like yet another significant disruption in school schedules that are already overly interrupted and crowded from waves of mandated testing. But, as one of us (Pai) explained from his perspective as a high school leader, the project was easy to support, particularly when there was a good match with the school's mission:

> It was very easy (you guys did so much of the work!), it was free (a sad but important part of any partnership for a poorly funded school), it had minimal interference with regular school activities, and it provided a ton of value added. Plus knowing Alex and having great references about you [Leigh], I knew your values were in line with ours. Partnering with a university is always appealing because it can lead to more down the road. The particular focus fit us, too—we have a lot of immigrant students. It seemed to be thoughtfully conceived.

What it takes for more youth to participate in spaces like these and for youth to create such spaces for themselves requires the most simple and challenging of work: leaders in education have to reimage how they think. First, they have to change their view of young people from one that attempts to predict youth's tendencies from outdated educational psychology frames. These frames, coupled with a reductive view of school-based competencies, will only see young people as a bundle of skills, and racial minority and low-income youth more specifically as in need of remediation. Through those lenses, there is precious little space for dynamic learning to occur, and certainly not across all participants in a contact zone.

Second, educators need to consider how existing institutional structures can be loosened to encourage dynamic learning so that, minimally, young people can be seen as something other than underperforming students. If educational leaders are truly transformative in their design of learning spaces, though, they will also see that young people are not the only ones in need of spaces to be fuller human beings. Adults would also learn and benefit from contact zones that are intentionally designed for transformation.

Finally, in designing sustainable spaces for transformation, educators cannot treat learning, development, and acculturation as simple, teleologic algorithms. In fact, there is no dynamism in theories of learning that ignore the vastly complicated interactions of human beings, and pedagogy always contains such complex interactions. Long-standing changes in our identities do not happen, largely, through singular events. Thick conversations about race, power, and oppression cannot and should not be collapsed into five-step lesson plans. They are longitudinal, ever-shifting, and necessary projects for individual and collective self-manifestation. In light of this, educators, minimally, must approach the young people they work with from a stance of inquiry rather than a prescribed notion of youth and adolescence and must then chip away at factory models of schooling that are inhospitable environments for the range of capacities and abilities youth hold.[19]

CODA

Pedro, the young man introduced at the beginning of the chapter, did not in one fell swoop of the internship permanently transform into the model young man. During the internship, his performance improved in school, and his teachers reported that he was more involved and less prone to disruption and that they, in turn, stopped dreading his attendance in class. This change, however, dissipated somewhat after the project ended and his normal daily school schedule resumed. One of us (Leigh) remains Facebook friends with Pedro and regularly cringes at his posts that are more than a little misogynist. However, it would be a simple and somewhat arrogant mistake to see this as a failure of the project or to consider Pedro a failure at all. A primary goal of transformative spaces is to simply provide space for transformation, with due humility to the observation that transformation is never a clean enterprise. Personal and collective identities are always complex, hybrid, contradictory, and impermanent ventures. The question should not be what one project can do but rather should be, where can these transformations occur? As Schott Foundation president, John Jackson, stated in a keynote address to educational researchers, "The entire system is one big effective intervention system for some kids. White kids. We keep making single interventions for our [low-income, racial minority] youth. When do we revamp the system so that it is one big, effective intervention for them?"[20]

6

Pedagogies of Race

Teaching Black Male Youth to Navigate Racism in Schools

Na'ilah Suad Nasir, Alea Holman, Maxine
McKinney deRoyston, and kihana miraya ross

RACE AND RACISM ARE core aspects of what youth navigate in their daily lives in schools and communities.[1] Even when people don't explicitly acknowledge the racialized nature of how young people are positioned in schools or how race operates in interactions within schools, race is nonetheless a powerful aspect of life in U.S. schools.[2] And while race is not a biological construct, it is indeed a fundamental social construct that organizes access, marginalization, and privilege in society.[3] Among the powerful pedagogies that can provide spaces of transformation for youth, one critical aspect of teaching African American and other youth of color is to support young people in navigating racism and racist structures in schools and society.

The research literature documents a myriad of ways that racism can influence how youth experience schools, including structural racism and access to high-quality schools and classes; interpersonal racism, whereby African American students are subject to racism and discrimination in their interactions with teachers, school administrators, or peers; and the pervasiveness of negative racial stereotypes in schools, leading to a lack of access to positive academic and racial identities in school settings.[4]

Further, these racial experiences in schools are gendered in powerful ways, such that black boys and black girls experience some overlapping but also some distinct forms of racism.[5] Ann Arnett Ferguson has documented the unique ways that elementary school African American boys and girls are racialized; boys are viewed as future criminals, and girls are viewed as future matriarchs who must "carry" the race.[6]

While the pervasiveness of race and racism in schools has been well documented, there has been little scholarly treatment of how students learn to navigate race in school. Nor is much known about how parents and teachers prepare students for successfully navigating racism in schools. The racial socialization literature does address the messages that parents convey to their children about race in general, which of course has implications for how they might discuss race in relation to school more specifically.[7] Another exception is the research about African-centered or Afrocentric education, which has illustrated the importance of addressing issues of race and reframing racial identity in African-centered schools.[8]

However, there is little literature on the available resources to help African American students, and more specifically African American male students, successfully manage racism and racialization. In other words, what pedagogies of race in families and in schools support students in positively navigating schools? In this chapter, we take up this question, drawing on data from two research projects on racial experiences in schools for African American students in middle and high schools in Northern California. The first project was an interview study (conducted by Alea Holman) that focused on the ways that sixteen black parents of adolescents racially socialize their children.[9] The second was a qualitative study of a new initiative in the Oakland Unified School District, the African American Male Achievement Task Force, which implemented all-black all-male manhood development classes in several of the district middle and high schools. The study involved interviews of forty students and five instructors over two years, as well as observation and videotaping of the manhood development class sessions.

One member of our research team, an African American man in his early twenties, collected the video and observational data. He positioned himself as an observer and occasional participant in the classes. Interviews were conducted by several members of the research team, all African American, one man in his early twenties and three women, ranging in age from early to late thirties.

This chapter focuses on ways that African American male youth experience race in schools and how parents and teachers teach these adolescents to navigate the treacherous racial terrain found there. We begin with a discussion of how black male students and their mothers describe race and racism in schools. Then we discuss two types of race pedagogies; one set enacted by parents in preparing their black sons to navigate race and racism in schools, and the other enacted by a teacher in an afterschool program for black male students, with a similar intent to help students navigate racialized structures and interactions in school. Our goal is to begin to describe the variation in pedagogies of race that parents and schools can provide African American students to support their healthy identity development and the most effective navigation of racism in schools and society. Given the negative stereotypes about African Americans that pervade U.S. schools, such pedagogies can indeed be transformational.

Thus, we view the pedagogies of race that we describe as quintessential pedagogies of possibility. They open up new frames for how youth can understand and position themselves in schools in ways that challenge negative stereotypes and narratives about black male students. This is critical because the internalization of such narratives can constrain opportunity and limit possibilities for youth.

THE SALIENCE OF RACISM AND RACIAL NAVIGATION IN SCHOOLS

Although some may argue that society is in an era of color blindness, where race has become a nonissue, black male students remain keenly aware of race and are often hurt by racism inside and outside school. Mothers also routinely recognize schools as racialized spaces for children in light of their children's discriminatory experiences and their own interactions with schools. Three core themes emerged in the reports from the aforementioned data samples of black boys and their mothers with respect to how they experienced race and racism in schools. First, both the mothers and the boys felt that teachers had low expectations for African American male students' academic achievement. Second, the mothers perceived that teachers did not care about them as parents, or about their children as African American male students. Finally, the students and mothers believed that African American male students were frequently subject to racist stereotypes and unjust disciplinary actions.

Low Expectations

A common theme in interviews with black male students and mothers of black sons was the perception that teachers held lower expectations of them than of their nonblack classmates. One boy noted, "My teachers have called me dumb to my face before. Since fourth grade. Just like that." While most students did not experience such explicit derogatory messages from their teachers, they often discussed how their teachers made them feel less capable academically. Another student discussed his feelings about receiving a different grade from his white classmate after submitting an identical assignment. When asked why he thought he received a different grade, he remarked, "I think, ummm, he has different expectations for me, than other people." Some students noted that while they had never been told by their teachers that the teachers had lower expectations for the boys, the students "just knew" their teachers expected them to fail.

Similarly, several mothers told stories of teachers holding low, disparate expectations of their black sons' capabilities. One mother remembered how her son, the only black boy in a predominantly Latino school, was treated in his kindergarten class:

> I began to notice, in the afternoon I would come, and the other kids were on a certain level, and he wasn't. He was put to play and build. And the

other kids were put to write. And I was like, "What is going on? He needs to be writing like the other kids." But as soon as my back turned, they would put him to build, and not write. And to this day . . . you know, when you start off with your kids, you start them off with the crayons and the pencil and for them to write. And that's what I get for . . . but I was working down the street . . . I should've put him somewhere else. As soon as my back turned, he was building. So even to this day, he has trouble writing.

Another mother of a son in a predominantly white school recounted an incident that prompted her to discuss the realities of racism and discrimination with her son:

When he was attending the school before this one, I think he was in fifth grade, fourth grade. It was an older teacher, and [my son] was struggling in a subject. I can't remember what subject it was; he was getting a C or D, something like that. We [the mother and her husband] were like, "What's going on?" So we came to see [the teacher]. I just felt like he wasn't focusing because he's been a good student all along. I said, "Well, some things are going to have to change. We might have to take some things away to get him to focus." And [the teacher] said, "Oh you don't need to do that." And I was like, "Whatever." But when [my son] talked to her, she told him, "You're getting a C or D." And he said, "Oh no, I can't do that." And she goes, "Oh that's not a bad grade; that's okay for you." Needless to say, I was like, "Oh no!" And so then we had that teaching moment.

In this incident, a teacher explicitly tells a black male student that a C is good enough for him. The message conveyed here is that the teacher had lower expectations for this student's academic performance.

Uncaring Teachers

Student and parent reports of teachers who held black male students to low expectations were often undergirded by the perception that teachers did not care about their students in a deep or personal way. For example, in the following excerpt from a black male ninth grader, the student articulated his perception that his teachers did not really care about him.

> INTERVIEWER: How do you know, what makes you think that they expect that of you?
>
> STUDENT: I know that, that's for a fact.
>
> INTERVIEWER: Do they say things that make you think, to feel that way? Do they do things to make you feel that way?
>
> STUDENT: It's like the way they act, I know . . . I'm not saying they don't care, but . . . like, the teachers, they just want the check; that's it. That's, that's, I think that's what they want. Some teachers, they say they care, but I really don't think they care.

The majority of black male students whom we interviewed did not believe their teachers knew them. Nor did the boys expect them to. Comments such as "they're just teachers" or "they're gonna get pink-slipped next year anyway" indicate that students were accustomed to not developing meaningful relationships with their teachers. In one instance, where a student felt that he should have been known for his academic prowess, he remarked that his teacher knew he played basketball, but was not aware of his academic strengths.

Mothers of African American boys also felt that teachers treated their sons with little care or concern. A mother of three teenage boys explained:

> I'm convinced that schools expect black children to underachieve. They don't push them as hard as they do the other kids. I'm convinced. The way I look at it is, I sent three very brilliant young kids to school, and somewhere along the way, they got messed up. They got discouraged. When they left my house to go to kindergarten, it was, "You can be anything you want to be." Somewhere along the way, they lost that. So, my oldest one, when he was in the fifth grade, he had done a paper one time, and it wasn't neat enough, and she took it and tore it up and made him

start over again. And I went up to the school about that because that was just ridiculous. So when I'm at the school and I'm explaining to them, "This is a child's . . . You have to know that you're dealing with a child's psyche. You know, their emotional state of being. You're the teacher! And there are certain ways to handle things. You don't just say this is messy and tear it up after they put all that work in it" . . . That was one incident with my oldest that to this day, he still remembers that incident.

Interactions like these made mothers feel as though the teachers were not treating their sons with positive regard and that, too often, the teachers were unable to provide a positive learning setting for them. In fact, the mothers worried that their sons were not only uncared-for, but also treated in outright hostile ways in schools. One mother remembered her son being openly disrespected by his gym teacher, in front of peers. "[The teacher] took the paper and basically threw it on the ground instead of handing it to [my son]. So he had to bend over and get it." This lack of caring left lasting impressions on the students, and parents felt that they needed to find ways to counter such negative interactions to protect their son's self-esteem and mental health.

Racist Stereotypes and Disciplinary Actions

Not only did black male students perceive a lack of care in their schools, as some of the incidents in the prior section suggest, but they also often felt outright racism. This frequently took the form of negative racial stereotypes and harsh, unjust discipline. One student noted that "teachers be stereotyping black people. Oh he's gonna be, he's gonna be a ratchet. He's gonna be a ratchet ghetto person." At times, students described how they perceived that these stereotypes affected their teachers' disproportionate disciplining of black students. One student noted, "When they send us out on a referral . . . sometimes when they write down stuff on the referral, they kind of like put a little extra on it, like you know like, even though we didn't do anything like that bad, they try to like seem like we did it a lot like worse." Another student described being overtly humiliated by being asked to pick up trash after smiling at his teacher:

> Okay, so the way it went was, so my teacher said, "Oh, so, you already know, you're on thin ice, so if you do one thing, I got a job for you." I'm like, "All right." So then he sitting there doing notes or whatever. I already finished them, so I'm sitting there like this, and I was thinking about something, and I smiled and I looked up, and he was staring at me. And he was like, "All right, buddy, I got a job for you." And I get up and I was like, ". . . What did I do?" So then, I went out. I went with him, I went to the hallway, and he was like, "You could start picking up all the trash in the hallway." I was like, "I'm not fina' do that." And he was like, "All right, or you could go see [the principal]." I was like, "All right." He gave me a referral because I refused to clean up the hallway.

This student felt that he was being punished for a seemingly benign act (a smile), and the consequence for his smile was to pick up trash in the hallway—a punishment the student perceived to have the intent of humiliating him.

Clearly, race remains salient for African American males in their schools. Confronted with highly racialized experiences, they felt that they were forced to navigate these situations alone throughout the day. While the boys acknowledged that African American girls are subject to racism in school, they were quick to report that being both black and male meant harsher treatment by teachers and administrators. Mothers also reported that boys had more racially salient experiences with teachers than did girls and that boys experienced these incidents at an earlier age than girls. Especially if the boy was larger, he was more likely to be punished for things other students (including nonblack males) were not.

PEDAGOGIES OF RACE

Student and parent reports about experiences of race and racism in schools for African American boys resonate with existing studies and illustrate the need for students to have systems of support, both at home and at school, for learning how to navigate the racialized terrain of schools. In this section, we offer two examples of pedagogies of race, or ways that parents (mothers in particular) and teachers support young black male students in making sense of their racialized experiences and develop strategies to minimize the harmful effects of racism in school.

Parent Race Pedagogies

All of the mothers of black male students interviewed reported that they engaged in conversations about race and racism with their boys. Mothers viewed these conversations as teaching opportunities, and they saw them as supporting their children in learning strategies that would protect the children from the potentially destructive forces of racist people and policies. Mothers employed three strategies and goals in their race pedagogies with their sons: (1) they worked to reframe boys' expectations and prepare them for discrimination; (2) they taught boys strategies to minimize racial harm; and (3) they intervened as advocates on the part of their sons, modeling for their children a proactive approach to combating racism.

Reframing Expectations and Preparing for Bias. Several mothers expressed that it was important for their sons to accurately detect racism and know when they are being treated unfairly. One mother explained that she wanted her son to understand "just how deviant and evil people can be. Know that it's out there. Not, you know, go looking for it every time you go to the grocery store or anything like that, but don't mislabel it and call it something else when it really is just that simple."

All mothers of sons in the sample wanted the boys to be aware of how they are perceived by society. Toward this end, the mothers provided various messages to make their children aware of the stereotypes and other biases that exist in society about black people and particularly black men. For example, the mother of the aforementioned son whose teacher told him that a C or D was a good enough grade for him recalled her response to this incident:

> [I told my son] "And this is the stereotype, son. Talking to her, I don't even think she's realizing what she's saying to you. But she's basically telling you, 'For *you* that's okay. If you don't get an A or a B, that's okay for *you*.' And I said, "That's not okay! You know that's not okay." And he said, "That's what I told her!" So that's when we started talking about, you know, you're going to come in contact with some people that feel like, because of their prior experiences think, as a race, "Well, you know, you may not be able to do it and if you can't, okay." And I said, "No, that's not okay, and that's not where you're from and that's not where you're going." And so he said, "Okay."

This mother was explicit in framing the incident for her son as racially motivated, and as being related to common stereotypes about black males. Another mother also conveyed the necessity of teaching her sons about racial bias: "I have to always tell them, you know, that it seems unfair. It totally seems unfair, but people are going to look at you differently, period. I mean, I hate to teach that at such an early age, but if they don't get it then, they're just totally blind." These conversations were intended to depersonalize the experience of racism and to frame personal interactions within a broader political and social context. This reframing and explicit instruction about racism both helped black male adolescents understand the racialized incidents that they encountered and recognize racism in the future, and not to see it as a personal affront, but rather part of the social context that they live in.

Teaching Strategies to Minimize Racial Harm. Given the biased and stereotypical perceptions that black boys encountered in their daily lives in schools and in society, mothers conveyed to their sons what the boys needed to do to minimize people's proclivity to apply these stereotypes to them. The mothers gave sons strategies and ways of performing in the world to avoid the harm of racism as much as possible. One mother told her teenage son:

> People are going to judge you based on your own behavior and then they will just lump you in a group with people who they think have that behavior. And then with rap songs and music videos, "Oh yeah, all black people act like that, and degrade women, and talk stupid and whatever." But you have to prove that you are not that and that's not who we are. And yes, there are some of us who are like that, but everybody's not like that and you have to prove it by the way you act and behave. Can you read? Can you learn? Can you speak with proper grammar? You make the difference.

Similarly, a mother whose son attended a predominantly white private high school explained to him:

> There is a certain demeanor that I think you need to have because they expect, for some, they expect the worst from us. I always tease him, "You got to go represent. You do." I am teaching him to have a relationship with his teachers because they tend to look at *us* as, "Okay, you are probably here under a grant. Are you here for sports?" I mean, it's human nature. So I encourage him to have a relationship with them—go in, ask the questions, be involved, be attentive.

Both of these mothers highlight the ways that young people's behavior and comportment can offset the effects of racism. They tell their sons that the boys do have some power over how they are being perceived and that there are tools at their disposal to minimize to some degree teachers' and others' racialized responses to them. One mother reported drawing on President Obama as a role model in managing racism, emphasizing that President Obama was able to maintain a calm demeanor even when he was being disrespected on the basis of race.

One particular strategy that mothers taught their sons was code-switching and what we might call performing "whiteness," in other words, altering one's language and comportment to be consistent with mainstream white ways of speaking and interacting. To teach her fifteen-year-old son the importance of code-switching, one mother compared his behavior to that of his twenty-seven-year-old brother:

> And [the younger son] is like, "I can't always say things to people and they just accept what I say." I said, "But it is also the way you say it. [The older son] knows how to code-switch and be very formal if he needs to, and that's something you still need to learn, because you have more attitude. People can be intimidated by your size. Your stature is totally different than [your older brother's]. You come off more manly, strong; your voice is even heavier than his, even at fifteen years old. And you don't necessarily know how to code-switch the attitude off to a more formal situation. So, yeah, people will be intimidated by you, and you will lose out on jobs and opportunities. And that is something you need to learn how to do from [your brother]. You need to be really aware of how you respond back to people."

Mothers also tried to make clear to their sons that while other people can respond and react freely, as black boys and men, they do not have this privilege in our society:

> One of the things I've always shared with the kids is, like in the workplace, we can never show our anger. I said, "Hear me when I tell you this: They can show their anger. They can have a meltdown and it's okay. But if we have a meltdown, they will call the police. They will never forget it; they will never forget it! It just is—it just is. It is a part of us assimilating." If anything, that's what my husband and I tried to teach our children. "We have to learn how to assimilate. It's not selling out. But if you want to get ahead, if you want to move in this circle, you have to know the rules and you have to play the game. And I don't mean be phony; you just need to know the rules. And when you are at home, you're at home. When you

are with your homeboys, that's a whole different thing. You have to know
when it's time." I think they're getting it.

Through messages such as these, black mothers hoped to offer their sons
strategies to minimize the extent to which the boys would be targets of racism and to minimize the effects of racism when they were targeted.

Intervening as Advocates. The preceding section showed that parents engaged their sons in conversations about the racism they were encountering
(or that they could face). However, parents did not stop at conversations
with their sons in response to racism. In anticipation of, and in response
to, problems in school, parents also advocated for students in purposeful
ways. The mothers in this sample were committed to being visible at their
children's schools as much as possible, particularly in the elementary years.
Across students' academic careers, parents met with teachers and administrators when their children were experiencing difficulty in a subject or with
a particular teacher. One mother explained:

> My husband and I did all of the parent-teacher things together whenever
> possible, because we wanted them to know that these kids come from
> a [two-parent,] middle-class . . . you know, these ain't no ghetto rats or
> nothing, and you're not going to treat them like that.

In addition to being visible at school to dispel stereotypes of black families for teachers and administrators, mothers made sure that their sons
knew that the parents were acting as advocates. In this way, the boys would
know that they were supported with respect to their struggles at school.
One mother put it this way:

> [I told him] "Yes, we do have your back, and wherever you go, you need to
> know that, that we care about you. Even if you feel like no one else does.
> We care about you, we love you, we're not going to leave you stranded out

here." So we basically had to meet with every single individual [at school], and it got to the point where we had to strengthen our family bond with him, just to make him know that, "You're loved, you're supported." So basically I was doing homework with him like every single night. You know, because he was feeling so low.

Mothers also modeled for children how to stand up for themselves and represent their culture in appropriate ways. One mother explained how she began doing the Black History Month exhibit at her children's elementary school, which she had been doing for the last twelve years. She identified this work in the classroom as important not only for changing the culture of the school community, but also for modeling for her sons that involvement can be an important aspect of changing the school and classroom setting to be more culturally inclusive. Similarly, another mother recounted her child's fifth grade class celebration of colonial day and the actions she took to challenge this district-wide activity:

So, I had to meet with the teacher. I said, "Why are you celebrating colonization?" She's like, "It's not a celebration. They're learning about this, and they have these different stations that they get to go to. And they get to write with quill pins and they get to eat Native American foods. They dress up." I said, "Do you realize that there was a trauma? This was traumatic; not just for black people, but the Native American people. I mean, are you serious?" She was like, "I'm so glad you told me that because I never thought . . ." She's been teaching in that school for twenty years; she never thought of that?! She never thought of it. But I thought about it, and I was like, when I pull my child out, these white kids are still learning this stuff. They are going to grow up in a society where they think that it's okay to colonize people and we can celebrate the fact that we colonized people. We don't even recognize the trauma. It's almost like I feel a duty and a responsibility to critique it because otherwise it's not going to be critiqued. Nobody else is going to do it. So that's why I said, "I want to make sure these things are talked about. And if you're talking about slavery, you're talking about it in different ways." [The teacher] pulled in a lot of resources, like outside supplemental readings about black slaves and free blacks. I feel like that teacher really did try to work with me because she kind of understood what I was getting at.

The race pedagogies employed by parents of African American male adolescents highlight how parents intervened to help their sons understand the racialized context of schools and successfully manage the racism that the students encounter there. In the next section, we consider the race pedagogies employed by an after-school program that was a part of a district-wide initiative to support the achievement of African American male students in the district.

Race Pedagogies in an Afterschool Program

In general, research has found that proactive conversations about race rarely happen in schools, and that schools and students find very few places of support to examine and discuss race.[10] In this section, however, we consider one program that deviated from that general pattern. The Manhood Development Program (MDP) at a middle school in Oakland, California, offered all-black, all-male courses, of which one explicit purpose was to foster a conversation around race with black male students to support them in navigating the racialization they experienced in school. We begin by providing an overview of the MDP, the school site, and the instructor that our analysis will focus on. We then share some classroom data and discuss the race pedagogy in the after-school program.

The African American Male Achievement (AAMA) Task Force was created by the Oakland Unified School District to address concerns about the high rates of suspension (23 percent) and chronic absenteeism (20 percent; defined as missing more than 10 percent of school in an academic year, including excused and unexcused absences) among African American males students in the 2008–2009 school year. The AAMA also sought to address the low performance indicators for African American male high school students in the district. For example, only 15 percent of African American male students tested at the level of proficient or above in English, and only 5 percent in math. African American males make up 17.3 percent of the district's student population, and 30 percent of the district's students (or 1,959 students) are enrolled in grades 9 through 12. The AAMA's mission was to increase attendance rates, lower suspension and expulsion rates, promote self-awareness, and help cultivate healthy identities among African American male students.

In the fall of 2010, the AAMA Task Force launched a program for adolescent male students in the district, serving middle and high school African American boys with classes at its school sites. The course's curriculum sought to address students' physical, emotional, academic, and social needs and to encourage students to learn more about themselves, their cultural and racial history, and their communities with the goal of helping the boys think differently about their education. African American male teachers, coaches, and community members taught the courses and developed their curriculum around the aforementioned goals, emphasizing students' agency toward shaping their own future, the future of their school, and the future of African Americans.

In this chapter, we focus on the manhood class at one middle school site, which we will call Baker Middle School. Baker is a diverse school with Asian, Latino, and white students each representing about 26, 15, and 11 percent of the population, respectively, with African American students representing over 40 percent. Nearly 60 percent of Baker's students qualify for free or reduced lunch. Baker attracts middle-class families because of its record of strong leadership, teaching, and student performance, as well as its stated commitments to maintaining a cohesive, supportive school community. The MDP at Baker was an afterschool program, combining the manhood curriculum with other resources such as homework support and tutoring.

The MDP instructor at Baker, Brother Jelani, was an experienced youth worker and was familiar with incorporating African American cultural and racial history and experience into his pedagogy. A self-titled artist educator, Brother Jelani had taught and been an artist in residence at a college, had led other after-school programs, worked at group homes and juvenile facilities, and raised his own sons and daughters. He expressed his concerns about racism within schools and about schooling environments where the only black adults present were the security guards, custodians, and administrative staff working for white administrators. Noting how he saw students taking up the racialized tenor within schools, Brother Jelani told us that some students were initially hesitant about joining the class, because when they learned that all the students were black and male, they automatically thought it was a "trouble class."

Brother Jelani felt that the MDP class was needed to address these kinds of concerns at the level of the student and the school by presenting counter-narratives and positive perspectives about black males and other black people. He termed this approach "cultural enrichment." He also saw the MDP class as supporting academic achievement:

> The reality of it is that if they go through manhood training, they become better in class and it raises their character, but if their grades are slipping, it's all bad. Now if their grades are good and they're into some craziness, that's all bad, too. So what we gotta do is balance it.

To facilitate students' positive self-identification as black males and as students, and to support them in navigating the racialized environments within schools, Brother Jelani's pedagogy was based upon several principles, including the following:

- Creating a safe, humanizing space for students within school
- Advocating for students and modeling how to deal with racialized stereotypes and other biases
- Teaching students about black history and culture, and developing positive racial and gender identities as African American males

Central to this work was the development of students as leaders and cultural and racial ambassadors to their school. In this section, we offer some examples of the nature of the race pedagogy in Brother Jelani's MDP at Baker, drawing on examples from a meeting he had with parents and from two class sessions: one early in the semester and one soon after the Trayvon Martin incident. In this nationally publicized racial incident that took place in Sanford, Florida, on February 28, 2012, an unarmed African American teen was shot and killed by a neighbor who was not immediately apprehended by law enforcement.

For Brother Jelani, constructing a safe, humanizing space and building community began with his personal methodology of believing in each student's potential and his investment in seeing "how high they can go." It also involved engaging with, and holistically cultivating, his students as individuals, as students, and as children. During a parent meeting, he drew a child on the board with several intersecting, overlapping circles around it. As he labeled the circles "school," "family," and "society," he explained that he works with "all that students bring to the class and all that they are and can be." Parents laughed and nodded as he shared anecdotes about each student's personality and asked them to give their children more food for the after-school program, because the school only provided "third grade snacks" for what were "grown-men appetites."

Brother Jelani's efforts went beyond simply recognizing his students as children and as unique individuals. He consciously framed his pedagogy within an understanding of the social realities of his students' lives as black males, as students, as children, and as persons living in America. The Trayvon Martin incident was a high-profile, contemporary example of these realities, and Brother Jelani took up the opportunity to reiterate to students the need to humanize each person and to develop community among African Americans. In discussing the case with his middle school students, he gave advice to his students:

Realize that Trayvon Martin is . . . a human being. That's a human being. Just don't reduce his name to a slogan; remember that's a human being. Pray for his family, his mother and father, and his family members. That's important . . . The same problems also happen in Oakland, and sometimes it's not somebody outside our race. It's us against us. We have to love each other, respect each other, not immediately fly off of the handle with each other. Have more empathy towards each other; it's not really that serious . . . We gotta be able to have that with each other . . . And one extra thing: we gotta be closer.

The Trayvon Martin case and the conversation following it also made students attend to the racialized environment within the school and highlighted the need for African American male students to have within the school a space that was devoid of stereotypes and disregard for their experiences being black and male. About a month after the incident, the principal announced that students could wear their hoodies to school the following day in solidarity with Trayvon. The next day, a couple of students began talking to Brother Jelani outside of the classroom right before the MDP class. After entering the classroom, one of the students went and sat in a far-off corner. Brother Jelani called out to him, "J! Come on, man. You're in your safe space now, so come on out your hood. Pull your arms out. I know that you had a rough day, but you're amongst family so everything is cool now."

Several students quickly began commenting that while most teachers were supportive, some still wouldn't let them wear their hoodies. Brother Jelani asked them, "Did your hoodie stop you from studying? Did it stop you today?! Did it . . . impair your ability to listen and learn today?"

When students responded that it hadn't, Brother Jelani went on to affirm them: "Okay, so now you get to see how they use something against you to try and play this authority thing. Stay strong, gentlemen . . . we're in the fourth quarter. You are going to succeed and make it through the rest of this year. Outta here. Those of you who are returning, you're gonna come back stronger, wiser, more able to handle everything . . . smarter, everything."

As the preceding scene indicates, the creation of a safe space and community extended beyond the physical bounds of the MDP classroom and modeled for students how to deal with the racism they encounter in school. In this instance, Brother Jelani went on to say:

> If you really want to get justice for Trayvon Martin, there's one thing that you can immediately do: stay positive, stay on your focus, handle your business, don't allow these teachers to start trying to mess with you and jam you up the way they're trying to mess with Jaquan [another student in the class] right now . . . Don't let it happen; don't let it happen. Be smarter than that . . . You all know that you can make it through the rest of the year. You know these teachers; overcome that. That's the first thing that you can do.

With these words, Brother Jelani encouraged the students to be resilient. He emphasized that they have the capacity to succeed in spite of the circumstances.

Much like the advocacy that parents reported, Brother Jelani positioned himself as an advocate for his students. This positioning involved actively identifying himself as a supporter of the students and working on their behalf when incidents occurred at the school. On the day of the hoodies, one student mentioned that a white male teacher had inappropriately joked earlier in the week that he might be a racist and that this same teacher wouldn't let them wear their hoodies in class on the day they were allowed to show solidarity with Trayvon. Several students remarked that these incidents had made them wonder if this teacher really was a racist. Brother Jelani quickly responded that he was going to go speak with that teacher and would do so while wearing his hoodie:

> Because that's what needs to happen. Your big brother—I'm your big brother in this case—needs to talk and find out if Mr. Graft is really racist. Because if he is, if you're [the teacher] joking and saying that, then we have an issue. Because how can you be racist and teach people that don't look like you? What are you teaching them? How do you feel about them? We have to talk about this.

Similar to the mothers, Brother Jelani also focused on strategies that would minimize students' being stereotyped by other teachers. In addition to reminding them to "stay on your focus, and handle your business," he frequently told the students to "organize themselves," and when they got too wild, he reminded them, "Gentlemen, discipline." During the end-of-the-semester interviews, one student described a sentiment that several students shared:

> Brother Jelani has really helped me with interacting with my teachers because he told me that when I have an argument with my teacher or something like that, the teacher is always right. There's really nothing, he said, they're getting paid whether or not you're learning. Learning is on you; the opportunity is there. You have to make sure that you take advantage of that. They don't have to come to you, ask you if you need help, or make sure, check on you all the time. Their job isn't to like you.

With this sentiment, Brother Jelani encouraged students to alter their behavior and expectations of teachers to minimize being the target of racism. A principle of self-discipline may be useful for all students, but given the racialized context of black male students' experiences and outcomes in schools, this principle also encourages students to act as self-advocates even where no such supports, whether intentionally or unintentionally, appear to exist.

Brother Jelani also viewed knowledge of African American history and culture as fundamental to helping students build the self-esteem necessary to navigate racism. He believed that to attain the balance that he talked about earlier, his students needed positive racial and gender identities as African American males. Brother Jelani tried to debunk racialized and gendered stereotypes about African American men and women and provided counterexamples that better reflected the breadth of the African American experience. This involved, but was not limited to, reminding students not to endorse or be limited to negative stereotypes of black men. Instead, he reminded students that they all had positive aspects to themselves and that "negativity [that they see or feel] is not all of you . . . You have more parts to yourself besides the negative stuff that you do." To this end, MDP students' accomplishments were publicly celebrated, and students were encouraged to bring in their academic and other honors because "we gotta lift these up, brothers!"

Brother Jelani also sought to develop positive racial and gender identities by teaching students about their history, namely, by providing them with a historical understanding that wasn't limited to slavery. This involved showing students movies like the *Black Power Mixtape*, a documentary about the Black Power movement; creating banners about the achievements and contributions of black men and women throughout American history; and randomly posting index cards containing, among other things, "Black Facts" around the school.[11] Brother Jelani challenged students to expound their understanding beyond Martin Luther King and other oversaturated, historic black leaders and to be proactive in teaching others and building a more positive culture in the school throughout the year, not just during Black History Month. He told the students, "Like I told you, the new generation is not just us. We need to be thinking about how a new generation can be a whole thing throughout this school. A new energy, a new vibe." Brother Jelani encouraged students to create artifacts and display them in the public spaces at the school.

To encourage students to draw on what they were learning to actively shift their peers' engagement with issues of race, Brother Jelani actively encouraged students to serve as ambassadors of black history within the school. He explained to students that they could approach people standing near the posters and index cards and say, "Hey, my name is ___, and I'm with the MDP. Let me introduce you to [some person on the banner]." He remarked, "That's how things get started; one person breaks form and others follow." The educator saw these artifacts, that is, the various posted pieces around the school, as opportunities for his MDP students to teach black history to other students, to serve as ambassadors to the larger school community, and to reshape notions about race within their school. He also used the artifacts to document what students learned and how much they developed over the course of the class. In another move designed to support students in changing the school community around issues of race, he created a Facebook page where students could engage one another and himself, and he set up meetings and "success" plans with individual students at different points in the semester. These activities created written records that the MDP student could later reflect upon or reuse.

The race pedagogy in the MDP class worked to help students name and understand the racism they encountered in their schools and develop new understandings of their racial and cultural history and context. It was also a space where they found community with one another and had access to advocates to intervene and model how to deal with racism in school.

THEMES AND LESSONS LEARNED

This chapter has offered a glimpse into the range of ways black male students experience racism in school and the strategies that parents and teachers can use to support them in successfully navigating that racism. As the data and analyses illustrated, several key strategies made up the race pedagogies we describe, some of which were consistent in the pedagogies of mothers and in the Manhood Development Program classes.

The first of these themes is that key to these pedagogies was the presence of trusted adults who acted as advocates for young people and, in doing so, modeled effective ways to respond to experiences of racism in schools. Both parents and the MDP instructor highlighted the importance of making sure that the young men had adults who cared about them and who were holding the school and teachers accountable for treating them fairly.

The second theme is that these pedagogies worked to deepen students' understanding of race, racism, and their cultural and racial history. In other words, the race pedagogies we described were not only reactive (in relation to events occurring in school), but also proactive, in that they sought to help students develop robust racial identities and build a positive sense of what it means to be African American to counter the negative images common in the media and society. Parents and the MDP instructor also deemed it important for students to understand the pervasiveness of racism and to locate this understanding of racism historically and politically.

In addition to helping students understand racism and develop the cultural knowledge to view themselves in ways that transcended racist encounters, another important aspect of the race pedagogies described here was offering young men explicit strategies to minimize their being targeted by racism. Strategies included encouraging young people to be on their best behavior and to conform to the accepted codes of comportment. Note that these strategies were conveyed not as criticism of the students' ways of being, but rather as a proactive way to minimize their experience of racism.

Given the profound experiences with racism and race that African American adolescents reported in this study, the race pedagogies offered by parents and teachers is critical to the young people's surviving and successfully navigating their school and classroom environments. The findings highlight the critical role that having access to pedagogies of race can play in black male students' developing healthy identities and surviving the racism they encounter in schools. Race pedagogies are indeed pedagogies of possibility in that they help youth reframe the negative ways they can be positioned in schools and support them in constructing and taking up identities as students and as learners. Realizing the potential of youth in schools requires pedagogies that create new possibilities for identity and new models for engaging school as African American students.

7

"It Is Best to Know Who You Are Through Your Culture"

Transformative Educational Possibilities for Native American Youth

Tiffany S. Lee and Nancy López

WHEN ASKED ABOUT HOW he defined an educated Native American, Bahii (pronounced "baa-hee"), a Navajo male high school student, did not hesitate: "It is best to know who you are through your culture."[1] Bahii's comments were emblematic of Native American youth's commitment to their cultural heritage as integral to what it means to be an educated Native American in contemporary U.S. society. The comments raise compelling questions about how Native American youth negotiate their identities across a variety of New Mexico public schools; they also beckon us to explore the cultural practices Native youth engage in to articulate their identities in contemporary U.S. society.

The objective of this chapter is to map the ways in which heterogeneous Native American youth exercise agency in navigating diverse public school contexts in New Mexico. We pay particular attention to their cultural practices and discourses related to their identities. We define youth as middle school and high school students, between the ages of eleven and nineteen.

In mapping the landscape of youth resistance and agency, it is important to conceptualize and document youth agency as independent from adult activism.[2] We look at how Native American youth have engaged and challenged the traditional power structures of school, which has historically marginalized Native American students both educationally and culturally. We draw upon Patricia Hill Collins and Linda Smith's theories about the dynamics of power to understand Native youth perspectives of their schooling experiences.[3]

Our data come from the study "Indian Education in New Mexico, 2025."[4] As two of the co-principal investigators for the study, we used Indigenous-based methodologies to investigate the state of Native education in New Mexico from the perspective of Native students, teachers, and community members.[5] The data included focus groups with eighty-three middle school and high school students in five public school districts and two charter schools in New Mexico from 2007 through 2009.[6]

We found that Native youth agency, resistance, and resilience results when youth position their cultural identity at the forefront for engaging with schools and developing relationships with adults and with one another. This positioning is a form of youth cultural practice where their heritage is utilized as a resource for resistance and agency. We argue that youth engagement with schools is both to defend their identity and heritage and to strengthen their connections and knowledge of their heritage language, history, values, and perspectives.

The chapter is organized into three sections. First, we discuss the key conceptual tools for mapping diverse Native American youth's experiences of resistance and resilience at a cross section of New Mexico public schools, from charter schools focused on Native American empowerment to the traditional public high schools that most Native American youth attend in the state. Second, we provide snapshots of social critique emanating from the youth and detail how they utilize their identities as Native American youth as sites of resistance to the marginalization of Native American culture, perspectives, and communities in schools in the United States. Third, we sketch pedagogies of possibility, hinting at what could be done by teachers, staff, school administrators, and policy makers as well as community members to transform the schooling system for Native American youth in the state and in the nation.

POSITIONING NATIVE AMERICAN YOUTH IN THE NEW MEXICO CONTEXT

New Mexico provides a valuable context for learning about the experiences of Native youth. Native American students in New Mexico are a highly visible, vibrant, and sizable population. New Mexico is a minority-majority state with the largest number of Hispanics or Latinos in the nation (45 percent), most of whom are nonimmigrants. With two million residents, New Mexico also has the fourth-largest percentage of Native Americans in the union, with about a tenth of the population identifying as Native American.[7] There are twenty-two Native and Pueblo nations in New Mexico. Specifically, there are nineteen Pueblo nations, the Navajo Nation, and the Jicarilla and Mescalero Apache nations.

The public school demographics mirror these trends. Of the eighty-nine public school districts in New Mexico, twenty-three are located on or near Native lands. Native students make up nearly 11 percent of the statewide student enrollment.[8] The twenty-three school districts serving Native students are largely rural, with very high concentrations of Native student enrollment in the particular schools within the district. Native students in twelve of the twenty-three districts make up more than 25 percent of the population, and in six of those districts, they make up more than 50 percent of the total population.

Native students have consistently performed at markedly lower levels on standardized tests in math, reading, science, and social studies than their white, Asian, Hispanic, and black peers.[9] The 2011 four-year cohort graduation rates of Native American students remain among the lowest of any racial or ethnic group in the state (56 percent) (figure 7.1).

This pattern or "achievement gap" is common across the United States among Native student performance levels as compared with white students.

FIGURE 7.1

Four-year cohort graduation rates for New Mexico public school students by race and gender, 2011 (including charter schools, N = 37,834)

Race or ethnic group and gender	Graduation rate (%)
American Indian	56
Hispanic	59
Black	60
White	76
Asian	78
Male	57
Female	68
Total student population (37,834 students)	63

Source: New Mexico Public Education Department (http://ped.state.nm.us).

Additional social, economic, and school-based conditions such as poverty, health disparities, under-resourced schools, and high student and staff mobility have added to the barriers of student "success" as measured and determined by state departments of education.[10] These conditions have often shaped a deficit framework for understanding Native student achievement in schools. Consequently, the educational experiences of Native students is laden with labels of "at risk," gaps, and scarcity. What is neglected are Native people's perspectives of their communities as places of cultural and community wealth, shared spaces, relationships, and resilience, as well as their experiences navigating existing power structures.

UNDERSTANDING YOUTH AGENCY

The experiences of Native students in public schools in New Mexico are varied, but a common pattern of intolerance, apathy, low expectations, and racial discrimination toward Native American youth and their communities has been found across many schools.[11] Regrettably, the six-year graduation rates for Native students at the University of New Mexico are the lowest of any group (21 percent compared with the total average of 44 percent).[12]

Despite the repressive conditions in many of these students' schooling experiences, Native students continue to negotiate schools in ways that resist markers that label them as deficient.[13] Native youth continue to exercise a sense of self that asserts a holistic definition of an educated Native person based on their cultural values, knowledge, experiences, and identity. Native adults express and promote their own definitions of Indigenous education and success as rooted in significant cultural characteristics such as knowledge of the Native language, history, and stories; participation in the community's ceremonial and cultural activities; and affective qualities such as being a helpful and caring person. These traits are only useful and recognized when used to contribute to one's community.[14] Greg Cajete and Angayuquq Kawagley discuss this characterization of an educated Native person as becoming a complete human being.[15] A complete human being is secure in his or her identity, has a strong sense of belonging, understands and fulfills his or her role in society, and thus serves the community for the betterment of all the people.

Research on Native student resilience, resistance, and agency has revealed how these students draw on their Native cultural resources, relationships, and values to confront negative school-based experiences. The students also seek out support and resources for expressing and strengthening their cultural identity and respect for their communities. Donna Deyhle shows how Navajo youth used music choices and performances to resist and challenge racial discrimination in schools. Navajo students engaged in break dancing to mobilize a group identity, express their uniqueness, and achieve their own kind of success in the midst of a negative school environment.[16]

In a study of a large urban public high school in New Mexico with a high percentage of Native American youth, Glenabah Martinez found that Native youth resisted and confronted the prioritization of dominant ideologies and the marginalization of their cultural heritage.[17] For example, when the local school district forbade youth from wearing their traditional

Native attire for the graduation ceremonies, students and the community protested by holding multiple meetings with school administrators and even taking their appeal to the local school board. After much public pressure and media coverage, the administrators agreed to "allow" Native students to wear their regalia, with one caveat: it had to be worn under the traditional cap and gown and could not go below the hemline. Martinez argues that this gesture was a compromise, which symbolically represented "giving in" to Native student demands. But ultimately, the system that set the compromise maintained its hegemonic control, which equated the experiences of Native American colonization and survival with that of any other "ethnic" group that wanted to wear its traditional clothing in lieu of the mandatory cap and gown. Although the youth acknowledged the compromise as a small victory, as one more battle in the 500-year history of colonization and oppression, what is important here is that Native American youth are not passive recipients of dominant and colonizing ideologies.

The 500-year history has resulted in dramatic language shift among Native communities, where English is replacing the heritage language as the first language of children. Over this time, Native youth today have been portrayed as apathetic toward their languages and blamed for this shift.[18] Yet, they long to be fluent in their Native languages and utilize communicative repertoires that include varied levels of Native language to express their cultural identity and consciousness.[19] A study by Teresa McCarty and colleagues found that Native youth's communicative repertoires "include different linguistic expertise (receptive, spoken, written) in diverse varieties of one or more Indigenous languages, English, and, in some cases, Spanish."[20]

The youth in Martinez's study demonstrated this connection of their communicative repertoires with their cultural identity and practices.[21] While the students in her study were largely being raised in the city, they were knowledgeable of the philosophies and values of their Native communities represented by linguistically significant phrases and terms. A group of Navajo students often referred to the tenets of Navajo philosophies of life and worldview when discussing what it means to be an educated Native person. These beliefs are represented in the phrase *Sa'ah*

Naagháí Bik'eh Hózhóón, which describes the principles for living one's life in balance and harmony. These principles "place human life in harmony with the natural world and the universe. The philosophy provides principles both for protection from the imperfections in life and for the development of well-being."[22] The students' understanding of the value of education was rooted in this worldview from their families and communities, not the rhetoric of the public schools. The youth's ideologies expressed here provide a sharp example of how youth engage in cultural practices linked to their heritage to confront schooling experiences and to define their own educational goals.

In *Black Feminist Thought*, Patricia Hill Collins provides a variety of useful tools for understanding the experiences of Native American youth in U.S. schools.[23] Collins poses a compelling question: what is the relationship between knowledge and empowerment? She defines oppositional knowledge as "a type of knowledge developed by, for and/or in defense of an oppressed group's interest. Ideally, it fosters the group's self-definition and self-determination." Collins defines agency as "an individual or social group's right to be self-defining and self-determining."[24] The last conceptual tool that helps us excavate moments of resistance among Native American youth is what Collins identifies as the interpersonal domain of power, which refers to the "discriminatory practices of everyday experience that because they are so routine typically go unnoticed or remain unidentified. Strategies of everyday resistance occur in this domain."[25] Each of these conceptual tools is anchored in Indigenous notions of sovereignty, self-determination, and social justice.

THE RESEARCH PROCESS AND ANALYSIS

This chapter is based on the analysis of qualitative data from the "Indian Education in New Mexico, 2025" study.[26] This statewide study focused on best practices in education from the perspectives of Native American students, their teachers, and Native American community members. Our analysis for this chapter focuses on the youth participants' perspectives and experiences; the participants were middle school and high school students who ranged in age eleven through nineteen.

To learn about Native youth perspectives, the research team, which included five Native and one non-Native co-principal investigators, anchored their work in Indigenous-based methodologies.[27] Our approach utilized methods informed by Navajo-, Pueblo-, and Apache-defined protocols, which, for this chapter, we generally call Indigenous-based methods. For example, prior to conducting the study in the Navajo Nation, the Navajo Institutional Review Board reviewed the entire research process before it was approved. While the Pueblo communities do not have a formal institutional review board, the protocol called for securing permission to conduct the study from the All Indian Pueblo Council (which represents the nineteen Pueblos in New Mexico) before obtaining permission from the public school districts to interview the youth. Our Indigenous-based approach for gaining access is context-specific and integral to Indigenous-based research.

After obtaining the necessary permissions, we found that gaining the trust of our participants was another integral aspect to an Indigenous-based process.[28] It involved drawing upon the experiences, cultural backgrounds, and language fluency of the co-principal investigators and research assistants to more meaningfully connect with our participants.

The analysis of data also exemplified Indigenous-based methodologies. For example, interpreting the results required culturally relevant knowledge, such as the ability to interpret Native language phrases used by participants and understanding the purpose and meaning behind culturally based activities described by participants. Additionally, we reported our results back to the community, school, and tribal authorities in feedback sessions to verify our findings and refine our understanding of the major issues they discussed before we wrote any final reports or made any presentations. Indigenous-based methodologies value reciprocity, respect, cultural relevance, and appropriateness, so our research incorporated methods to privilege those values while honoring the specific procedures determined by the tribal communities and schools in each context.[29]

Because we wanted to capture the experiences of a cross section of diverse Native American community contexts, our study included a total of thirteen schools (eleven public schools and two charter schools) located within seven communities. We conducted thirty-one focus group discussions and fourteen interviews with 205 participants, 83 of whom were Native youth, primarily in high school. Three focus groups included middle school students. The majority of youth participants were Pueblo and Navajo, and a small number were Apache. A little more than half of the youth participants were female. The focus group discussions and interviews lasted about one to two hours each. We coded the transcriptions according to seven critical areas reviewed in the literature prior to data collection. Those thematic areas included participant perspectives and experiences with school climate, pedagogy, curriculum, accountability, language, and meanings of student success, and their visions for an ideal education. Our analysis revealed an eighth area, which focused on relationships.

During the focus group and interview sessions, we found a strong pattern of youth expressions of resistance, resilience, and agency across the aforementioned key thematic areas. We identified patterns of responses that demonstrated those three characteristics and have combined them under the thematic areas described below. The quotes are primarily represented by Navajo and Pueblo youth.

For the next section, we provide snapshots of the experiences and cultural practices of Native youth across a variety of schools in New Mexico. Those experiences and practices showed a common thread of youth agency and resistance. We organized their experiences and perspectives as follows: (1) cultural and linguistic relevance in school; (2) critique of false or hypocritical inclusion of Native knowledge and experiences; (3) affirmation of youth intelligence and abilities; and (4) youth's negotiation of the regional intolerance and racism penetrating school contexts. We conclude with a discussion of transformative possibilities as envisioned by the youth at one charter school that was anchored in the importance of cultivating Native youth leadership and resilience through cultural practice and activism.

CULTURAL AND LINGUISTIC RELEVANCE IN SCHOOL

Native youth recognize what counts as knowledge in their schools, and they are aware that their people's history, stories, and ways of life are not included in the curriculum. The following quote reflects how a student used interpersonal power to challenge the structural arrangements at a school that marginalized, ignored, or misrepresented Native American experiences:

> We did a paper on slavery, and it was interesting to learn about other people's struggle, but I would like to learn more about Native American history. I asked our teacher if we could do an activity on ourselves, and the teacher said Native American history was not a requirement in the curriculum, and I told her it's a Native American school.

This student exercised her agency by shining a light on the contradiction that exists when a school may have a significant percentage of Native American students, but when the official curriculum does not reflect this reality.

Similar to the Native students at a large public school in Martinez's study, the student we spoke with rejected the mainstream approach that marginalized Native American experiences in the "official" curriculum, dictated by the standards-based assessments that were used to assess the achievement levels of any schools.[30]

The middle school and high school youth in our study also articulated counterhegemonic criticism of the lack of Native American language courses available to students throughout the K–12 pipeline. Students spoke fondly of the ability to take language courses in elementary and some middle schools, but they were very disappointed about the lack of courses available at the high school level. This was less of an issue among Navajo students (because there were many Navajo language courses taught in the high schools), but it was common complaint among Pueblo youth. The students recognized the language shift occurring in their communities, and they desired to learn their ancestral languages as a way of contributing to language revitalization and the resiliency of their communities.

Language is an indicator of a person's close connection to his or her heritage. Youth understand the significance of language as a cultural marker for identifying as a Native person. One student discussed her interest in learning her language so that the authenticity of her identity could not come into question:

> I guess that's what you could say I really, really want to do. I want to learn how to speak Navajo. I don't want to be a fake Native, you know what I mean? I mean, for example, you go to a different reservation and they are like, "Yeah, I'm Native." You say, "What kind of Native are you?" and they are like, "Oh, I'm part Cherokee and Winnebago," and you are like, "Do you know anything about your past?" They don't exactly know their language or—I don't really want to be like that.

She later explained her value for the language: "If I could speak Navajo, I'd definitely speak it twenty-four/seven. I do kind of understand it, and I can sort of speak it, but it's not as good as my grandma's." For this student, learning Navajo was tied to her cultural identity, and she recognized the level of fluency she felt was necessary for speaking Navajo, which was at the level of her grandmother's fluency, to authentically call herself Navajo.

This student highlights one struggle that Native youth experience with regard to the connection of their cultural identity to the languages they speak. Often, youth come to school without fluency in either academic English or their Native languages, thus creating an image that Native youth are "semilingual." The stereotype of Native youth as "semilingual" because of heritage language shift and low achievement on standardized academic English tests is untrue. As stated earlier, McCarty and colleagues showed that youth's communicative repertoires represent the complex linguistic experiences and expertise of Native youth.[31] These communication abilities can offset heritage language shift and strengthen youth's ties to their heritage.

Despite the variations of fluency and comfort in understanding and speaking Native languages for the youth, our participants demonstrated how their Native languages served as a resource for confronting hostile school environments. A Native American college student who participated in the focus groups we piloted among college students before interviewing high school students described how speaking Navajo served as a site of resistance to the racism he encountered when in high school:

> [Hispanics are] New Mexicans, and they have been there for like, you know, like the fourteenth generation of New Mexicans. They really hate Navajos. There would be fights, and the principal, he would suspend and expel the Indian kids, and then one day later, the [Hispanic] New Mexicans would be back after a fight. What we would do is stand against the wall and we start talking our language back and forth between us.

Notably, this young male student's cultural practice was to use his Native language deliberately; it created a blanket of protection and resilience in a hostile and oppressive school context. Most importantly, this act of defiance actively created community and simultaneously contributed to the resiliency of his community through language.

Other students discussed learning about American history and Native American history in culturally relevant ways. The cultural life of New Mexico Native communities is thriving and is carried out continually every day. Native people's artistic creations express the worldview and beliefs of Native people, and students wanted this type of expression represented in their courses. "If we're learning about Americans," said one Native student, "we should [also] be, like, allowed to do an activity in our own [cultural] way—like sing a Native song, bead or make jewelry, make pottery, baskets."

While the youth shared with us their desire for more culturally and linguistically relevant and experientially based education, they also demonstrated their agency and interpersonal domain of power. These attributes, grounded in their cultural identity and heritage, helped the students express their discontent and confront the power structures in their schools. In this way, they set the conditions for achieving the self-definition they desired.

CRITIQUE OF FALSE OR HYPOCRITICAL INCLUSION OF NATIVE KNOWLEDGE AND EXPERIENCES

Youth identified insensitive school administrators as creating barriers for the students' full participation in Pueblo ceremonial obligations. This involved a paternalistic relationship with Native communities. One Pueblo student said, "The dean of students told us that if we were to take part in a dance and stuff for the feast, that we had to specifically go to the governor and ask for a letter." The governor is one of the highest-ranking of the Pueblo leaders, equivalent to the president of the United States for a Pueblo nation. This institutional climate created an unwelcoming environment for many Native youth across New Mexico schools.

When schools include Indigenous histories and perspectives into the curriculum in disingenuous ways or pay mere lip service to the inclusion of students' opinions and perspectives, it creates a distrusting environment in which youth are unwilling to respect and participate. One student discussed this type of duplicitous inclusion in regard to how much their voices count in decision making: "It's like they tell you, 'We want to listen to anything you want to say to us,' but then when you want to say something, it's like you get in trouble for saying it. So there's no point in saying it in the first place."

This type of insincere community engagement is only perfunctory. Providing a forum for Native American voices may be reduced to window dressing, which makes it appear that democratic principles are being practiced. However, if Native Americans continue to be a demographic minority, the underlying power structures can continue to marginalize these voices and experiences under the guise of democracy.

Another student commented on the preconceived, judgmental behavior of some educators toward Native youth: "I don't know, it just feels like a prison sometimes. It's like some of the teachers, they act like they just know you so well when they don't even know your name." Students consistently reported that they were subjected to negative treatment, which assumed that youth were doing something wrong. This reality has created a prison-like school climate for some youth. As this student portrayed, they can read between the lines when they hear the school's rhetoric of inclusion but then experience the actual exclusion of their voice and the negative preconceptions of them and their families and communities as people.

Youth did not mince words in sharing their criticism of colonial education embodied in the standard curriculum, which marginalized the experience of Native Americans in the United States. The inclusion of Native experiences is minimal and again perceived as insincere by the students. A high school student explained: "Well, my freshman year, they didn't really teach us anything about it [Native American history]. We only go, like, probably one section of Native American history." Another student echoed: "Like in New Mexico History, they just talked about how the Spanish took it over and that's it." These social critiques of the disempowering history are akin to academic violence as it denies Native American students the right to recognize their own people's history. Cornel Pewewardy discusses this type of disempowering history, which includes everyone's perspectives and experiences but the students' own, as a form of miseducation of Native youth.[32]

In her ethnography of the experiences of Native American students in one of the most diverse schools in New Mexico, Martinez also unearths critiques of the politics of education that muted and erased Native American experiences from the "official" curriculum.[33] In particular, the high school students interviewed by Martinez were keenly aware of the difference between the "core" courses and the "elective" courses, where Native American content courses were generally housed. Students even criticized the politics of admissions at prestigious colleges that only looked at advanced placement in math, English, French, or Spanish courses as evidence of the "merit" and potential success of students.

AFFIRMATION OF YOUTH INTELLIGENCE AND ABILITIES

Besides criticizing the disempowering curriculum, youth across the middle schools and high schools had a unanimous criticism of banking education. In *banking education*, students are considered empty vessels to be filled with the knowledge of the omniscient teacher.[34] Worksheets devoid of any engagement were particularly problematic. A high school student expressed a common sentiment: "The first semester, we had a teacher—she never taught us anything. So we basically missed out on biology. We used to just like sit there, and she would give us pages out of a book . . . worksheets. And she'll ask us to have them done by the end of the class period. So we try to do them, but we really wouldn't understand any of it." At one of the Pueblo schools, a middle school student lamented, "They give you a piece of paper [a worksheet], and expect you to do it." Another student continued: "I don't like the way they teach. They don't know how. They don't do anything."

We were appalled by the frequency of this complaint; however, students were actively engaged in resisting these oppressive dynamics. For example, student shared with one another which teachers to avoid. The youth also recognized and appreciated teachers who were engaging in transformative pedagogies like relationship building, experiential methods, and making connections with the students' families and community. At one high school, for example, the youth made every effort to take the Navajo language courses because the teacher created caring, reciprocal relationships with the students and created a classroom environment based on respect, trust, and high expectations for learning Navajo.

It is important to juxtapose these youth narratives with those of school administrators who frame students as unengaged, apathetic, or troublemakers. Youth recognize this unfair, often racist, treatment toward them and confront it:

[Staff] talk down to you. Like the other day, we came back from a field trip, and we got back early. We weren't supposed to get back for another two hours. We got back right before the [last class], and some of us had to call our parents to tell them we're coming home at three instead. Well, they stopped us and said, "What are you guys doing out of class?" We asked if we could borrow the phone, and they were just being so rude. I said, "You know what? We just got back from a field trip. Our parents don't think we're getting back 'til five, and she needs to use your phone to call her parents." I had to tell her like that, [because] she wasn't gonna [help us]. And it was rude, I know. But if you're not gonna listen . . .

When this young female student was faced with an administrator who assumed that she and a classmate were skipping class, she had to convey an authoritarian (resisting) stance to garner the respect and attention she needed. She was apologetic because most Native youth are taught not to disrespect those who are older, particularly educators.

Similarly, another youth described the low expectations one teacher expressed for Native American students. Again, drawing on his interpersonal domain of power, this young man challenged those negative assumptions:

We had one teacher that said us Indians would never amount to anything. Mr. X, he is anti-Indian. He would say all Indians are going to be the people who fry burgers. Serious, he would say us Indians will never amount to anything. I got mad. We will prove you wrong. There was another Anglo teacher, and she threatened one of the boys. She said we'd never make it to college. And I told her, "Well, we'll prove you wrong."

These examples of how Native American youth actively resist the controlling images of them as lazy, incompetent, and low-achieving youth are a key reminder of how Native American youth responded to these moments of racist microaggressions. The youth described how they would work toward "proving" the racist wrong by becoming leaders firmly anchored in their identities as Native youth.

YOUTH'S NEGOTIATION OF THE REGIONAL INTOLERANCE AND RACISM PENETRATING SCHOOL CONTEXTS

This theme extends from the previous three by focusing on the particularly anti-Native and otherwise racist environment present in border towns (bordering Native land and non-Native towns). The toxic atmosphere then permeates the school culture.

The racist environment in towns surrounding Native nations has been well documented in the news media over decades. Yet, these towns would not survive without the Native business they garner. In June 2012, the New Mexico secretary of education denied a petition to propose a split of one of the school districts that would have effectively contributed to de facto segregation.[35] The proposal would have created two districts: one that was mostly Anglo and Mormon, and the other mostly Navajo. The proponents of the split included Anglo residents who worried that the current district focused too much on Native culture and traditions instead of math and reading as mandated by the state-based assessment tests. Non-Native parents supporting the split argued that the split was justified because Navajo students were bringing down the overall scores on these tests in their children's schools. Native parents rejected this assertion and instead argued that the split would lead to further marginalization of Native American students through the creation of a de facto segregated school district.

Racial tensions have affected relations between youth, and between adults and youth, in school settings. Native youth were up-front in describing the racial discrimination they experienced. One high school student explained:

> It's all about race here, too. Like some people think Native Americans just get free money and they're stupid and stuff, and you hear other kids down the hall making fun of us and stuff. And that's not right. And the teachers don't do anything about it. Like my freshman year, this kid was—I just called him off because he was making fun of Indians. And he hit me, and I didn't hit him back, and so I got suspended for saying stuff back to him. And he didn't get in trouble. I got in trouble. And it's just all race here, like that's all they think is [that] Native Americans are stupid and stuff.

Another student who attended a border town school located just outside the Native nation's boundaries summed up the climate of the town and the school: "Most people are racist so it's kind of hard here. Like in the community, they're really racist."

Native youth had many stories of bigotry shown to their parents and other community members in the border towns. A focus group with Anglo teachers in one middle school showed its own intolerance and ignorance of the surrounding Pueblo communities. One teacher went as far as to suggest that all his Native students be removed from their homes to attend boarding schools to speed up a Western assimilation process. Another teacher expressed a concern for Native American students who remained ensconced in their Pueblos, as she feared that they would not learn how to be tax-paying members of "mainstream" society.

Youth articulated their experiences against the backdrop of environments that were frequently hostile to their cultures and identities. This was evident in the low expectations among some teachers and school staff who neither understand nor respect Native youth and their cultural heritage. Despite the antagonistic environments many of these youth navigated, they were unafraid and uninhibited in describing the negative interactions they experienced.

Native youth's sense of agency is not only demonstrated in their resistance to these expectations and negative labels. They also recognize the need for attending school and becoming educated to achieve economic and social upward mobility for themselves and their communities. Youth were not satisfied by conventional definitions of what it means to be an educated person. For them, being an educated Native American student meant remaining firmly committed to their identities as Native youth who were actively contributing to the well-being of their communities.

TRANSFORMATIVE POSSIBILITIES: VISIONS OF NATIVE YOUTH

This last theme represents the sense of agency, self-determination, and resilience that Native American youth have for utilizing school and their education for positive change. Notwithstanding the frustrations and microaggressions navigated by the youth, they recognize the school as a vital place for upward mobility for themselves and for their communities.[36]

Realizing that their education can be utilized to transform their communities, they withstand the negative experiences and utilize a grounded cultural identity from which to draw strength and to maintain hope. They want their schools to reflect and respect their culture, and they want to see the school transformed. These students have life goals to serve their communities and want an education that is relevant to those communities.

Native youth envision their education and life goals in communal ways—as service to their communities. A community-oriented purpose in life is a strongly held value in Native communities in the Southwest. It is also related to becoming whole, compassionate, and a true human being in Indigenous philosophies.[37] An aspiring young woman talked about how her connection to her grandfather had solidified her goal to stay in the community:

> I'll probably stay in the community because I want to keep my traditions alive. Like, I don't want to lose anything. Because my grandpa, he's like the one next to the head chief, so like I'm always there for him whenever he needs anything. No questions asked, I'll do it . . . I just want to keep my tradition alive.

Similarly, several youth were asked about their future plans and expressed their aspirations as unequivocally tied to their unwavering commitment to their communities:

- "I wouldn't mind working here. I know it—it probably wouldn't even be the best pay, but I'd still want to come here and support my community here."
- "I want to be, like, an engineer. Maybe if it was for me, and I had time, I'd come and help out with things, like maybe even teach, and donate money or anything that I could to help, just to get something going."
- "I actually want to become a doctor so I can help."
- "I don't know, give something back. Like give back to the community, my community."

Even when youth are unsure about their own future ambitions, as noted in the last quote, their intention remains the same. Their goals are community-minded. Although our study spanned several schools districts across the state of New Mexico, we found that a deep commitment to community and the survival and resilience of Native sovereign nations was a common thread among all the youth we spoke with.

ONE YOUTH PERSPECTIVE: BAHII'S VISION OF HOLISTIC EDUCATION

This section is a portrayal of youth resilience and agency through the experiences of one young man, Bahii. We quoted Bahii in the title of this chapter, and we return to his perspectives and experiences now because of the tremendous insights he shared with regard to what it means to be a successful Native person and how schools should respond to their students' lives and needs, rather than youth conforming to schools' expectations. His experiences highlight the youth resiliency we discuss throughout the chapter.

Bahii lives on the Navajo Nation, was sixteen years old at the time of the study, and lived in a very rural region of the nation. His mother had to commute sixty miles one way to work each day, so Bahii was left with many family responsibilities, such as caring for his younger brother after school, fixing his mother's vehicle when it had problems, cooking for himself and his siblings, hauling wood for their wood-burning stove (the only source of heat in his home), and feeding and training their family's horses, including baling hay for the horses. While some might consider his life to be characterized by poverty and isolation, he presented himself with confidence, strength, and incredible insight. In discussing the responsibilities in his life, Bahii discussed it as maintaining stability and balance; he said, "I keep everybody moving forward instead of moving them back," meaning he does not let any hardships affect their lives negatively.

Bahii recognized the change in Navajo society in terms of the influence of Western society, such as language shift. He also discussed the disconnect he experienced between his school and his life at home and the changing ways and needs of Navajo life. He felt his courses were limiting. He enjoyed courses that taught him skills, such as AutoCAD, a drafting computer program, because he felt it had no boundaries and it allowed him to express his creativity to its full extent. He said he joined the school's Navajo club and participates in its cultural activities as a way to affirm his identity. His school only has one Navajo language teacher—a situation Bahii said is a result of the school's promoting assimilation and positioning Navajo culture as part of the past. But he felt this was wrong: "There's a lot to be learned from Native culture." In explaining the disconnect between school and its relevancy to his own life, he discussed it in terms of the limited ways school influences his learning. Coming from a background of many responsibilities and skills associated with those responsibilities, he discussed school as concealing and stifling:

> It's like there's a different world for me here. It's like school world. It's like your mind's more covered, concealed at school. You're worried about letters and alphabets. But when you're out there, you're worrying about the whole thing. Not only from A to F, your alphabet, but you're looking for A to Z out there.

His goals are to utilize his education to continue to help his family and community. He exercised his agency and commitment to his cultural identity through his desire to become a human being who can transform negative stereotypes and other racist, controlling images of his people.

> I like to go out there and be the best as I can, to show my family proud, to get us out of people thinking that we're nothing but drunks. That's also what I'm getting determined by is to show, to prove to them that actually Native Americans actually have good ideas and intentions instead of thinking in the wrong way. I mean, that's mostly every first impression they [non-Navajos] see when they enter the rez is seeing [Navajo] people that cause the negative thinking towards them. But I guess the world says that once I did good, no one remembers, but once I do bad, no one

forgets. It's like that . . . I could say I'm trying to prove to them I'm not like that, savages.

Bahii acknowledged that the social problems that some of his people experience and that are related to the poor socioeconomic conditions of the communities leave negative, lasting impressions. But he wants to challenge that limited notion of his people and set an example. Bahii's hopes and desires may not be supported in his school, but we found through another school that when the cultural identity and experiences of students like Bahii are understood and utilized as a resource, instead of as a deficit, youth flourish in these settings; they enjoy school, see its relevance to their lives, and recognize how their education can be applied to their communities.

TRANSFORMATIVE EDUCATIONAL POSSIBILITIES: EMPOWERED YOUTH AND COMMUNITIES

Sovereignty Charter School (SCS) provides one example of the transformative possibilities for Native youth. SCS was founded to provide a holistic education for Native youth, mirroring the tenets of Indigenous philosophies discussed earlier.[38] Its goals are as follows:

- Build youth to be confident in their cultural identities.
- Encourage youth to persevere academically.
- Support physical, emotional, and spiritual wellness in youth.
- Prepare youth academically and emotionally for college.
- Strengthen youth to take their role as leaders.

SCS promotes core values for all students and staff to embody and practice in all activities and courses at SCS. Those values include respect, responsibility, community service, culture, perseverance, and reflection. These values directly relate to Native communal values and goals for using one's education to contribute back to one's community. The wellness philosophy of the school is practiced through courses (personal wellness), the food (healthy foods policy), and the wellness wheel, where students relate their growth to academic, physical, social-emotional, cultural, and spiritual indicators. Youth spoke excitedly about student-led conferences, where they used the wellness wheel to demonstrate their growth to all their family and other significant people in their lives, not just immediate family members. One student explained the student-led conference and the use of the wellness wheel:

> [The student-led conference is like] a parent-teacher conference, but it's way better 'cause we get to do it our way, to where it's not really just with your mom or dad, or your parents. You can have different family members or friends come in. You talk about your grades. You talk about what you like here at school and what you don't like, and how you can fix it. You have goals of yourself or for yourself. And you talk about how you want to reach it. You also have a wellness wheel—it talks about how you're feeling in academics, physical, intellectual.

Native perspectives and knowledge are also integrated across the curriculum. Unlike the majority of youth we spoke with, youth who attended SCS described a number of examples of this empowering approach. One student explained:

> The school year is different than many others that I went to. The classes here, there's studies that's focused around Native culture. And, like, we refer the classes, such as math, like the way Native Americans did math in their way . . . We're studying how the Mayans did their math. Like their predictions.

Similarly, students described pedagogical practices at SCS that were anchored in acknowledging students' and their families' experiences and knowledge. Those experiences are significant inclusions to learning about Native people's history and lives today. One youth discussed how she was able to utilize her grandmother's experiences when learning about the history and impact of boarding schools:

> We're [studying] Indian boarding school or, basically, Indian schools. And . . . then the teacher's kind of like encouraging us to go like interview people from our families, not to just take it from, like, Web places and books and stuff. So I'm actually getting to, like, read my grandma's journal before she passed away.

All of these students spoke very excitedly about how they draw on their identities to create their paths. The extracurricular activities are driven by student interest, such as the Powwow Club, Comic Book Club, and SCS Rocks (a rock-and-roll history and music course). This culturally enriching environment is aligned with high expectations for attaining higher education beyond high school. Students take dual-credit courses in their junior and senior years with the University of New Mexico and Central New Mexico Community College. SCS arranges whole-class college campus visits and created a staff position, director of college preparation, to assist students with applications, test preparation, and social and emotional readiness for college. Of the first graduating class of twenty students, two students were Gates Millennium scholars. Collectively, the graduates earned over $500,000 in scholarship funding to support their higher education.[39]

Students repeatedly described SCS as truly a student-centered school. Despite the pressures of meeting standardized testing levels, the school found a way of providing a culturally and linguistically responsive education, while also holding high expectations of students for a college education. At the same time, the students at SCS have performed at higher levels on standards-based assessments in reading and writing, and at similar levels in math as their peers in traditional public schools. For example, SCS students outperformed the state average score for Native American students in all five subject areas tested.[40] These results suggest the student-centered, culturally relevant approach is aiding students' performance on state tests.

We have learned from the perspectives of Bahii and the examples from Sovereignty Charter School that youth understand and appreciate an education that recognizes their prior knowledge and experiences. They appreciate and find meaning in education that is directly relevant to their families, communities, and heritage. This approach in education is rigorous and holistic. Educators can be assured that an education that is centered on their students' experiences and values can motivate those students, and those students will achieve. There is less meaning in an education that is centered on standards and curriculum with little or no connection to the realities of students' lives.

This chapter began with a powerful quote from Bahii, a Navajo male whose repertoire of cultural practice was anchored in knowing who he is through knowing his culture as a young Native man in contemporary U.S. society. Throughout the rest of the chapter, we ground Native youth's perspectives of education by illustrating how they engaged in resistance to negative labels that frame Native American youth as deficient. Instead, we found that Native American youth find ways to seek out support and resources for expressing and strengthening their cultural identity and respect for their communities. They carve out their identities by honoring their cultural values and demanding an education that respects and includes Indigenous knowledge and experiences.

The youth in our study demonstrated the multitude of complex experiences they have in and out of school. They teach us that to truly understand their lives in meaningful ways, it is important for all educators to view their lives holistically and to recognize how they resist and confront the notions of deficits. One youth offered a powerful transformative example of how he would go about mapping the complexity of experiences Native American youth have in New Mexico schools:

If you really, really want to understand it, spend at least a week here. And you will find out every little thing—when kids are being harassed, when kids are being told that they're no good, they're not gonna go nowhere. And when kids are being avoided by teachers, and how teachers have their favorites—I would say that you have to spend a week. At least spend one day in our shoes and see what we go through every day.

As a leader in his school setting, this young man articulated a counterhegemonic definition of the dominant and racist narratives of underachieving Native American students who do not value education. His statement compels educators to confront those inequities, as the youth in this study have shown. They face and tackle the labels and persevere. When Native youth are recognized as human beings and their growth is facilitated with Indigenous goals and values in mind, such as the way the Sovereignty Charter School does, youth become excited about the possibilities education holds for them. They are then supported to achieve their goals of transforming their communities in meaningful and positive ways.

8

In the MAC

Creating Safe Spaces for Transgender Youth of Color

Ed Brockenbrough and Tomás Boatwright

FOR TRANSGENDER YOUTH of color, finding safe spaces can be a complex endeavor. While their multiple identities afford potential membership in various racial, gender, sexual, socioeconomic, and youth communities, their multiple forms of difference may place them in the margins of the myriad social and cultural contexts in which they exist. As these young people negotiate shifting identity politics and arrangements of power in their search for places to call home, what strategies can they and their allies employ to create spaces that are fully inclusive and supportive of transgender youth of color? In this chapter, we explore this question by examining the factors that enabled and challenged the inclusion of transgender youth of color at the Midtown AIDS Center (MAC), an HIV/AIDS prevention center in a midsize city in the northeastern United States.[1] Despite its mission to serve lesbian, gay, bisexual, transgender, and queer (LGBTQ) youth of color, the nonprofit MAC struggled at times to create an inclusive space for transgender youth. Interviews with two transgender youth, along with other study data, reveal not only how transgender marginalization was produced at MAC, but also how the two transgender youth used MAC to create transgender-supportive networks. Thus, this chapter illuminates the need for spaces that are inclusive of transgender youth of color and points to strategies for creating such spaces—strategies that engage transgender youth of color and their allies in anti-oppressive pedagogies of possibility.

Throughout this chapter, *transgender* and the abbreviated *trans* refer to persons who, in any number of ways, do not fit neatly into traditional gender binaries of male or female. This includes people who undergo hormone therapy or reassignment surgery, or both, to *transition* from one gender to another, as well as people like drag queens, drag kings, and genderqueers who do not undergo such procedures but identify and express themselves in ways that may *transgress* the boundaries between conventional Western definitions of male and female.[2] The two trans participants whose interview narratives are featured in this chapter were born as males but identified as females and were at various stages in their transition to womanhood.

TRANS YOUTH MARGINALITY AND AGENCY

Transphobia—the construction of trans individuals and communities as aberrant Others, and the discriminatory cultural attitudes and institutional practices that follow suit—requires transgender youth in the United States to negotiate a number of obstacles.[3] Many trans youth struggle to come out to, and find acceptance from, their parents or guardians, and the American Psychological Association's ongoing classification of transgenderism as "gender identity disorder"—a sickness—continues to pathologize and endanger transgender children.[4] For those seeking hormone therapy or surgical procedures, a lack of financial resources, combined with age-of-consent barriers within medical institutions, can prevent them from accessing services.[5] Trans youth as a whole experience alarming rates of suicidality, and for trans youth of color, their location at the intersections of multiple oppressions make them especially vulnerable to threats of violence, homelessness, employment discrimination, and the HIV/AIDS epidemic.[6] As all of these factors make clear, trans youth must contend with a litany of challenges to their safety, sanity, self-determination, and freedom.

The reach of transphobic encounters across familial, medical, and other contexts of trans youths' lives makes access to safe educational spaces all the more important. While a growing body of scholarship has explored the educational experiences of LGBTQ youth, attention within this literature specifically to transgender youth remains scant. Several texts offer potential strategies for trans inclusion, but these strategies are based primarily on anecdotal evidence or theoretical literature.[7] To date, the analysis of transgender youths' responses to the Gay Lesbian Straight Education Network's (GLSEN) 2007 National School Climate Survey provides the most insightful snapshots of trans youths' educational experiences, specifically in K–12 schools.[8] As noted in GLSEN's report, almost all trans respondents reported enduring verbal harassment, over half reported enduring physical harassment (being "pushed or shoved"), and a quarter reported enduring physical assault (being "punched, kicked, or injured with a weapon") over the previous year in their schools. This in-school harassment occurred at higher rates than those reported by nontrans students.[9] Furthermore, trans students who reported high levels of harassment were more likely to skip school than other students because of safety concerns, and when compared with their less frequently harassed trans peers, these trans students had lower grade point averages and more tentative aspirations for enrolling in college. While more research clearly is needed on the educational experiences of transgender youth, the GLSEN report—the most illuminating source to date—suggests that transphobia pervades American K–12 schools, compromises trans youths' safety, and undermines trans youths' academic achievement and aspirations.

The obstacles facing trans youth, though formidable, are not necessarily insurmountable. While much of the literature on trans youth emphasizes the transphobic constraints imposed on their lives, Megan Davidson's study of activism by queer youth of color reminds us that trans youth of color have the agency, as well as the support of allies, to make space for their own existence.[10] As gentrification of New York City's West Village—a longtime haven for trans and queer youth of color—made these young people vulnerable to increased surveillance and police harassment, Davidson chronicled the collective organizing of trans and queer youth of color to assert their right to occupy this space. More studies like Davidson's are needed to understand how trans youth of color resist the repressive regimes that shape their lives, and how their allies can support their resistance. This chapter's focus on the politics of trans inclusion at the MAC is one attempt to address those aims, with a particular eye toward informing educational spaces that engage trans youth of color in developing and deploying pedagogies of possibility.

THE STUDY

This chapter reports a set of findings from our study of how LGBTQ youth of color addressed their educational needs by utilizing resources at a not-for-profit HIV/AIDS prevention agency in Midtown, a midsize city in the northeastern United States. In order to delve more deeply into the agency's current and potential function as an educational space, we employed qualitative research methods to illuminate the embedded meanings of study participants' perspectives on their experiences at the agency. Data collection, spanning from January to July 2011, consisted of the following: an audiorecorded and transcribed, in-depth, one-on-one interview with each study participant (the interviews lasted 1.5 to 2 hours); observations and field notes on youth-oriented programs and events; and collections of the agency's reports, newsletters, fliers, and other relevant material. Using a grounded-theory approach, each data source was coded line-by-line to generate initial codes, which were examined across data sources to create categories and subcategories for organizing the data. Additionally, analytic profiles of each study participant were created to illuminate the relevance of various codes to each participant's narrative and to reveal themes that may not have been fully captured by coding schemes. Throughout these iterative phases of data analysis, we analyzed data sources independently and then jointly to generate and refine codes, and we shared preliminary reports of findings with multiple audiences to solicit feedback that further refined our data analysis.

Given our interest in exploring alternative educational spaces for LGBTQ youth of color, the MAC—the only space in Midtown that featured a specific emphasis on programming for LGBTQ youth of color—was chosen as the site for this study. As queer male educators and scholars of color with a commitment to social justice, we felt strongly that our presence at MAC could not be limited to data collection for our research, especially given the educational aspirations of MAC youth and the center's limited resources to fully support those aspirations. Thus, we volunteered at MAC for a year prior to initiating our study and continued to help out after data collection by tutoring MAC youth, serving as panelists on MAC-sponsored college and career forums, and providing support to staff during several MAC youth workshops. Not only did these activities enable us to build trusting relationships with MAC staff and youth, but they also allowed us to give something back to those who had graciously and courageously invited us into their lives.

In all, eight adult staff members and volunteers and ten youth who regularly participated in MAC's youth programming enrolled in the study. Youth participants ranged in age from seventeen to twenty-two, and among the youth participants were two trans youth: Binky, a nineteen-year-old black and Puerto Rican trans female who was enrolled in community college; and Nicole, a seventeen-year-old black trans female who was a high school junior. Because of this chapter's focus on the politics of trans inclusion at MAC, Binky and Nicole's perspectives receive particular attention in the analysis that follows.

CHALLENGES TO TRANSGENDER INCLUSION

While trans advocates have increasingly situated the struggle for trans justice over the past two decades within LGBTQ communities and advocacy initiatives, transphobic blind spots within these contexts have frequently placed trans voices and concerns on the margins.[11] Mirroring this broader resistance to trans inclusion, the center presented several challenges to the full participation by trans youth of color in its programs and institutional culture. Two of the biggest challenges were the limited funding for trans-specific programming and the tensions surrounding trans female sex work.

Limited Funding for Trans-Specific Programming

The MAC's youth programming did not target all of its youth constituencies equally. Out of 148 programs and services listed on MAC's events calendars from January to June 2011, only 6 had a specific focus on transgender issues. While all 6 of these programs were open to trans youth, only 2 were part of the 108 youth-oriented programs and services offered over that period. One reason for the scarcity of trans-specific programming was MAC's reliance on restrictive governmental funding. As one senior staff member explained during an interview, the erosion of federal funding streams had left MAC heavily dependent on state grants that funded HIV/AIDS prevention efforts specifically targeting young black men who have sex with men (MSM), a population that had recently seen severe spikes in HIV infection rates throughout the state.[12] Under strict state surveillance of grant implementation, MAC staff members were obligated to rigidly tailor state-supported programs toward young black MSM.

The narrow focus that typified MAC's advertised programs and services did not go unnoticed by trans youth. As Binky stated during her one-on-one interview, "I saw that when I came here, a lot of the funding was just for MSM and didn't include transgender. To me that's a sign of loopholes, and I don't believe that's fair, because transgender groups are only on Saturdays now. So I definitely saw a problem and I want to fix it." While retaining a belief in her ability to remedy this dilemma, Binky still understood that funding for young black MSM HIV prevention initiatives had produced lopsided programming at MAC and had pushed transgender issues increasingly to the margins. Binky's criticism, along with the senior staff member's explanation of funding stream constraints and the lack of trans-specific events on MAC's calendars, pointed to the center's programming as an important arena for understanding the challenges to trans inclusion.

Tensions Surrounding Trans Female Sex Work

Limited state funding for trans-specific programming at MAC was symptomatic of a much broader set of social and economic circumstances that produced trans marginality. Pathologizing medical discourses, job and housing discrimination, and violence are among the myriad factors that make up the transphobic landscape of American culture.[13]

As researchers in public health have noted, the lack of social acceptance and support networks, economic hardships due to transphobic barriers to employment, and other structural and cultural hurdles have led a number of transgender women, particularly transgender women of color, to rely on sex work to earn money for survival.[14] This reliance on sex work starts in adolescence for some transgender females of color as family rejection and homelessness lead them to this survival strategy.[15] Binky and Nicole, the trans youth who were interviewed for this study, were not engaged in sex work. However, some of the other trans female youth at MAC, in the face of limited employment opportunities and other challenges, were relying on sex work to make ends meet. Aware of this predicament, some young gay males, or "butch queens," as they were commonly called at MAC, engaged in transphobic discourses about trans female sex work that created explosive tensions among their peers and threatened the trans inclusiveness of the space.[16]

The most animated examples of the opprobrium for trans female involvement in sex work emerged in a workshop that we facilitated at the beginning of the study. During the session, we invited MAC youth to discuss, unpack, and question the meaning of *LGBTQ*. To elicit youth perspectives, we posted large sheets of paper on the walls of a meeting room. Each sheet had one of the LGBTQ identity labels written at the top of it, and youth were asked to write lists of whatever came to mind when they saw each identity label. In the case of "Transgender," endearing colloquial terms for individuals who might fall under the trans moniker, including

"T-girls" and "Fem Queen" (friendly colloquialisms in LGBTQ circles for trans females), were joined by pejorative descriptors, including "Craigslist Whores," "Prostitutes," "backpage," "Back list," "Broadway," and "Broadway bitches."[17] All of these responses "outed" the participation of some trans females in the sex industry. Along with disparaging descriptions of sex acts, "Craigslist Whores," "backpage," and "Back list" were specific references to Web sites where some trans females who were involved in the sex industry would advertise their services, and "Broadway" was the name of a Midtown street frequented by trans female sex workers. In contrast to the friendlier set of colloquialisms, the latter terms were clearly intended as insults.

As a mix of excitement and contempt swelled in the room, several trans females who were participating in the activity added pejorative terms to the list of descriptions of "Gay," such as "will always be a faggot," "Vogue every day," "aldutry [sic]," "Escorts," and "Confused."[18] These descriptions, like the derogatory terms on the transgender list, attempted to denigrate the gay male butch queens in the room by associating them with scandalous sexual acts. Additionally, responses like "Vogue every day" and "will always be a faggot" depicted butch queens as engaged in frivolous activities that destined them to remain worthless individuals. The antagonistic nature of the terms written on both the transgender and the gay lists became painfully apparent as we attempted to facilitate a whole-group discussion on the responses. A shouting match erupted between the trans females seated on one side of the room and the butch queens seated across from them, with each group accusing the other of ill intentions, wrongdoings, and indecent acts. After ten minutes, several youth walked out, and a few more were asked to leave by staff to prevent further conflict. The entire episode sadly yet poignantly underscored the sharp animosity between some trans females and butch queens at MAC.

Binky, one of the trans participants in this study, was present during the tumultuous workshop session and actually defended her butch queen friends against attacks from other trans females. In an interview, she elaborated on the tensions between the trans females and butch queens who had participated in the workshop:

No shade, they've gotten beat up by almost every youth in here 'cause [the transgender girls] have a lot of mouth . . . I'm not saying all the transgender girls, the main group. There's about six, and . . . they have a lot of mouth and they think that butch queens are disgusting and all that. But I'm like, "Well, you used to be a butch queen and you used to do the same things. You used to be in the back room of MAC voguing, so why are you all high and mighty? You're women now, okay, I respect that, but don't forget where you came from. You used to be here with us, chilling and everything, and because you became a girl and now you are 'working women,' you're all high and mighty. News flash, you can't claim your job on your taxes if it's illegal." So I feel that they need a reality check and they need help—not mental help, maybe—but you know, there's something in them that they're unhappy about and they're taking it out on anyone else. So there's a lot of tension between the girls [the butch queens] and the T-girls that aren't humble.

Binky's references to prior physical altercations between the trans females with "a lot of mouth" and other youth underscored the severity of the tensions between the groups. Since the trans females described by Binky in this passage agreed to participate in the opening workshop but did not volunteer to be interviewed, we were unable to explore their perspectives on why and how hostilities had emerged between them and their butch queen peers. Nevertheless, pejorative terms from the workshop like "Craigslist whores," along with Binky's interview remarks about "working women" who could not claim their illegal work on their taxes, indicated negative attitudes toward trans female sex work as an ongoing source of tension among the youth at MAC.

Revisiting this dynamic later in her interview, Binky offered insights that illuminated her own strained relationships with other trans females at MAC:

Unfortunately, the older girls—I wouldn't say older, the generation before me of T-girls, maybe in their twenties—don't like me or the other new girl, Nicole. They don't like the newer girls, because they feel that we're competition to them, and it's like the crab-in-the-barrel effect. They're going to pull you down so that you won't go ahead of them . . . So and then I've always tried to give a helping hand, whether it's name change, food help, clothing, doing hair, if you need help with school. I always try to help, and they feel I'm being stuck up because I'm trying to help you. "Oh, you got your name changed, you think you're all that." No, it was for me, not for you all. I don't care. So a lot of them don't like me and that's a relationship I wish I could mend.

As she mentioned in this excerpt, Binky had managed to complete the legal process (which could be lengthy and costly) for changing her name. She noted elsewhere in her interview that she also had secured a job, enrolled in community college, and rented an apartment with a few of her butch queen friends (with support for some of these activities from MAC staff, as discussed later). By contrast, some of her slightly older trans female peers—the ones engaged in sex work—had not achieved some of Binky's accomplishments. With employment status, educational access, and other factors protecting her from a reliance on the sex industry, Binky found herself at odds with some trans females on the other side of the sex work divide.

Binky was not the only study participant who noted the fallout from the tensions surrounding trans female involvement in sex work. Aaron, a gay male youth study participant, noted his reticence toward being associated with some trans females because of their dubious reputations:

I think that transgenders, they set a bad name for the gay community because of the way they come out of the house looking, the way they carry themselves overall . . . Say, for example, I walk down the street with a transgender who gets around and who is a whore; they're going to look at me the same way.

Echoing Aaron's anxiety toward being associated with "whorish" trans females, Peggy Lee, a MAC staff member, noted that tensions between trans female and butch queen youth were affecting attendance patterns at MAC events, with each group trying to avoid the other. Both Aaron and Peggy's interview responses revealed that even when trans and gay youth were not engaged in direct confrontations with each other, the tensions between the two groups could discourage ongoing associations.

While Peggy attempted to support trans female sex workers by facilitating workshops on safety precautions and offering tips on how to eventually exit the sex industry, negative attitudes toward trans female sex work continued to fuel volatile divides between trans females and butch queens, and among trans females themselves. Without a clear resolution, this recurrent point of tension continually complicated youth interactions at MAC, posing a serious challenge to the center's capacity to be fully inclusive of transgender youth.

TRANS-SUPPORTIVE NETWORKS

Although the Midtown AIDS Center faced major challenges to becoming fully inclusive of trans youth, the potential for trans inclusion was not completely lost. Family studies scholar Ramona Oswald explains that gays and lesbians often establish intentional, family-like networks with others who support them in overcoming the marginalization they experience because of their sexual orientations.[19] These relationships are useful for redistributing resources and information and establishing emotional support, particularly if biological familial support is strained or nonexistent. Mirroring what Oswald characterizes as a gay and lesbian phenomenon, both Binky and Nicole, the two trans participants in this study, drew upon the LGBTQ-defined space at MAC to establish trans-supportive networks with youth peers, trans mentors and role models, and staff members. Having tenuous relationships with their biological families because of their affirmed trans identities, Binky and Nicole used their trans-supportive networks to make MAC more responsive to their needs as trans youth.

After recalling her biological family's rejection of her because of her trans identity, Nicole detailed the intricate support system that she had developed to help her navigate her life experiences:

> My support comes from all over. My support really comes from my family and friends. Not like biological family or friends, but my family and friends. Like biologically, I don't have that many. I have family, but my support doesn't come within my family . . . My family comes from all over. For example, [MAC staffer] Peggy, I consider her family 'cause she does a lot for me. Or Binky, she's family because I can trust her. Or [MAC gay male youth] Skittles, I can trust him. Like, family is someone, if you came to my circle and made it clear that you're pro me and not against me, you're more than an ally. You're just like you want to be in my circle and you're family, and that circle is a family circle. You could be on the outside, which is an ally. You could be outside the ally, which is an enemy or a friend.

For Nicole, the trans-supportive networks that she identified as family consisted of individuals who were invested in her life. Critical of conventional definitions of family as just biological relatives, Nicole reached beyond her own biological family unit to redefine family as inclusive of MAC youth peers like Binky and Skittles (and MAC staff members like Peggy, who will be further discussed later), whom she could truly trust. For Nicole, MAC became an appropriate setting to develop relationships with peers she believed would support her and understand her experiences.

In addition to establishing a trans-supportive network with MAC youth peers, Binky and Nicole sought out older trans women of color as mentors and role models. Through the formation of these connections, MAC again served as a space for cultivating trans-supportive relationships. In some cases, trans mentors provided vital firsthand knowledge of the realities of simply existing as transgender women. Binky elaborated on this as she described her relationship with a trans woman of color named Symone, her "gay mom" and a former member of MAC's Lead Team, a peer leadership group that helped to shape MAC's youth programming:[20]

Symone was a member of the Lead Team, and she's my gay mom. Symone, nonstop helping me, encouraging me never to settle for less, never to get punked, always go for the real surge. And she definitely encouraged me to get my name changed. She was the first one to tell me, "Hey, your makeup using, stop it." So, like, she helped me with a lot. She helped me, like, "Hey, this is how you can make your chest look like yours even though it's not there," and "This is the clinic you can go to for hormones," and "This is how you get your health care."

Binky's description of the care and advice she received from Symone illuminated the importance of having a trans mentor with trans-specific experiential knowledge. By offering advice on how to enhance the quality of one's gender presentation as female, where to receive hormone therapy for gender transitioning, and the importance of undergoing legitimate gender transitioning procedures—or "the real surge"—instead of more accessible yet dangerous alternatives, Symone played an invaluable role in Binky's MAC-mediated, trans-supportive network.

Like Binky, Nicole also described the importance of older trans women of color as mentors and role models. In addition to attending youth programs at MAC, Nicole participated in the house/ball community, a national network of social groups—or houses—that provided familial, intergenerational support within black and Latino LGBTQ communities. The network recurrently convened at social events called balls.[21] Nicole reflected on how meeting one of her idols, a popular trans woman of color in the house/ball scene, at a MAC-sponsored forum on the history and politics of the house/ball community, inspired her own future aspirations:

Just recently I met an individual who was my idol, who is a transgender woman who's famous in the ballroom scene but has a PhD. I felt like, well, she wants to get a doctoral degree and I want my doctoral degree. And she's also pretty, and I thought I'm pretty—well I know I'm pretty—so I believed her, and she really made an impact on my life. Like I was a flower in the process of growing, and I feel like seeing her was that last step in that process for my blossoming, and I felt like I blossomed to a rose now.

For Nicole, meeting this highly regarded trans woman of color who was about to earn a doctoral degree enabled her to envision the possibilities of her own future. This woman's impact on Nicole's educational aspirations is another indication of the importance of trans female role models for trans youth like Nicole.

Along with connecting them to youth peers and older trans female role models and mentors, being involved at MAC enabled Binky and Nicole to recruit one more important constituency into their trans-supportive networks: MAC staff members. Both Binky and Nicole described how MAC staff members supported their physical and emotional development as young trans females. Nicole reflected on her attempts to gather information about puberty, ultimately finding knowledge and support from staff member Peggy Lee:

> MAC offered help [during] my process, my mental process of my gender role and identity, I guess, and also therapy sessions with Peggy helped me a lot. For example, I recently had a session with Peggy about puberty 'cause I was going through a lot of stuff. I didn't know what it was, and she was somebody I could relate to. She kind of gave information about what I was going through and kind of helped me with it—young female puberty . . . Like if I had a mother, I would ask my mother, but I have a sister, but she wasn't here at the time, you know. But it's information which I could get from anywhere, but I'd rather get it from Peggy.

Nicole pointed specifically to Peggy several times as a reliable source of support for her around trans-specific issues. Likewise, Binky identified Peggy as an especially supportive MAC staffer in several interview responses, including the following:

> I came back to MAC right before my transition. I met Peggy and I poured my heart out to her for some reason. Like I told her that yeah, I'm transgender, and then we were like sitting there talking about it. And I'm like, "'Well, I don't know this bitch and she don't know me,' but I was sitting

here telling you my life story because I'm enjoying you," and she became my mom. And like I became a Lead Team member, like, two weeks later. I started attending events regularly. I started throwing events and really becoming an active member.

For both Nicole and Binky, Peggy's responsiveness to their need for trans-specific supports positioned her as a go-to person on MAC's staff, and for Binky, Peggy even became a mother figure at MAC. Strategically testing the waters during moments of trans disclosures, Nicole and Binky were able to identify Peggy as someone who could be trusted to support and care for them as young trans women of color.

Although Peggy emerged across interview responses and other data sources as the point person of sorts for trans support and advocacy, other staff members were also identified as part of the trans-supportive network at MAC. Binky cited all of the staffers as she described how MAC had supported her during her gender transition:

> MAC is the only organization I feel comfortable with because they helped me throughout my transition. Bernard, Peggy, Tina at times, even Collette, Graham, Greg, Kyle—all of them. They helped me understand different types of sexuality, making sure that I was really transgender, [that] I wasn't a transvestite or just a drag queen and under the umbrella term *transgender*. They really helped me find a job, résumé building. So this is the one place I know where yes, I may be transsexual, but they see me still as Binky. They don't see me as Brandon anymore, even though it was like an overnight process. Like, I came in, July 9 was my last day at work as a boy; July 10, I came back with a full head of weave. So even though it was an overnight thing, they still saw Binky. They accepted me for me.

By being in Binky's corner in a variety ways during her trans coming of age, MAC staffers positioned themselves to varying degrees as members of Binky's trans-supportive network.

In sum, Binky and Nicole's perspectives on their MAC experiences revealed that their participation in the space connected them to their peers, older trans mentors and role models, and staff members who supported their development as young trans females. The trans-supportive networks developed via MAC did not obviate the challenges to trans inclusion described earlier in this chapter, but did create meaningful opportunities for Binky and Nicole to locate valuable resources. While these networks reflect positively on the individuals who willingly offered trans-sensitive support, they also speak volumes to the mix of courage, self-awareness, and intuition that enabled Binky and Nicole to confidently articulate their needs and strategically identify individuals who could respond to them. In this way, the trans-supportive networks described above can be understood as a co-creation of MAC stakeholders and the trans youth themselves, reflecting the agency of all parties in creating space at MAC for trans youth of color. These networks also suggest what pedagogies of possibility for trans youth of color might look like in youth-serving institutions, an implication that is discussed in the section that follows.

STRATEGIES FOR TRANS INCLUSION

A growing body of educational scholarship over the past decade has emphasized the importance of creating safe spaces for LGBTQ youth.[22] Like all young people, LGBTQ youth deserve access to spaces where they can exist freely and safely. However, creating a safe space for all LGBTQ youth is not necessarily a simple undertaking, especially when the diversity of identities that may occupy such a space is taken into account. Education scholar Lance McCready has examined how one high school's gay-straight alliance, predominated by white lesbians, struggled to include black gay and gender-nonconforming males.[23] Similarly, this chapter spotlights the transphobic blind spots that left trans youth on the margins of a center designed to serve LGBTQ youth of color. Though disheartening, these blind spots should not be surprising, given the history of trans marginality in LGBTQ communities and politics.[24] As educational stakeholders and youth advocates continue to push for safe spaces for LGBTQ youth, they must do so with a more sophisticated understanding of safe space—one that accounts for, and responds to, the internal deficiencies that can make LGBTQ youth-defined spaces more responsive to some youth over others.

Through a more nuanced understanding of safe space, educational stakeholders and youth advocates can nurture pedagogies of possibility that seek to address the specific needs of transgender youth of color. While not generalizable to the experiences of all trans youth of color, the findings presented in this chapter do provide a starting point for identifying specific strategies that may create safe spaces for this particular population. In light of our study findings, the following strategies seem worthy of further consideration:

1. For health-focused community agencies like the Midtown AIDS Center, which often rely heavily on state and federal grants to provide youth-oriented programming, it may prove beneficial to tap into additional funding streams that would allow more flexibility to address the needs of a range of participants, including trans youth of color.
2. Agencies like MAC and other youth-serving institutions, including schools, might consider having trans people of color on staff or available as mentors, thus affording trans youth of color with access to role models who possess firsthand experiential knowledge on trans issues (as Binky and Nicole's role models did).
3. These institutions might also consider having professional development sessions on issues facing trans youth of color so that all staff— even those who are not trans people of color (like MAC staffer Peggy Lee)—can provide some measure of support.
4. Institutions working with trans youth of color could consider having specific resources in place to help the youth who are transitioning. These resources might include a network of trusted and culturally sensitive medical providers, legal supports for changing one's name, and educational or career counseling to help trans youth of color like Binky and Nicole (who were quite ambitious) to pursue their professional aspirations while undergoing major personal transformations.

Again, these strategies are offered as starting points for ongoing considerations of pedagogies of possibility that might better serve transgender youth of color. Reflecting an understanding of pedagogical work as opportunities for exploration and empowerment in and beyond school settings, these strategies have the potential to benefit trans youth of color across the multiple contexts of their lives.

Lastly, it is essential that future pedagogical efforts in support of trans youth of color center the voices and agency of these youth through assets-oriented lenses rather than deficit-oriented ones. Despite facing a daunting array of challenges, Binky and Nicole developed their own strategies for locating resources and building trans-supportive networks. Discourses that linger on the burdens of trans marginality will miss the resourcefulness of these marginalized youth—a resourcefulness that can actually guide allies toward genuine collaboration and meaningful action with transgender youth of color.

9

En Mi Barrio

Building on Cuban Youth Culture, Hip-Hop, and Reggaetón

Ezekiel Dixon-Román and Wilfredo Gomez

THE COMMUNIST ISLAND OF Cuba is witnessing many structural evolutions today. Indeed, the political leadership is aging and ideologically departing from some of the political practices led by Fidel Castro. Under Raúl Castro, the government has attempted to be more responsive to the interest of the people (e.g., introducing cell phones or allowing Internet use in hotels) while also trying to create a sustainable socialist economy under global capitalism (e.g., expanding the private market or investing in oil and natural resources). Despite the numerous successes that the Cuban Revolution achieved in education and health care, many Cubans continue to live under austere conditions; increased inequality, materialism, and consumerism due to tourism; and a fractured moral economy.[1] However, Cubans are not ideologically monolithic, and their desires and interests are diverse. Thus, the focus on political and economic changes runs the risk of missing the social, cultural, and ideological shifts that materialize in Cuban everyday practices, particularly for the youth (i.e., Cubans between the ages of fifteen and thirty). How might the Cuban youth make do (i.e., act, adapt, and survive) in the face of the current conditions of austerity and rapid political and economic changes? How might youth cultural productions create opportunities for engaging critical and transformative dialogue? How are pedagogical processes present within the dialogue of these youth cultural productions, particularly for the marginalized? And, how might the transformative possibilities in youth cultural productions be galvanized for cultural change? These questions will explore the meaningful pedagogy in the creative and adaptive everyday practices of youth living in conditions of social and economic austerity. Moreover, the questions will help show how others can employ these youth cultural practices and productions for transformative possibilities.

This chapter is part of a larger program of research investigating the multiplicity of Cuban youth cultures. Much of the Cuban government and the rest of the world have broadly depicted the youth of the Caribbean communist nation as homogeneous (e.g., the Cuban government outlawed a documentary that exposed the multiplicity of youth culture and perspectives on G Street in Havana). Our work seeks to demonstrate not only that a monolithic perspective of Cuban youth culture is far from the only narrative to be told, but also that youth's cultural movements like hip-hop and reggaetón represent spaces where one can engage Cuban youth and the multiplicity of perspectives on their current living conditions. We analyze the cultural productions of hip-hop and reggaetón in Cuba and their transformative possibilities for the reenvisioning and remaking of young people's futures.[2]

Specifically, we focus on En Mi Barrio, a community project founded and directed by Cuban hip-hop artist Lourdes Suarez. En Mi Barrio uses the medium of hip-hop to raise funds for communal libraries where information can be accessed, while conducting workshops and other programs that are safe spaces where participants can talk about issues of identity, gender, tolerance, difference, and the like. The program operates year round and travels from neighborhood to neighborhood, attempting to raise awareness of these matters in Cuban society. This project is key in creating cultural change among the youth in Cuba via hip-hop culture. As described later in this chapter, the cultural change En Mi Barrio seeks to forge does not radically depart from the Cuban Revolution but reinforces ideas of equality, literacy, tolerance, and, ultimately, a commitment to Cuban history and culture.

One cannot do work in Cuba today without situating it historically within the political and economic context of the post–Special Period. The hardest economic time of the Cuban Revolution, the Special Period (in a time of peace) was brought on by Cuba's weakened political and economic relationship with the falling Soviet Union in 1988 and continued through 1994, when the island turned to tourism for national income. As will be discussed, the Special Period created social and economic austerity and generational gaps in how the revolution was perceived. The youth growing up during, or after, the Special Period began to become increasingly more disenchanted with the revolution. As many Cuban young people have put it, the Cuban Revolution was their grandparents' and parents' revolution, not their own. The youth not only imagined something beyond their current living conditions, but also found a form of cultural production in hip-hop, which enabled them to articulate their own perspectives and questions. In particular, hip-hop provided the youth with a cultural space and practice to critically question, within the ideological interest of the revolution. Questioning was deployed within the rap lyrics as a way to engage in a state-sanctioned critical discourse that would go unnoticed by the panoptic gaze (i.e., surveilling and policing practices) of state institutions.[3] This posture of questioning aligned with Fidel Castro's first cultural policy of the revolution, "Inside the Revolution, everything; against the Revolution, nothing," while still being critical of the revolution.[4]

In other words, hip-hop provided the medium, form, and opportunity for critical expression that was interested in change within the existing revolution and the language play that, through the use of double entendres or local street colloquialisms, could also go unread by the censoring eye of state institutions. We refer to state institutions rather than the state to emphasize that the state is not a monolithic entity, but rather made up of many bureaucratic institutions.[5] The degree of social control and censorship materializes in government rhetoric, surveillance by video cameras and the police, and the embodied surveillance by the people. The state institutions' panoptic gaze engenders a sense of paranoia for most Cubans. Thus, hip-hop emerged as a cultural practice and production, a heterotopic space that enables "something like counter-sites, a kind of effectively enacted utopia in which the real sites are simultaneously represented, contested, and inverted" for marginalized youth of Cuba.[6] In this chapter, we will point out that present in both hip-hop and its variant of reggaetón are transformative pedagogical possibilities, what we refer to as *pedagogías marginal* (marginal pedagogies). We also describe a community project that uses the medium and media of hip-hop culture for transformative pedagogical possibilities. Through this chapter, we seek to describe the pedagogical richness and importance of hip-hop culture and how it can be employed in a community project for transformations of youth culture.

The current research is based on ongoing ethnographic work in Cuba that began in the winter of 2008. We made at least one or two visits each year since 2008, each visit between two and four weeks long. We obtained data in various ways: interviews with hip-hop artists, visual ethnography, and observation of youth participants in their cultural spaces such as Calle G (G Street) in Central Havana (located outside a hangout space for youth). Observation and interview sites included the privacy of the interviewees' homes, underground hip-hop clubs, the office of the Cuban Rap Agency, and the Malecón (famous eight-kilometer sea wall where youth hang out). Lourdes Suarez was interviewed regarding the community project En Mi Barrio.

THE POST-SPECIAL PERIOD IMAGINATION

The Special Period has been the most trying time of the Cuban Revolution thus far. Many foreigners thought that Cuba was the next communist country to fall, behind East Germany and the Soviet Union. While the revolution continued its social priorities to provide universal access to education and health care, the Cuban society also lost a substantial amount of capital in its moral economy after the Special Period.[7] Prior to this time, the economy of Cuba was well resourced and healthy. The country's economic and political relationship with the Soviet Union maintained a substantial amount of national income and resources despite the U.S. embargo on Cuba. During these times, the top two professions to aspire to and occupy were those of doctors and teachers.[8] There were good reasons to go to college and to contribute to the revolution, because the revolution was providing for the people.

However, when the Soviet Union fell in 1991, these forged relationships were severed alongside ties in national resources. The economy dropped and the government had to turn to tourism to save the country. Unfortunately, tourism gave workers in the tourist industry access to currency beyond what they were being paid by the government.[9] In short, the turn to tourism and access to the U.S. dollar began to shift the prescribed and perceived financial value inherent in occupations in the labor market. Thus, the country began to see many doctors and teachers leaving their respective professions to work in tourism. As hotel staff and taxi drivers began to make more money than their doctor or teacher counterparts, the prevailing wisdom began to question the necessity of higher education for many people. Because there was no financial incentive imbedded in the system itself, the cultural capital derived from the pursuit of higher education began to erode at the seams.

The shift to tourism and the unequal access to the dollar produced increasing inequality in income. In 1986, Cuba's Gini coefficient—a measure of income inequality, where 0 signifies complete equality and 1 signifies complete inequality—was estimated at 0.22 and, in the late 1990s, increased to 0.41.[10] The Special Period also brought increased activity and dependence on *la bolsa negra* (the black market), along with increased remittances from Cuban families abroad and greater numbers of *jineterias* (street hustlers, including sex workers).

The demographics of the service occupation of tourism also shifted dramatically. Although Fidel Castro declared on April 1, 1959, that racism was not of the revolution and that to be racist was to be *contra la revolucion*, racism continued to manifest and remanifest itself culturally, ideologically, and in practice. One material manifestation of these racialized practices was in the shifts in the labor market toward tourism. Prior to the legalization of the U.S. dollar and turn to tourism in 1993, over 38 percent of the workers in tourism were of color.[11] When Cuba legalized the U.S. dollar and opened its borders to tourism, many people then wanted to obtain employment in the formerly less desirable sector of the labor market. The remnant and reproduced ideologies that *los negros* (blacks) were "lazy," "inefficient," "ugly," "dirty," "smelly," "unintelligent," and "defiled" seemed to materialize once again in the hiring and firing practices of tourist labor. The rationales given were that *los negros* lacked the physical and educational attributes, including good presence, proper manners, and *nivel cultural* (cultural level), to interact properly with tourists.

In addition to these racialized labor market practices that contributed to increasing racial inequality in income, there was already an inequitable distribution of remittances from family members abroad since an overwhelming majority of the Cubans who fled the country were white. Both of these processes substantially contributed to the demographic shifts in the labor market and increased racialized income inequality. The dynamics of inequality and the living conditions of the Special Period structured the living conditions of youth, particularly marginalized black youth, who because of both implicit and explicit manifestations of prejudice and discrimination were seemingly locked out of employment opportunities in the tourist industry. Rap music affords these young people a space from which to vent their frustrations, desires, needs, and sense of self—all activities not readily permitted by state institutions. Thus, hip-hop in Cuba was predominantly a socially and economically marginalized and black-cultural production.[12] And, despite the changing complexion of artists in more recent years, hip-hop (which encompasses rap) is still a youth culture that is considered black, deviant, and radical.[13]

Cuban Youth and the Special Period

One of the profound effects of the Special Period was on the youth. Those who grew up in, or were born during, the years of the Special Period did not experience the more well-resourced days of the Cuban Revolution. The Cuban government declared the end of the Special Period in 1998. However, the residual effects continued to manifest themselves socially, economically, culturally, and politically, as seen in the 2006 Gini coefficient. Youth had become increasingly disenchanted with the revolution and frustrated by the system in which they were living. While tourism provided substantial national income, it also exposed youth much more to *extranjeros* (foreigners); foreign cultures, styles, and ideals; and the privileges that were being allotted to these outsiders. In fact, a 1994 survey in Havana and Santiago found that generational differences were the primary factor determining perceptions about the revolution, its achievements, its shortcomings, and the impact of the Special Period.[14] Youth were becoming increasingly disillusioned.

Hip-Hop and Reggaetón in the Revolution

The confluence of these historical social and economic conditions, the racialized ideologies and practices, and the disillusionment toward the revolution birthed hip-hop in Cuba in the early 1990s. What started as a simple practice whereby youth who lived north of Havana used clothes hangers to pick up Miami's hip-hop radio station, 99 Jamz, then morphed into everyday practices of youth not only consuming but also reusing, reproducing, and reappropriating material to produce their own forms of media and cultural productions. That is, by working with the resources that they had—initially a radio or tape recorder and later the computer or laptop—Cuban youth began to produce their own forms of hip-hop that focused on particular themes. For instance, in "Musica Infantil," underground Cuban rap group Los Aldeanos use personification and the metaphor of Disney characters to speak about the everyday experiences that Cubans are living and the possibilities and choices they are confronting. The group speaks of challenges such as desires to leave Cuba and bring one's family to the United States, or a critical indictment of love, beauty, and relationships in the context of a state that is supposed to be beyond matters of racial difference and inequality.

Indeed, the transnational flows of hip-hop produced Cuban hip-hop as a unique reappropriation of U.S. hip-hop.[15] Those transnational flows have also influenced U.S. hip-hop. Artists such as Mos Def, Dead Prez, Common, Talib Kweli, the Roots, and many others have visited the island and produced songs inspired by Cuba. Two popular examples are Mos Def's "Umi Says" and Common's "Song for Assatta" (for Assatta Shakur, a Black Panther who escaped to Cuba for political asylum). In fact, these outside interests by U.S. hip-hop artists; U.S., Canadian, and European academics; and consumers have maintained a market for Cuban hip-hop.

Reggaetón, initially born out of Puerto Rico, Panama, and Jamaica, emerged as a new musical genre in the early 1990s. The fusion of salsa, rumba, reggae, and rap was infectious throughout the Americas. With its fast rhythm and use of salsa, reggae, dance hall, and rumba, reggaetón incites the body to move and dance. Although the genre existed in Cuba prior to 2002 it was primarily an *extranjero* cultural production. However, because of its infectious form and its clear commercial viability, reggaetón has surpassed hip-hop in popular consumption. It is in part for these reasons that former rap group Primera Base then made the conversion to reggaetón.[16] The popularity and consumption of Cuban reggaetón then began to spread rapidly as more artists began to either emerge or make the switch for the more commercially viable genre. The popular advent of reggaetón in 2002 eclipsed rap's popularity and put into question rap's place in Cuba, particularly given its commitments to being critical and political. As twenty-year-old female rapper Hermana (pseudonym) says, "Rap es para pensar o expresar, reggaetón es pa basilar" (Rap is for thinking or expressing, reggaetón is for partying).

Hermana's words are more than the sum of their individual parts. She sets the tone for how Cuban rappers have framed their creative, expressive, embodied, projected, and performed positionalities and ways of being. Although a dialectical relationship is established to differentiate the two genres of hip-hop and reggaetón (the latter of which seemingly dominates the popular imagination of Cuban youth), it is precisely the discursive framing between the two that produce two distinct relational experiences.

The relational experience between hip-hop and reggaetón is defined not by mere definitions of degree, but rather by the distance between the two. Rap and reggaetón in Cuba may represent distinct practices of the sonic, aural, genealogical, and, by extension, geographical type. They address realities that provide both context and subtext to the sounds that inform and are informed by the political, as well as the individuals who embody it. Furthermore, the two genres help define youth culture through conversations about insiderism/outsiderism, everything/nothingness, mind/body, and the mainstream/underground.

Simultaneously, the genres do not overlook matters of kinesthesia, access, presence or lack thereof, and the relationship of these (overlapping) issues in the multiplicities of Cuban youth culture and popular expression following the Special Period. Rightfully so, a superficial reading of such a positioning of perspectives may signal a crisis, a fragile fault line, or an outgrowth as much from internal disagreement as pertaining to the moral and ethical high ground of particular forms of Cuban youth expression. In other words, on the one hand, rap is for thinking and expressing the critical and the political; on the other hand, reggaetón is for dancing and partying, a freeing of the mind from the body through bodily movement. Thus, while rap cultivates expression and reggaetón claims ownership of the body, both do so transcending the scope and jurisdiction of the state.

In establishing the parameters for defining the complex realities of what constitutes rap and reggaetón in Cuban society, several perspectives speak to how the genres manifest themselves, but more importantly what their function is. One of our ethnographic informants, Hermana, is an MC for whom rap and reggaetón represent distinct goals and obligations for their respective constituents. In this capacity, Hermana asserted that rap allows for the expressive possibilities of being in its penultimate form. Not only does rap serve as a vehicle from which to say what one cannot articulate (whether censored or not) vis-à-vis other musical genres, but it is also a musical form whose function and value come from its liberatory effects and its ability to elicit an affective disposition of freedom. Rap is at once individually therapeutic. It is indicative of the collective suffering of the youth who remain marginal yet choose not to acquiesce to the silence that sometimes threatens to engulf them.

Hermana explained that reggaetón is diametrically opposed to the commitment of broader social, cultural, and political realities (particularly regarding social control and censorship). These same realities are seemingly both a residual factor and an outgrowth of the failure of the Cuban Revolution to eradicate societal inequality across racial, gender, and class divides. Although Hermana suggested that reggaetón shares space with rap, rap ultimately does not welcome reggaetón within its parameters. While many of Hermana's ideas are shared by many in the hip-hop community, there are also clear departures by other participants; some of these departures have to do with their relationship with the government.

LA AGENCIA CUBANA DE RAP

The Cuban Rap Agency (La Agencia Cubana de Rap), a government-created and government-sponsored institution, is dedicated to preserving, promoting, producing, and advocating for hip-hop-centric programming, concerts, and other initiatives across Cuba.[17] While it adheres to articulating a viewpoint that differentiates rap from reggaetón, the agency does so by offering a critical genealogy of both the roots and the routes of hip-hop and reggaetón. The agency argues that the genre differentiation is embedded in the temporal, spatial, political, and cultural push-and-pull factors that collectively can be called history.

In this context of La Agencia, it is difficult to neatly position rap within a discourse of revolution and radical change. Nevertheless, rap, critically examined under this lens, constitutes a postrevolutionary musical genre, one that both carries on the revolution and embodies an inherent (critical) unpacking of it. (We discuss an example of both hip-hop and reggaetón below.) Rap also symbolically establishes a real and imagined historical link between, and a symbiotic investment in, the Cuban government on the one hand and the 2002 founding of La Agencia Cubana de Rap on the other. While the employees of the agency, themselves rappers, speak to similar qualities shared by rap and reggaetón in Cuba, they suggest that reggaetón goes along with what comes easy, the movement of the body. Despite the genres' similarities, their differences are expressed in the words of La Agencia's employees; in rap's ideological commitment to the critical, "a lo fuerte, a lo underground" (a commitment to the hardcore, to the underground); and reggaetón's incitement for dancing and partying. Not only is there a difference of substance and content informing both genres, but rap's commitment to a certain extent is also wedded to a conscious positioning that is present, yet beyond the scope of the panoptic gaze of state institutions.[18] Indeed, rappers operate independently of, yet indebted to, the decisions and complex web of forces that collectively make the Cuban Rap Agency an agent and extension of state institutions.

For an example of these differences in subject matter and genre, compare Los Aldeanos' "Hermosa Habana" (www.youtube.com/watch?v=eLHtukfQkDc) and Osmani Garcia's "Chupi Chupi" (www.youtube.com/watch?v=IMDIdbvheW0). In a song that conveys a certain nostalgia for the Havana past, in both its visual and its audio formats, the cinematography and aesthetics of "Hermosa Habana" are a montage of alternating palimpsest images that visually create the dichotomy expressed in song. The song itself waxes nostalgic for the Cuba of the past, with the presence of history manifested in the present. To this effect, Los Aldeanos, through the grainy framework that is the camera, attempt to juxtapose the ideal of revolution with the nostalgia and aftermath that is revolution in practice. Los Aldeanos speak of two Havanas, one a Cuba ripe for consumption, a still image of pleasure, women, beaches, and tourism, the other, a glimpse of potential in that which seems tangible, yet unobtainable, where prostitution, hustling, and the respectability of professionalism and education have given way to survival and the conditioned response of schizophrenic behavior. Where possibilities of better are best juxtaposed by revolutionary images captured on postcards destined for foreign lands, and ambitions of travel with no return in sight, unknown, perceived to be a reality, yet received as something akin to a paradise, one created in the image of new Cuban realities.

If the literal and the metaphorical can be said to represent two paradigms, rhetorical rhyme schemes that embody reggaetón and rap, "Chupi Chupi" is a manifestation of the former rather than the latter. If Los Aldeanos' use of visual images conveys a myriad of narratives structured by layers, both in film and in lyrics, "Chupi Chupi" lacks those conventional methods. The song itself is a rather atheoretical treatise on oral sex, and the visuals accompanying the track further augment those claims. Scantily clad women are not seen gyrating, but gaze toward the camera and, presumably, the eyes of the viewer, suggesting an intentionality of sexuality only heightened by the consumption of ice cream pops. At one point, this feeling is further corroborated as a woman rubs the ice cream in between her cleavage. The lyrics are suggestive of the rampant sexual conquest of women by the most virile of men and of an insatiable thirst for oral sex. The only female voice on the track inverts the narrative by placing the woman on the receiving end of the exchange of oral sex; however, it does little to subvert the power dynamics and male-dominated, patriarchal, and heteronormative content of the lyrics and the visuals that exists alongside those lyrics.

As can be observed in the stark contrast between these two songs, there is a cultural canyon in the lyrical content of rap and reggaetón. In "Hermosa Habana," we see the overt commitment to the critical and the political, whereas in "Chupi Chupi," the body and partying are the central tropes of interest.

The perspectives of Hermana and the Cuban Rap Agency on hip-hop and reggaetón; the similarities of, and differences between, the two genres; and the commitment to the critical and the political nature of rap are each markers of critical pedagogy and transformative possibilities.

PEDAGOGÍAS MARGINAL

Embedded in the artists' perspectives expressed above are examples of larger material practices of critical dialogue that also constitute *pedagogías marginal* (marginal pedagogies). Both hip-hop and reggaetón are two forms of marginal pedagogies, or what one of us (Ezekiel) refers to as indigenous cultural repertoires.[19] Indigenous cultural repertoires are those practices labeled and sanctioned by the dominant society as deviant. They are often overlooked and shunned—practices that not only serve as cultural currency and legitimacy in marginalized communities, but are also processes of complex pedagogical experiences. The term *repertoire* refers to the cultural tool kit of acts, practices, skills, and styles.[20] Ezekiel argues that these cultural repertoires include complex and meaningful experiences of learning and development.[21] Indigenous cultural repertoires appropriate a politics of deviance that seeks to move so-called practices of deviance to the mainstream while appreciating the rich pedagogical experiences in these practices.[22]

Hip-hop and reggaetón and the critical dialogue between their culturally constructed binary natures exemplify indigenous cultural repertoires for Cuban youth. On the one hand, the production of both genres requires great technical, creative, and linguistic skill, a kind of bricolage and poaching of other forms of cultural productions within and beyond the symbolic boundaries of Cuba.[23] The reappropriation, for instance, of the beat or style of a U.S.-produced hip-hop track by adding Cuban signifiers of sound and very politically situated lyrics enables Cuban youth not only to make do with their own resources, but also to begin to learn and master the art of cultural productions. They start to learn and use technologies in fundamentally new and different ways from what these tools (e.g., the turntable or laptop) were originally purposed for, ultimately reusing what they have consumed to become producers of their own creative products.[24] For instance, youth may use a laptop to remix two or more songs to create a new and different song or beat to rap to. The adding of poetic lyrics that express aspects of life particular to Cuban youth and their living conditions ultimately produces a new musical product for consumption both within and outside of Cuba.

On the other hand, the culturally constructed binary of the two musical forms, contents, and genres also produces social interstices of critical dialogue that implicitly questions the role of musical form after the Special

Period moment of the Cuban Revolution and the future of the musical forms of hip-hop and reggaetón. Nelsito (pseudonym), a Cuban underground hip-hop artist, could not agree more. Nelsito would like to see more of an amalgam between hip-hop and reggaetón:

> They [Cuban rappers] are trapped in making good music with subpar music to accompany it. And they want to do things with high music [culture] playing alongside topics, themes, subject matter that is very serious. Playing themes that in reality the people need to hear, to hear what you have to say. But you have to do it in a particular mode of how things are allowed to be said. It's not what you want to do, or how you want to say it. It's the mode in which you say it so that the people can understand.

The dialogue works out to be a kind of critical questioning of the function and identity of both genres, the state and the revolution, and the contradictions in living conditions—questions that would not be asked in other musical genres. As a form of reflexive questioning, the critical dialogue also insightfully considers the future possibilities given what is recognized and understood of the tastes and aesthetic desires of the consumer base and, moreover, a radical critique of the existing society. This critical questioning enables transformative pedagogical possibilities that would not exist under the panoptic gaze of the state.

Undeniably, the indigenous cultural repertoires of hip-hop and reggaetón are forms of marginal pedagogies with transformative possibilities. To be sure, the pedagogical experiences of rappers and reggaetóneros range from technological skills to literary and poetic creativity. These skills are not insignificant in a society where resources are limited and much of what is available must be reimagined and then refashioned. Thus, through the cultural medium of hip-hop, many pedagogical experiences can be galvanized for transformative possibilities toward new desired social and cultural futures. The potential for social and cultural change is realized via various community and youth projects such as En Mi Barrio.

A TRANSFORMATIVE COMMUNITY PROJECT

The marginal pedagogical experiences present in hip-hop culture can be and are employed for community and youth projects. One example of this in Cuba is En Mi Barrio (Spanish for "In My Neighborhood [or 'Hood]"), a project founded by Lourdes Suarez, who is currently its director. En Mi Barrio is a community project that seeks to teach youth about the history and ideologies of hip-hop and, in particular, to use the media of hip-hop and rap as a way to engage in a public discourse about other societal issues that the youth in the community raise. The project originated in the Casablanca neighborhood, which Lourdes is proud to call home. The project has its roots in directly addressing the growing need for cultural spaces whereby Cuban youth can be creative, self-reflexive, and connected to the cultivation of communal ties and expansion. Furthermore, En Mi Barrio promotes the arts alongside an agenda that values an awareness of self and the happenings that inform one's sense of community. The project seeks to strengthen the connection between youth, community, and their culture by offering a series of programs, concerts, and other initiatives that value the pulse of Cuba's young people and their energy, passion, creativity, and, ultimately, desire and need for self-expression.

Throughout Cuba, En Mi Barrio works in different communities that lack the cultural education on hip-hop. The program initiates each community engagement with a concert to attract the community youth with what they are familiar and involved with. Within this context, the first concert arises with the ambition of transforming the culture by conducting a public discourse. It is a communal project that purposefully seeks to expand on the meaning of community by partnering with other projects whose underlying goal is empowerment and development in their own locales. En Mi Barrio uses hip-hop as a strategic vehicle that is conscious, youth driven, and popular as a means to cultivate a broadened discourse about the real-life subject matter that is spoken through the music. Hip-hop provides a cultural text that can enable a public and community discourse that critically questions both one's social reality and their understanding of it. Through this public discourse, new understandings are potentially developed and alternative possibilities revealed—alternatives rooted in context and the particular needs and desires of community youth.

En Mi Barrio draws on rap and hip-hop to directly connect to the cultural lives and sensibilities of the youth participants of the community. It is precisely because of the existing misunderstanding of societal issues at large and the genre's role in Cuban society that hip-hop is introduced as a medium through which to tackle sensitive subject matter deemed taboo for public engagement and critique. These topics include racism, sexuality, desires to leave Cuba, lack of employment opportunities, and inadequate wages. The project has garnered attention for its ability to convey to a Cuban public an understanding of the medium of hip-hop, while simultaneously, via donations, helping to expand libraries and programming specifically geared toward children and youth. In the process, Lourdes is adamantly clear about the goals and vision of En Mi Barrio, which exists outside the purview of the Cuban government and thrives beyond the pursuit of money. En Mi Barrio is committed to community building and is firmly entrenched in ideas of social justice and public service. To this effect, the project's fundamental objective stresses the integration of each participant to his or her community, with the intention of creating leaders and encouraging a culture of activism.

During the project's most nascent stages, Lourdes took on the responsibility of organizing everything: the identification and organizing of communal space, speaking and appealing to local voices, and being ever mindful of popular sentiment and current trends. These responsibilities befell on Lourdes as a direct result of the first project's being located in her neighborhood. With this in mind, Lourdes pays attention to the particular nuances and distinctions of every locale, with the intention of focusing her message and pedagogical lens on the issues of concern in that particular community, be they questions pertaining to race, sexuality, family, young people, or something else. Some of these locations are the streets, parks and plazas, vocational schools, secondary schools, and prisons. As

Lourdes noted, the emphasis on these spaces are directly tied to a vision of regaining a heightened awareness of the spaces through which conversation needs to take place:

> Our fundamental objective in each and every neighborhood and locale is to seek converts to the tenets of activism. It is for this reason that we seek to gauge the relevance of programming and pulse of each individual as it relates to the particularities of their location. That is why we have baptized the program with the name En Mi Barrio. The program seeks to ferment the precise feelings of relevance and need because it has been lost in many persons and locations.

En Mi Barrio events take place as conferences, seminars, and public debates. On each occasion, the Cuban flag is featured prominently, not as a symbol to project the political (something that is looked upon with much skepticism), but rather as a sign of identity and nation, shedding light upon the idiosyncrasies of what it means to embody, remember, and live *Cubanidad*, or Cubanness. The members, those who collaborate in the setting up of programs, are usually managers, depending on where the community members are working. For this reason, the project was christened En Mi Barrio. The name is an attempt to engender feelings of relevance within the communities, because the dominant perception was that the community participants had lost such feelings.

A second objective of En Mi Barrio consists of the building of communal libraries that can unpack cultural and educational awareness in Cuban neighborhoods. The program also incorporates activities dedicated to the dissemination of information on the prevention of sexually transmitted diseases, including HIV/AIDS. Information on the latter is specifically tailored to male members of the community that have sex with other men, be it for monetary gain or otherwise. En Mi Barrio seeks to emphasize the importance of prevention throughout all neighborhoods in Cuba, because there are many taboos and misunderstandings with regard to public health, sex, sexual orientation, and sexually transmitted diseases.

Lourdes shares her passion and interests with those who accompany her, and her ultimate goal is to reach every corner of her country, giving back to the community, even if that means searching for the one person who needs any type of help: "It is from my interests and those who accompany me to reach every area of my country, while there is at least one person suffering who is in need in any capacity."

Her ambitions are to highlight the culture of hip-hop so that all may know it, in all its realities and manifestations and its capacity to transform the life of every Cuban. Above all, En Mi Barrio stresses the real history of Cuba: the profound contributions and history of Afro-Cuban descendants, aborigines, and women. The organization is dedicated to doing; it is receptive to the collaboration of all who consider themselves Cuban.

Even as these descriptions vividly construct the work and activism of En Mi Barrio, the project itself and the articulation of its goals fundamentally confront the assumptions, the politics of respectability, and the misinformation that guides Cuban society. For example, in her articulation of the founding and goals of En Mi Barrio, Lourdes addresses children as apart from youths or adolescents, by speaking of *niñ@s*, rather than *niños/niñas* (boys and girls). To this effect, it can be argued that En Mi Barrio has subtle goals at the forefront of its objectives. By recognizing, acknowledging, privileging, and voicing a sensitivity to, and heightened awareness of, the gendered, nongendered, ambiguous, and in-between gender identities, Lourdes seeks to critically examine the innocence and implication of the Cuban Revolution in the minds of its youngest and most vulnerable sectors of society. All of this, nuanced within a larger discourse of marginalization, lack of information, and propensity for revolutionary ideals, takes time to be internalized in the national consciousness of a Cuba very much in flux.

Similarly, any discussion of sexuality, the act of sex, and the prevention of sexually transmitted disease has a common foundation when the target audience is men who engage in sexual relationships with other men. While homosexuality is considered taboo in Cuban society, Lourdes views

En Mi Barrio as a critical tool for engaging community members toward multiplicities of identity. She highlights these multiple agents of change and activism:

> The motto of our program is "in my neighborhood or 'hood, we say doing." This project was founded in the Casablanca neighborhood where I grew up and [is] rooted in the circumstances of our experiences. From here we offer a cultural space for youth. We organize seminars dedicated and tailored to the experiences of young people. We also include health programming centered around the prevention of HIV/AIDS and other sexually transmitted diseases with the primary audience being men who engage in sexual relations with other men and/or men who engage in sexual relations where some sort of transaction is occurring.

A commitment to such an ideal about public health arguably disrupts the politics of respectability in relation to commonly held assumptions about relationships. The discourse transcends the prevailing attitudes on sexuality and moves the dominant conversations about sexual relationships beyond the panoptic lens of the state and its satellite surveyors—dominant conversations represented by people who may oppose a focus on same-sex acts and sexually transmitted diseases among Cuban men. Without question, the explicit and implicit goals of En Mi Barrio activities on this subject use the marginal pedagogies of hip-hop culture to expand an appreciation of the possible, the real, and a future Cuba that is progressive in its embodiment of revolutionary change.

Despite the social and economic austerity that was imposed during and after the Special Period, Cuban youth have found ways to express their own voices, critically question, and creatively make do. The shifting Cuban youth cultures we see are especially found in hip-hop culture and the discursively constructed binary between rap and reggaetón. Present in the youth everyday practices and cultural productions of hip-hop and reggaetón are meaningful pedagogical processes and experiences—what we have referred to here as *pedagogías marginal*. Moreover, it is through community projects like En Mi Barrio that the pedagogies embracing hip-hop culture can galvanize toward social and cultural change. For educators and youth advocates, En Mi Barrio provides a model for engaging youth in culturally relevant and meaningful ways. En Mi Barrio structures itself to enable expressions of Cuban youth toward their desired futures.[25]

10

Documenting Youth Engagement with Digital Music Production in Australia

Andy Brader and Allan Luke

MANY AUSTRALIAN YOUTH leave school in early adolescence, dropping off the official radar of educational systems. There is of course some dispute as to whether to refer to children and youth who have left school as *at risk*, *marginalized*, or *disengaged*, as the fields of education and social welfare shift from deficit connotations of the term *disadvantaged*.[1] However we name it, the consequences of educational, social, and economic marginalization are significant. Youth who leave school are more likely to experience or have experienced poverty, substance abuse, homelessness, teenage pregnancy, language and learning difficulties, mental health issues, and legal problems.[2]

Flexible education programs to reengage students who have left schooling have become a burgeoning sector in Australia, the United Kingdom, and Canada—involving schools, social-welfare groups, churches, and nongovernmental organizations. These programs aim to provide alternative and more flexible pathways for those young people failed by the universal state system. For the past five years, we have been using digital music production to work with disengaged youths in five of Queensland's most economically marginal suburbs and in urban Brisbane, all with high migrant and Indigenous populations. These areas are home to many young people and adults with low levels of formal education, high youth unemployment, and elevated levels of violence, crime, and drug use.[3] Our research partner is the Flexible Learning Centre (FLC) Network—which manages FLCs nationally, through a range of funding agreements at national and local levels, alongside its affiliation with the Christian Brothers' Edmund Rice Education Australia. According to promotional flyers, the Edmund Rice network offers "teaching and learning . . . characterised by small class sizes, a flexible curriculum that draws on the individual interest and needs, and a democratic pedagogical approach that encourages empowerment and autonomy."[4]

The network employs over one hundred teachers, youth support personnel, arts and social-welfare workers, counselors, and psychologists. Besides the everyday challenges of curriculum and pedagogy, the FLCs' broader policy and funding push for accountability via increased assessment of student outcomes. In response to these challenges, we developed a social networking site for students to publish and critique their original music productions.

The student body described in this study is diverse. The students' reasons for leaving school include alienation from schooling, family breakup and inadequate foster care, domestic abuse and violence, identified learning disabilities, mental health conditions, bullying peer relations, poor academic performance, behavior problems, and so forth. Currently, there are two major technologies for the assessment of at risk youth. The *psychometric and educational* approach is represented by standardized norm reference achievement tests, and the *clinical and psychotherapeutic* approach uses mental health diagnostic risk assessments. The former consists of tests of basic skill, behavior, and knowledge in the areas of literacy and numeracy. The latter consists of face-to-face diagnostic inventories and written assessments of psychological health and development, resilience, at-risk and self-harming behavior, and depression. In these students' educational files, there is documentation of test score performance, school grades and attendance, and, where it has been undertaken, developmental diagnostic and psychological profiling undertaken by speech pathologists, counselors, and school psychologists. Additionally, official records include relevant reports from police, courts, and welfare officers.

Reliance upon these two kinds of instruments for generating value-adding data raises theoretical and practical problems. First, many of these students score in the lower quartiles of achievement on standardized tests, well below grade level or age-equivalent performances. Second, anecdotally reported improvement in these settings often focuses on self-confidence and social skills, peer relations, cultural engagement, and creative performance. And accordingly, a final point is that neither psychometric nor clinical technologies can show how growth has occurred in creativity, performance, and affiliated social, peer, and audience relations.

The flexible education field therefore faces a concrete dilemma in evaluation policy and practice: documenting improvement and development in nontraditional domains beyond the academic grids of schooling.[5] The literature and the cases that follow offer compelling evidence that digital music production can form a central tool in reengaging and sustaining participation among youth. The research question we explore here is this: How can we document and "make accountable" the reengagement, development, and performance gains achieved through multiple audience evaluations of students' music productions in online social networks?

In what follows, we review selected key literature on reengagement of youth through digital arts production. We outline our development of a social network interface to set the grounds for peer and mentor evaluation of student productions. We then turn to two cases drawn from our current work across a flexible education network. Our aim here is to raise questions about the adequacy of conventional measures of educational achievement and engagement to describe creative works—and outline possible directions for research and development in authentic digital assessment.

THE HOOK: REENGAGEMENT THROUGH DIGITAL ARTS

Arts-based interventions can reengage youth who have left schooling. David Buckingham and Julian Sefton-Green describe a prototype of reengagement through the arts.[6] In a Tottenham secondary school—music, drama, and art production provided a nonschool, informal learning environment where young people could work through issues of identity and social and peer relations and engage in skill development and learning. It stressed the power of popular cultural forms—which remain on the margins of conventional secondary curricula—as focal objects of critical literacy, technical mastery, bricolage, and creativity. Studying U.K. arts education, Shirley Heath, Edward Boehncke, and Shelby Wolf argue that both studio-based arts and scientific laboratory work generate rich interactional exchange, collaborative problem-solving, and affiliated linguistic and cognitive development.[7] At the University of Chicago Charter School, Nichole Pinkard and colleagues have used digital production of rap music, advertisements, and poetry with African American youth in after-school programs.[8] The researchers worked with local poets, musicians, and other artists to set up the Digital Youth Networking project. It established the I-Remix social networking Web site, which blends YouTube-styled video and artistic work with peer and expert evaluation and ratings. Its aim is to blend artistic expression in the media arts with learning to constitute an online community with regional, national, and international audiences.[9] After exchange visits with the Chicago I-Remix team, we posited that I-Remix creates a social field of exchange where peers and experts engage in collaborative exchange, evaluation, and judgment and discuss artistic products.[10] Within that field, students literally earn peer and institutional recognition, awards, and I-Remix "dollars" for performance pieces.

There is sufficient qualitative, case-based evidence from diverse regional and cultural settings that digital arts and music-video production can make a difference in reengaging educationally disenfranchised youth. There are, of course, varied theoretical models for explaining how this digital-aesthetic "hook" works. The social, psychological, educational, and economic situations of these young people are so varied, experts point to numerous reasons, and have developed models to explain, why digital arts can assist the nontraditional student. Many of these explanations are featured in this volume.

This is, indeed, yet another brave new world that the twentieth-century industrial school has struggled to come to grips with. There, the "arts" remain in school subjects, with variable classical-canonical and progressivist-expressive orientations. The high-stakes push for measurable literacy, numeracy, and technical and scientific skills has narrowed the curriculum, subordinating the arts even further. At the same time, in many state curricula, the digital has been appropriated as a mode of technical-scientific instrumental rationality, rather than as an aesthetic-cultural phenomenon. Yet despite first-wave attempts by the math and science curriculum to control the definition and use of information technology, the digital arts have become a key site for educational development and innovation. This has been accelerated by the diffusion of inexpensive, cross-platform, and open-source software for music and video production. In state economic and cultural policy, furthermore, there is an emergent nexus of digital arts and "creative industries," with Australia, Finland, and Singapore setting GDP targets for productivity in gaming and software design, animation, music and media production, fashion, and other areas of design.[11]

Indeed, digital technologies enable a host of other cognitive and representational learning opportunities in the social and creative relations between human subjects, and mentor-apprentice-tool relations that are not part of the DNA of print-based, industrial schooling.[12] Our view is that the combination of the digital and the arts enables a reconstructive space for learning and power-knowledge relations, which are clearly distinguishable from those of traditional schooling.

REPRESENTING AND VALUING MUSIC PRODUCTIONS ONLINE

We designed the Workspace, an online assessment tool that captured more than five hundred digital productions from FLC students. It augments the I-Remix approach with principles of "authentic assessment."[13] The online interface is constructed as a transparent learning zone where experts and apprentices view and judge performance—from conventional academic assignments to digital music productions and video performances.

For the past five years, we have been working in five of Queensland's most economically marginal suburbs and in urban Brisbane. All these areas have high migrant and Indigenous populations. Our research project, funded between 2009 and 2012, is called Sustainable Selves, and our aim is to document and translate digital performance into digitally acknowledged cultural and social capital. The publicly available home page of the Workspace tool (http://workspace.edu.au/home) comprises a social networking interface for a content management system driven by individual profiles. The system provides a means for students to compile their art and to present their portfolios of (cultural) capital for exchange and evaluation. It enables either restricted or open access by peers, teachers, experts, and the public, encouraging display, distribution, consumption, and remixing and jamming. The Workspace's digital display of artworks and their metadata (total number of views and comments) constitute a field of value—a live site where artists and audiences interact, exchange critique, analyze, and respond. These peer and audience responses are interactive online social and aesthetic evaluations of performance. The online social network is, then, a site for the exercise of taste, for the allocation of distinction by a virtual community.[14]

The Workspace site is also a practical attempt to provide teachers with tools to document students' achievement. This documentation entails the conversion of both immediate and asynchronous judgments from peers and mentors for symbolic recognition of performance and achievement into archival material or digital capital. This capital in turn may be used as evidence of artistic achievement for future employment and training pathways.

The students used the interface's ability to circulate their work to an inner circle of peers and mentors. Our aim was for peer and expert feedback to guide revisions of the performance and its formal description prior to a moderation process that allows for public circulation. As the work's comments and viewings accrue, they act as quantitative and qualitative indicators of capital value, which educators can learn to identify and treat as evidence of learning and exchange for credentials. Our focus is on the ways these interactions reflexively are used to further build the quality of the students' productions, their self-confidence, and their literacy practices. In what follows, we outline two cases where youth reengaged through music production. Both of us are musicians who have worked with youth in studio settings. The narratives are recounted by one of us (Andy), a youth worker and teacher at FLCs from 2003 to the present.

Case Study One
Name: Mark
Gender: Male
Age: 20
Tagged with: albert park hip hop music
Sustainable Selves URL: http://workspace.edu.au/profile/ayreton
Bio: im 18 i got to albert park flexi school in brisbane and i produce hip hop.

Mark's previous school reports labeled him as lazy, but he was adamant that he just wanted enough time and equipment to make music. He came from a white Australian, single-parent family that survived on the government-set poverty line ($22,000 per annum).

Mark's records show that his truancy began in elementary school. Yet none of the standard psychometric or clinical tools showed any significant learning or behavioral problems. Mark had struggled with what he construed as the authoritarianism and limited course offerings at several high schools. His literacy and numeracy test scores were only fractionally below state age-equivalent averages. Mark stopped attending school regularly during ninth grade. Some three years later he met a youth support worker, who referred him to the FLC.

Mark enrolled in the Certificate II in Music: a vocational education certification in Australia. He quickly acquired the basic composing, sampling, and arrangement skills required to produce authentic hip-hop and rhythm-and-blues instrumentals of a reasonably high quality. After he attended school for a few months, the school's music studio got a computer upgrade, and so Mark was allowed to take an old PC with music sequencing software home with him. Over the next six months, Mark produced and uploaded twenty digital music productions to the Workspace site. We retrace Mark's online interactions, his revisions, remixes, and original creative works.

Mark's First Music Production

http://workspace.edu.au/work/view/325/ayreton

Mark's first music production, uploaded August 24, 2010, was titled "Watchya Know"—an original instrumental hip-hop piece lasting 3.02 minutes. It sampled four bars of a classic Memphis/Stax soul recording "Do What You Gotta Do," by Clarence Carter, from the 1968 album *This Is Clarence Carter*. Mark carefully captured and spliced his vinyl sample; layered his own drums, bass, and keys; and rearranged the composition so it followed an industry standard for hip-hop instrumentals. The technology enabled him to jam with the famous Muscle Shoals rhythm section, which was responsible for work by Carter, Aretha Franklin, and others. Mark did not initially reference his source sample in the meta-data he associated with this first upload. The following is an online comment that one of us (Andy) made referring to copyright responsibilities, with Mark's response:

ANDY [*01:10 p.m., August 24, 2010*]: nice work mate, where is the sample from? you need to reference it . . . but i like it v. much . . . what tools did you use to create this? is it all ableton? is this a vinyl sample? how did you get the sample into the digital domain?

MARK [*01:52 p.m., August 24, 2010*]: cheers dude appreciate it! the sample is by someone called clarence carter, that's about the extent of my knowledge as far as the sample goes haha. and im not to sure what you mean by reference it, or is that what i just did? i got the sample and imported it into acid pro actually, and chopped the sample in that, also partially laid the drums in it, and then finished off the drums and laid bass in ableton at home. dont have a midi at home so i actually had to use literally a keyboard, the type with letters on it, to lay the bass haha. and yes it is a vinyl sample. not too sure what that last question means but i think you mean how did i get it to the computer? just used a cable connected to a computer via a mixer and recorded into ableton. all the beatmapping etc was done in acid.

Mark's practical music sessions at FLC led to mastery of music production software (e.g., Acid Pro, Ableton) and midi and keyboard recording. Over the next eleven months, the audit trail shows Mark's improved literacy and visual representation skills and his improved music production acumen. In the passage above, note his use of a face-to-face conversational register (and his anticipation of audience and interactive response), his description of technical procedures, and his use of specific music recording terminology (e.g., beatmapping).

Mark's Second Piece

http://workspace.edu.au/work/view/328/ayreton

Mark's second piece, "Tomorrow," was uploaded one month later, on September 22. In his second entry, Mark offered a fuller description of the processes that led to his final mix. His extended textual description attracted four feedback comments, each of which he responded to. The piece generated over a hundred views from other members of the Workspace groups. Note that his brief description for his initial upload had received only two comments and thirty-five views. A strong correlation exists in all our online exchanges between lengthier student descriptions, total views, and frequency and length of comments. This follows the pattern described by Shirley Heath and colleagues, where face-to-face studio interaction and creative processes generate increasingly sophisticated levels of description and exposition, technical discourse, sociolinguistic exchange, and tool use.[15]

Peer and public views and qualitative validations are central to what counts as evidence of skill acquisition and achievement in our model. The following examples of Mark's feedback to students from other FLCs show that he engaged with and encouraged his peers' music productions in a similar manner to the feedback offered by Andy.

> [*07:18 p.m., August 5, 2010*] hey this is heaps good! im from albert park flexi in paddington, brissy. Sounds real clean and well done

Mark offered peer comments about a group music production at another site, after he had been advised about a female student singer for possible collaboration.

> [*01:57, June 3, 2011*] this is cool man:) like the piano rifts [sic]!

Note also Mark's peer comments about the work of Phil, the student featured in the second case study.

Mark's Third Piece

http://workspace.edu.au/work/view/538/ayreton

The third piece is a collaboration born from the previous track "Tomorrow," remixed and uploaded by Mark eight months later, on May 23, 2011, after he had left Albert Park. This was converted into real, economic capital: Mark received a reward for this piece, hard cash paid to him by a local MC for use of his instrumental. After his first uploads, Mark was encouraged to use the Creative Commons licenses to share his productions so that others could record vocals over his instrumentals. The move appeared to provide additional motivation. Mark made a more concerted effort to describe his work, and he also answered all the additional questions. His prose texts were lengthier. He soon began to use a copy-and-paste strategy to respond to our recurrent question, What use is this work? His answer: "For other MC's or to sell."

Mark's Latest Production

http://workspace.edu.au/work/view/549/ayreton

Mark expanded his repertoire to add visual aids to extend the audience's understanding of his music. His last production switched from a straight music upload to a visual how-to instructional genre, as a way of explaining the processes that gave rise to his composition. This part of the feedback trail, over a one-month period, led to a visual representation of Mark's music production. It also marks out the emergence of metacommentary and technical elaboration on his work—rather than performance per se. Over this period, then, Mark had shifted his position in the field from performer, student, or apprentice to teacher or mentor of others, providing running metatextual commentaries on his production and technical and artistic decisions to assist others. Note the tenor of the exchanges about this work with peers:

> STEVE@#@ [*11:06 a.m., June 17, 2011*]: AWESMUNGUS!!! hey mate, I'm listening to this on my PC at work which only has crappy little speakers but it sounds big and fat like a movie theme. It would be really good in a movie (I think). You should make really creative kinda slow-mo movie clip to go with it, it needs visuals! (I think). It's a great piece maybe it could use a kinda bridgey bit or some sort of change somewhere, but it is a great theme melody.

> **MARK** [*04:23 p.m., June 26, 2011*]: haha i know nothing about movie editing at all! thanks though! really appreciate all the feedback!

> STEVE@#@# [*05:28 p.m., June 29, 2011*]: movie making is easy on a PC or Mac, no really, if I can do it, I'm sure you could do better.

> **MARK** [*03:01 p.m., July10, 2011*]: I didnt make a movie clip as such, but if you look at my most recent vid, I had a crack at making a "the making of" beat video haha

The four music productions described here constitute an *e-portfolio* of Mark's accomplishments as a producer, musician, and digital artist. In total, Mark's twenty digital productions received 497 unique viewings over eleven months, approximately half of which were anonymous views of public work, half from registered FLC users. His work received fifty-three positive feedback comments, the technical and musical quality of his productions showed improvement, and his written online descriptions became more elaborate and more specifically targeted to audience.

Mark did not complete his Certificate II in Music before leaving the FLC to pursue full-time employment. In addition to the small amount of economic capital his material yielded, our aim was to make them count as evidence of skill acquisition and the value-added experience of flexible learning. Mark continued to engage with the Workspace well beyond his official school enrolment. His most prolific period of digital music production occurred in the six months after his official attendance ceased.

Case Study Two

Name: Phil
Gender: Male
Age: 18
Tagged with: 1993, music
Sustainable Selves URL: http://workspace.edu.au/profile/jdsuperstar
Bio: I write music. i Love to play music with a few people together jamming.

Phil was fifteen years old when we conducted the study, and both he and his sixteen-year-old friend were musicians. As outreach participants, they only managed to access the local school-based music studio one afternoon per week for rehearsals, until we introduced them to digital music production. When asked about his local area, Phil contrasted it with the urban scene, stating that it was more dangerous to express yourself in his local suburb because of violent youth gangs. On his school experiences, he replied:

> Well, at first I was perfect. I was, like, a straight B student in primary school, and then I hit high school . . . and um . . . I first went to C___ high, and I was getting picked on and stuff, then I was getting into fights and stuff like that, and then I was too scared to go back inside so I just never went and I stayed away from . . . I never went to school for, like, four months, and I was just sitting at home . . . and I went to T___. I went there for about a month and then just never went there either. I don't know, it was just like the sense of different people being around me, it's just weird.

His official records offered no explanation of Phil's low attendance, but his literacy and numeracy test scores were well below average. Andy gave Phil a two-month intensive course in music sequencing because Phil was digitally literate and highly motivated. Phil acquired an inexpensive music-sequencing program for his home computer and began six months of composing and recording at home. He transitioned from the outreach program to full FLC enrolment in 2010. During that period, Phil was encouraged to use the Workspace tool to showcase his home productions. In the second half of the year, teachers reported that he had hooked into other school activities, with special interest in a YouTube-style visual presentation technique we were demonstrating online. This technique, which he soon mastered, allowed him to combine still images, transition effects, and moving text with his original music.

In an examination of Phil's digital collection and its learning trail as a whole, the data tells us he was taking particular note of online visual demonstrations. Between July and May 2011, Phil joined four Workspace groups (three music related, one English), and he uploaded four original music productions (two audio, two video).

1. "Jackhammering Bass" (audio), uploaded July 23, 2010
   (http://workspace.edu.au/work/Updated/295/jdsuperstar)

   Description: a heavy bass trace/electronic/techno song i made from scratch to get u jumping!:)

2. "Secret Life" (video), uploaded November 15, 2010
   (http://workspace.edu.au/work/view/389/jdsuperstar)

   Description: A song i made to remember me of my house burning down and of the love i have for my family. please rate and tell me what u think!

3. "RnB Mastered" (video), uploaded November 15, 2010
   (http://workspace.edu.au/work/Updated/390/jdsuperstar)

   Description: a song i wrote when i was bored!! i used fl studio to make this track.

4. "Incredible Lives" (audio with moving graphic), uploaded May 21, 2011 (http://workspace.edu.au/work/view/537/jdsuperstar)

Description: [see below]

In mid-2010, Phil's family home burnt to the ground in a tragic accident. No one was seriously injured, but the family lost everything. Through sustained participation in our virtual community, Phil learned to combine photos of his home with his music to deepen his account of the accident. He not only added his own scrolling credits and transitions to his song, but also gave a very personal description of the work (see his notes about "Secret Life," earlier).

Three pieces of online feedback about the final piece ensued over a period of nine months. Adib and Steve are project researchers, and John is an FLC teacher.

> **ADIB** [*10:24 a.m., November 16, 2010*]: Hey Phil, great sounds and nice film clip—thank you for sharing. This really communicates the extent of the fire and its impact. Thanks also for sharing your story, it's inspiring to know that your bravery kept everyone safe. You won an award for this right?

> **STEVE** [*03:32 p.m., November 25, 2010*]: Hi Phil, this cool, it's strange how we develop an affection for a building huh? I guess that really it's just about the people inside, but it feels like house-love sometimes. Really I think it's just home-love though.

> **JOHN** [*12:59 p.m., June 24, 2011*]: wow . . . i just watched this track. I had only listened to the music before, but this time i read all the text and looked at all the photos . . . Phil I'm shocked by the photos of the damage, but also stoked that you managed to write about it with words and sounds . . . this is tops . . . I'm gonna make it public.

Phil's digital productions incorporate the audience feedback, as his third and fourth pieces experiment further with scrolling credits using variations in tempo, font, and size.

Phil was hooked at this stage in our project. Like Mark, he used the Workspace mainly during out-of-school hours. His sustained engagement with digital production and communication tools generated original music and visual compositions. The quality of these works of art is not yet professional, but their authenticity is affectively rich and powerful.

Song: "Incredible Lives"

Description: This song has a cool story behind it . . . i was almost fast asleep in my bed, and i had these piano chords playing over and over that i've made up. So i get up and start making it, and before you know it, it was finished, 3:00am in the morning and on the net!:) (made with fl studio 9)

Describe the best features of this work? I'd say the best feature of this work is the piano. im totally in love with the piano and yeah just makes u relax!:P

What did you find easy and/or difficult in completing this work? what i found difficult in this song is finding small sounds to put in the background to make the song sound good.

Who helped you complete this work? me myself and i!

We've included Phil's description of his fourth piece of music, "Incredible Lives," because it demonstrates his sophisticated integration of art and literacy to connect audiences with his emotions. This extended literary description is a direct result of the feedback he received from audiences.

In both "Incredible Lives" and "Secret Life," targeted feedback from multiple sources acted as a catalyst for revisions and the generation of new designs over an extended period. It is worth contrasting the duration of this design work with the time frames for student work demanded by conventional lessons, assignments, and units. In conventional schooling, opportunities for a young person to compose, revise, and expand a piece of work over a full calendar year would be rare. These exchanges allowed Mark and Phil to better understand how a single piece of their work can be experienced and valuated more than once, especially when they combined audio with visual modalities. For Mark, peer feedback was brief, basic, and informal. We found four examples where Mark offered feedback about Phil's work, and vice versa (the "like the piano rifts!" feedback from Mark, noted above, was directed at Phil's production "Incredible Lives"). These students never met face-to-face. But this instant, public peer feedback formed a scaffold and incentive for continuous revision.[16]

What follows is a typical expert-student e-mail interaction.

> **EXPERT:** if you write fuller descriptions in the student description part, they will make all your stuff public (i.e. anyone can view it without logging in). You should get a lot of interest that way from people all over the place . . . those who have done this already have seen massive increases in the views of their work . . . I'm saying this to you because i think your work is excellent, and it could help to inspire others.
>
> **MARK:** Haha I completely forgot I had to do that, cheers for reminding me. I went back and added them all and wrote descriptions for them, thanks a lot for making them public! And thanks heaps for the compliments, appreciate it!

This private exchange between Mark and a music industry expert is an example of how audience validation and expert feedback led to the rearticulation of Mark's cultural product descriptions (see http://workspace.edu.au/work/view/549/ayreton).

EXCHANGE AND VALUE

Rock and roll, digital resources, and social networking provided an educational hook for disenfranchised youth. The social fields of the digital Workspace constituted a site where students' performances were validated through various exchanges with peers, teachers, mentors, outside experts, and anonymous others. This composite, virtual, and real audience marked out rules for distinction and value, leading to self-reflection, revision, and rearticulation of multimodal performances. Like the digital-cultural studies interventions described at the onset, the Workspace interface successfully reframed school-based, vocational learning activities as the production (and reception) of popular cultural genres and creative works. Our colleague Stephen Connolly refers to this as an "e-field": a digital social field for moderated peer and expert assessment.[17]

As on YouTube, Reverb Nation, I-Remix, and other open-access online sites, value in the field is governed by the tacit and stated rules and the dynamic critical criteria exercised by an anonymous and, in some instances, known audience who have actual 24/7 access. These fields of exchange are, quite literally, reshaping the political economy of popular-music creation, marketing, and consumption.[18] In conventional school assignments, criteria for academic performance are made explicit to varying degrees before the actual design or performance activity, and they follow the rules of genre pedagogy. In contrast, the rules for exchange and valuation on online sites are movable feasts—created, critiqued, and re-created by audiences on a continuous, evolving, and unpredictable basis. In these fields of attention, audiences literally vote with their eyes, ears, and fingers, choosing to click or view, or not, and then deciding whether the performance is worthy of blogged comments and critiques.

In these two case studies, we identified four sources of audience validation for digital productions: peer comments, teachers and instructors, external experts, and anonymous audience ratings. First, we found that comments from known peers, both from within and from outside the flexischool network, readily validated the earlier demo versions of students' music. Second, teachers, youth workers, and support staff contributed verbal and written feedback on these students' acquisition of technical and prerequisite skills, particularly where the students met the requirements of the competency-based vocational certificate. This type of targeted feedback led to more-visible improvements, revisions, and rearticulation than what came from peer comments. The third source of support, experts from the field of music production, offered external validation beyond the FLC institution. The fourth type of validation came from the anonymous public audience that viewed students' revised and moderated work published on the Workspace home page (e.g., total hits, star ratings).

Taken together, these validation sources constituted a moderated or negotiated assessment of what were, inter alia, artifacts of the work produced under the mentorship of teachers and youth workers. Further, once these rules of exchange were constituted and enacted online—the student-artist took up the role of critic and mentor of both others and his or her own work. In theory, the student-artist evolved an online-constructed aesthetic habitus, embodying expert knowledge and judgment.

The cases demonstrate that digital studio work in music or other arts, combined with social networking tools, generates rich interactions that suggest not only artistic and technical, but also linguistic and cognitive development. Both students' blends of informal and formal text communication with online audiences demonstrate nuanced understandings of the context of their messages and how the messages will be received. Students responded positively to the moderation filter we put in place, and they accepted the general premise we presented to them on the Web site: "increased public views of your cultural products can be traded as industry currency, and it also counts as recognition of prior learning." Over the eighteen-month period of FLC student engagement, students became increasingly sensitive to the demands of the field, referring to their music industry reputation or currency in the "views and comments" section of the Workspace. They also became more astute commentators in the acquisition and exchange of capital—often extending and replicating the criteria that others had used to judge their work in their own comments on their peers' work.

Several patterns we observed have practical implications. First, the re-engagement hook worked best when at least half of its most crucial interactions took place outside the time-space constraints of official FLC activities. In both case studies, the students experienced a limited number of face-to-face music studio tutorials, with sustained engagement through home and mobile use of the Workspace interface after hours. Their asynchronous trails of audience feedback often continued for months after the students' initial upload and, in many instances, after they had formally left the institution.

Because the interface offered a flexible way to view, comment on, and publish media content, it therefore altered what counted as participation in learning activities—augmenting, appropriating and supplanting traditional face-to-face FLC assessment. At the same time, these student-artists perceived the valuations of this field as more authoritative than those provided by teachers and other students in classrooms. Simply put, the work morphed from an institutional activity into one with a life outside the confines of the institution, where the participants owned and exchanged performances. There was, then, a shift from an inside-school activity to an outside-school, 24/7 digital community in this particular digital/social field of exchange.

Second, the Workspace represents students' digital productions and the interactional traces they leave behind as evidence of their developing cultural and social capital. Distinct audiences engaged with the work at varied stages of its conception to provide feedback. This constitutes artifactual or textual evidence of learning and the conversion of products into other forms of cultural capital (i.e., credentials) and social capital (e.g., online reputation, friendship, access to other virtual and real communities, community status), with the single instance of conversion into economic capital (i.e., the MC's payment to Mark).

The culture-specific music knowledge each student brought into this schoolwork from wider social groups (music technology forums, blogs, and open-source information), and the number of public views and comments the works received from expert music producers, increased the students' cultural capital—knowledge and performative resources—but these forms of capital are not currently recognized as legitimate by school systems. In other words, the project was successful at enfranchising and appropriating artistic work that had little value in official school-like settings into a broader educational field that blended both teacher and school relations with peer artistic and cultural relations. These FLC students developed commodities that, theoretically at least, had potential value in open digital markets of popular culture via YouTube, Reverb Nation, and other open-access media.

The populist networking features of the Workspace bring social capital into play in the construction of what counts as evidence of learning. The interface's online music groups, where students shared their work, engaged a broad and diverse range of viewers and critics. For example, we engaged an academic and music colleague who offered online feedback to these students. He was a highly acclaimed music producer with an international reputation. His expertise served two purposes: aesthetic feedback about the quality of the work and potential transfer of this currency to the music industry proper. Not surprisingly, students responded even more favorably to the feedback once they had confirmed the expert's capital for themselves by checking his status online via *Wikipedia*. The expert's involvement upped the total reputational and symbolic value of the field. It also enhanced the students' reputational portfolios (e.g., via citations of expert endorsement) as they branded and presented their work to new audiences.

In terms of improvement of the students' actual productions, students frequently emulated the expert's language in their online descriptions of remixes and referred to music concepts the expert had commented on—such as "compression" and "reverb." This was part of the developmental expansion of the students' technical vocabulary. The expert's reputation added value to the students' work; the endorsements both validated and became part of a visible learning trail. Furthermore, the students' musical products and the pieces' associated descriptions, comments, and views provided FLC staff with new, unconventional evidence of achievement for the standardized certificate courses in the music industry.

Third, while neither Mark nor Phil completed his certificate course, classroom teachers and youth workers confirm that both made cognitive, technical skill, and social gains, much of which the educators attribute to multiple audience validations. These interactions with audience set the grounds for improvements to students' artistic performances; increased levels of attention to technical problems, software, and musical form; and led to extended online reading and writing.

CONVERTING DIGITAL ART INTO CULTURAL CAPITAL

We began this chapter with a practical and theoretical problem: How do we demonstrate the artistic, cultural, developmental, and educational growth of students whose work with popular cultural and digital designs falls outside the metrics and criteria of schooling? Working in an alternative setting with disenfranchised youth, our model encouraged several students and their teachers to informally present, acquire, and exchange their social and cultural capital through the Workspace interface. The learning trails and the automated aggregates of comments and views that their music and videos generated built and sustained the cultural and aesthetic hook of digital music production—and it did so, well beyond students' official attendance and FLC participation. These two cases—and several of their peers—demonstrated that the students spent extended periods on task during, after, and outside official school hours. The students experienced concentrated attention to design; extended textual interactions with an anonymous audience, experts, and peers; and sustained and multiple revisions of their work. When framed in such conventional educational terms, the result clearly has educational value, even though it cannot be measured by achievement tests, curriculum exams, and classroom-based assignments.

Notably, the mastery of digital tools and the intersubjective exchanges between artist and audience, student and teacher, occurred without the prerequisite of traditional schooling: a shared, disciplined, physical time and space. In this study, digital production and social-network tools acted as mediating points for an educational and aesthetic hook. Youth with histories of alienation and exclusion from the official social fields of schooling generated expressions of self, culture, and community and mastered skills with both digital technology and traditional expressive media (e.g., keyboards, voice, written and performed lyrics). This growth occurred via the development of performances which, in turn, were validated both within and outside the institution by multitiered audiences. These online social networks act as microfields of exchange: dynamic "attention economies."[19]

The development work described here was used by FLC staff for purposes of institutional assessment. The alternative and conventional evidence was used to augment achievement data for standardized, competency-based training credentials. Music industry representatives considered the evidence as a potential verification of artistic achievement suitable for future employment and training pathways. But we did not manage to implement the Workspace as an operational instrument across the FLCs, despite our efforts to encourage students and teachers to upload traditional written assignments and tasks, now common practice in university study. Simply put, many of the participating teachers struggled with the transition from traditional pencil-and-paper assessment to online exchange.

It is almost a curriculum cliché for twenty-first-century educational systems to call for an emphasis on digital technology and on creativity, variously and contentiously defined.[20] But the response of schools, teachers, curriculum developers, and educational bureaucrats has been to push for accountability narrowly based on conventional print measures, reinforcing the predominance of face-to-face didactic teaching and explicit instruction. Students like those presented in the case studies represent a challenge, a prospect, and, indeed, an anomaly facing educational systems: young people deemed at risk by the criteria of traditional testing and grades can reengage through a curriculum premised on an idiosyncratic architecture of digital and popular cultural forms. Such an architecture is built on and acknowledges the students' community and cultural resources and background knowledge and can convert these advantages into performances that have verifiable capital in nonschool social fields. We believe that digital arts production, combined with social networking tools, is an effective hook for disengaged youth. Yet at present, information and communication technologies in secondary education remain strongly affiliated with the science and technology curriculum, a legacy of its expansion in the

1990s.[21] This remains an impediment to the opening up of digital spaces for creative work in schools.

The welding of digital music and video production with social networking described here offers a *curriculum technology* of enormous potential. This can be done when schools, teachers, school leaders, and curriculum designers acknowledge the robust and vibrant social market for online music, art, and video. University, polytechnic, and vocational courses have begun to make such a move through the integration and institutionalization of creative industries, design, and multiliteracies paradigms. For schools, the historical shift of the means of assessment and exchange of value is proving a much slower and reactionary process—back to the basics indeed. It is a matter of creating institutional spaces and fields of exchange for cultural capital that is already embodied, lived, and experienced by students—but remains invisible to those working within the paradigms of industrial-era, print-based schooling.

ACKNOWLEDGMENTS

This research was funded by a grant from the Australian Research Council, 2009–2011. We thank coinvestigators Val Klenowski, Stephen Connolly, and Adib Behzadpour for their input and work on the project; Phil Graham and the Institute of Creative Industries, Queensland University of Technology, for technical support in the development of the Web interface; Dale Murray and the students and staff of the Edmund Rice Flexible Learning Centres, Queensland, for their support and participation in the project; and, of course, Mark and Phil for their generosity and creativity.

Afterword

Shirley Brice Heath

THE AFTERWORD, A RECENT genre in the publishing world, reflects the urge of the present generation to look beyond the here and now to what lies ahead. Neither conventions nor norms have, however, been firmly set for the genre. Thus to those authors who have recently asked me to write an afterword for their book, I feel obliged to caution that my strategy in looking ahead is to consider where the book points readers and how future scholars might build from the current work.

Thus, after a brief summary of key indicators for the future suggested by the book's contents, I try to provoke readers to think of what the volume does *not* say about the central questions or issues raised. For the current volume, we may ask what questions remain for readers who see possibilities of transformations in the contexts they currently study. Who are the central initiators of transformative contexts discussed in this volume, and what circumstances of local history and timing created the environments reviewed here?

For any volume whose focus is learning, an examination of methods and their contribution to comparative analysis is essential. An additional imperative question seeks to determine the theoretical contributions of any volume that addresses learning.

What do we learn from this volume? Three contributions seem central. The first is the strong reiteration of a fundamental of anthropology: the most beneficial contexts of learning derive from the felt needs of learners. In every case study included here, learners were not targets toward which outsiders directed their curricula or methods. In spite of struggles and setbacks among the learners, the framers of the contexts described here knew enough to step back and let the learners themselves work through their internal differences.

A second contribution coming from most of the cases concerns the effective role of the arts in promoting a sense of transformational learning for insiders and outsiders. The arts have never respected boundaries of any kind. All borders and constraints eventually give way through the force of the arts. The young in particular find the unbounded possibilities of the arts welcoming. Hybridity, crossover, mixing and remixing, multimodal and multimedia, classical and cutting-edge: these terms characterize all the arts. Just as hip-hop grew simultaneously through four art forms (break dancing, graffiti art, rap, and DJ-ing), so will future genres of art created by the young mix and remix, eluding boundaries. Thus, spoken-word poetry morphs into film, taking musical and layered visuals with it.

A third theme running through the cases of this volume points to the need to acknowledge that young people see no reason for "academic" learning to be viewed as centrally owned or controlled by formal schooling. The individuals and groups reported here sought not only their transformations of identity, but also a means of creating and managing organizations and their operations. They planned, scheduled, and critiqued events of their own making. Throughout the transformative learning experiences detailed here, individuals were in part motivated by the need to prepare realistically for the certainties of facing homophobia, racism, and other prejudicial judgments and injustices. Yet the cases assuredly indicate ways that transformational learning includes much that is also at the heart of social science courses in psychology, modern history, biology, and the arts.

What gaps of coverage in this volume might other researchers work to fill? Across fields, the case study method is most frequently used to report transformations, whether in education, medicine, environmental studies, or engineering failures. All such fields of application need an accumulation of cases in order to compare patterns of co-occurrence. Otherwise, case studies can contribute only minimally to the generation of theories concerning the phenomena of focus. Case studies typically address only limited stretches of time or single instances or events (such as the collapse of a particular bridge). Hence, they generally do not undertake explanations of causal or continuative factors. The vital task of cases is to provide description and factual data related to a defined phenomenon.

This volume points to the need for future researchers to examine an extensive collection of cases of transformative learning that have in common factors described in the instances given here. Questions raised here include the following:

1. To what extent does transformative learning across the life span reflect common features? For example, do middle-aged individuals who lose their jobs during economic recessions join together in their transformative learning toward new identities or acceptance of an altered status, and if so, how do these instances compare with those of younger learners?

2. What then do the cases here (and in related volumes) suggest that is unique about the transformative learning of adolescents and young adults? Could their heavy reliance on the arts and on their own life stories reflect that (1) the young are early adopters of technologies and (2) learners of this age have generally cast off dependence on their parents and have not yet found stable life partners? In other words, does their limited life experience mean that they need organized contexts for the exploration of multiple identities more than do middle-aged workers, who have extensive life experiences on which to draw as the older individuals realign themselves throughout life transitions?

These questions suggest several theories relevant to the cases presented in this volume.

Stance theory, though often loosely defined across disciplines from sociology to linguistics to the neurosciences, helps explain the successful learning experiences reported here. Reports from disciplines using stance theory consistently indicate one feature of the learning that takes place when individuals assume roles or take stances other than those to which they are usually assigned. Emotional commitment engages learning that becomes embodied. Individuals use and hold their bodies in ways that differ from their normal postures. They speak differently and view their language in metacognitive ways that relate to how they see themselves within different roles and stances. Moreover, taking on a different persona or function within an organization or a group forces individuals to look into the future, to imagine what they must do and how they will comport their new selves. The heightened enlistment of different brain centers helps promote long-term memory of what it is like to participate beyond the ordinary self.[1]

We have much to gain from studies of what happens when individuals who perceive themselves as assigned particular roles or stances by others take on new stances. Such "assignments" harm, block, and imprison individuals. This is the case whether the assignments are innocent (e.g., the assignment of the role of student, child, or teenager) or maliciously directed (e.g., the multiple forms of name-calling addressed to individuals of specific races, religions, ethnic groups, disabilities, or sexualities).

A final arena of theory suggested and worthy of more consideration in relation to the cases within this volume has to do with the holding power of transformative learning experiences relatively early in life. Literary artists have often addressed this issue. Both autobiographies and biographies have, particularly since 2000, addressed the transformative learning that came with rapid stardom and an early life of drug addiction. Similarly, autobiographies from individuals whose transformational learning came through specific historical events, such as civil rights legislation, indicate the lasting effects of this kind of learning. However, we know relatively little about the life course of younger individuals, who entered puberty during the late 1990s and the first decade of the twenty-first century. In these years, a near-constant stream of coverage of "diverse" identities came in the public media and arts world. Moreover, during this same period, the young took control of new technologies and independent modes of production to represent themselves, effectively thumbing their noses at representations created by mainstream channels.

In looking beyond this volume, this afterword raises questions unlikely to fit easily within the confines of education research if institutional powers continue to be driven by current values of standardization and prediction. The field most likely to move forward from this volume is that of learning sciences, where the focus is firmly on context, conditions, actors, agency, self-directed learning, multiple identities, and performance. This volume has the potential to push recognition of the imperative to understand all these variables in interdisciplinary ways and to acknowledge their role in generating new theories and directions in practice not for schools and schooling, but for life-wide learning.

Notes

Introduction

1. Maxine Greene, *The Dialectic of Freedom* (San Francisco: Jossey-Bass, 1988).

2. Maxine Greene, "Toward a Pedagogy of Thought and a Pedagogy of Imagination," 2007, www.maxinegreene.org/articles.php.

3. William Ayers, "Doing Philosophy: Maxine Greene and the Pedagogy of Possibility," in *A Light in Dark Times: Maxine Greene and the Unfinished Conversation*, ed. William Ayers and Janet Miller (New York: Teachers College Press, 1998), 3–10.

4. Roger Simon, *Teaching Against the Grain: Texts for a Pedagogy of Possibility* (Toronto: Ontario Institute for Studies in Education Press, 1992).

5. Henry Giroux and Roger Simon, "Schooling, Popular Culture, and Pedagogy of Possibility," in *Popular Culture, Schooling, and Everyday Life*, ed. Henry Giroux and Roger Simon (Toronto: Ontario Institute for Studies in Education Press, 1989), 219–235.

6. Henry Giroux and Roger Simon, "Schooling, Popular Culture, and Pedagogy of Possibility," *Journal of Education* 170, no. 1 (1988): 9–26.

7. Ibid.; Peter McLaren, *Life in Schools* (New York: Longman, 1988).

8. Roger Simon, "Empowerment as a Pedagogy of Possibility," *Language Arts* 64 (1987): 370–382.

9. Paulo Freire, *Pedagogy of the Oppressed* (New York: Continuum, 1970); Paulo Freire, *Pedagogy of Hope: Reliving Pedagogy of the Oppressed* (New York: Continuum, 1992).

10. Jeffrey Duncan-Andrade, "Note to Educators: Hope Required When Growing Roses in Concrete," *Harvard Educational Review* 79, no. 2 (2009): 181–194.

11. Ibid., 190; Lisa Delpit, *Other People's Children: Cultural Conflict in the Classroom* (New York: New Press, 1995); Shawn Ginwright, *Black Youth Rising: Race, Activism, and Radical Healing in Urban America* (New York: Teachers College Press, 2009).

12. bell hooks, *Teaching to Transgress: Education as the Practice of Freedom* (New York: Routledge, 1994).

13. Geneva Gay, *Culturally Responsive Teaching: Theory Research and Practice* (New York: Teachers College Press, 2000); for related terms and discussions, see Gloria Ladson-Billings, *The Dreamkeepers: Successful Teachers of African American Children* (San Francisco: Jossey-Bass, 1994); Django Paris, "Culturally Sustaining Pedagogy: A Needed Change in Stance, Terminology, and Practice," *Educational Researcher* 41, no. 3 (2012): 93–97.

Chapter 1

1. Korina Jocson, *Youth Poets: Empowering Literacies in and out of Schools* (New York: Peter Lang, 2008).

2. Lawrence Lessig, *Remix: Making Art and Commerce Thrive in a Hybrid Economy* (New York: Penguin, 2008), 76.

3. Paul Miller, *Rhythm Science* (Cambridge, MA: Mediawork/MIT Press, 2004).

4. K. Wayne Yang, "Kutiman: It's the Mother of All Funk Chords," in *Art and Social Justice Education: Culture as Commons*, ed. Therese Quinn, John Ploof, and Lisa Hochtritt (New York: Routledge, 2012), 11–13.

5. James P. Gee, *What Video Games Have to Teach Us About Learning and Literacy* (New York: Palgrave Macmillan, 2003).

6. Anne H. Dyson, *The Brothers and Sisters Learn to Write: Popular Literacies in Childhood and School Cultures* (New York: Teachers College Press, 2003), 108.

7. Mikhail Bakhtin, *The Dialogic Imagination* (Austin: University of Texas Press, 1981); Norman Fairclough, *Language and Power* (London: Longman, 1989).

8. Gunther Kress, "Multimodality," in *Multiliteracies: Literacy Learning and the Design of Social Futures*, ed. Bill Cope and Mary Kalantzis (London: Routledge, 2000), 182–202; Gunther Kress, *Literacy in the New Media Age* (London: Routledge, 2003).

9. Gunther Kress and Theo Van Leeuwen, *Multimodal Discourse: The Modes and Media of Contemporary Communication* (London: Arnold, 2001).

10. Robert Hodge and Gunther Kress, *Social Semiotics* (Cambridge, UK: Polity, 1988).

11. Louie Althusser, *Lenin and Philosophy and Other Essays*, trans. Ben Brewster (New York: Monthly Review Press, 1971); Michel Foucault, *Discipline and Punish*, trans. Alan Sheridan (New York: Vintage, 1977); Stuart Hall, "Encoding/Decoding," in *Culture, Media, Language*, ed. Stuart Hall, Dorothy Hobson, Andrew Lowe, and Paul Willis (London: Routledge/Center for Contemporary Cultural Studies, 1992), 128–138.

12. Douglas Kellner, *Media Culture: Cultural Studies, Identity and Politics Between the Modern and the Postmodern* (New York: Routledge, 1995).

13. Linda Charmaraman, "Media Gangs of Social Resistance: Urban Adolescents Take Back Their Images and Their Streets Through Media Production," *After School Matters* (2008): 23–33; Erica Halverson, "Film as Identity Exploration: A Multimodal Analysis of Youth-Produced Films," *Teachers College Record* 112, no. 9 (2010): 2,352–2,378; Glynda Hull and Mira Katz, "Crafting an Agentive Self: Case Studies of Digital Storytelling," *Research in the Teaching of English* 41 (2006): 43–81; Theresa Rogers et al., "From Image to Ideology: Analysing Shifting Identity Positions of Marginalized Youth Across the Cultural Sites of Video Production," *Pedagogies: An International Journal* 5, no. 4 (2010): 298–312.

14. Catherine Burwell, "Rewriting the Script: Toward a Politics of Young People's Digital Media Participation," *Review of Education, Pedagogy, and Cultural Studies* 32 (2010): 382–402; Korina Jocson, "Unpacking Symbolic Creativities: Writing in School and Across Contexts," *Review of Education, Pedagogy, and Cultural Studies* 32, no. 2 (2010): 206–236; Douglas Kellner and Gooyong Kim, "You Tube, Critical Pedagogy, and Media Activism," *Review of Education, Pedagogy, and Cultural Studies* 32, no. 1 (2010): 3–36.

15. Robert Ferguson, "Media Education and the Development of Critical Solidarity," *Media Education Journal* 30 (2001): 37–43.

16. Len Masterman, *Teaching the Media* (New York: Routledge, 1990).

17. Steven Goodman, *Teaching Youth Media: A Critical Guide to Literacy, Video Production, and Social Change* (New York: Teachers College Press, 2003); Ernest Morrell, *Critical Literacy and Urban Youth* (New York: Routledge, 2008); Jeff

Share, *Media Literacy Is Elementary: Teaching Youth to Critically Read and Create Media* (New York: Peter Lang, 2009).

18. Steven Schneider and Kirsten Foot, "Web Sphere Analysis: An Approach to Studying Online Action," in *Virtual Methods: Issues in Social Science Research on the Internet*, ed. C. Hine (Oxford, UK: Berg Publishers, 2005): 157–170.

19. For an analysis of "Slip of the Tongue," see Korina Jocson, "Remix Revisited: Critical Solidarity in Youth Media Arts," *E-Learning and Digital Media* 10, no. 1 (2013): 68–82.

20. Elizabeth Moje, "But Where Are the Youth? On the Value of Integrating Youth Culture into Literacy Theory," *Educational Theory* 52, no. 1 (2002): 97–120; Stanton Wortham, "Youth Cultures and Education," *Review of Research in Education* 35 (2011): vii–xi.

21. Kress and Van Leeuwen, *Multimodal Discourse.*

Chapter 2

1. National Endowment for the Arts, "About Us: Highlights in NEA History," accessed May 2, 2013, http://www.nea.gov/about/40th/act.html.

2. Mark Bauerlein and Ellen Grantham, eds., *National Endowment for the Arts: A History 1965-2008* (Washington, DC: National Endowment for the Arts, 2009), 14–15.

3. For more information on these and similar collaborative community projects and events, see the following organizations' Web sites: Life Is Living (www.lifeisliving.org), Living Word Project (www.livingwordproject.org), Youth Speaks (youthspeaks.org), Yerba Buena Center for the Arts (www.ybca.org), Intersection for the Arts (theintersection.org), Brett Cook (www.brett-cook.com), and Theaster Gates (www.theastergates.com).

Chapter 3

1. Vanessa Diffenbaugh, *The Language of Flowers* (New York: Ballantine Books, 2011), 63–64.

2. Django Paris, "'A Friend Who Understand Fully': Notes on Humanizing Research in Multiethnic Youth Community," *International Journal of Qualitative Studies in Education* 24, no. 2 (2011): 137–149; Django Paris and Maisha T. Winn, eds., *Humanizing Research: Decolonizing Qualitative Inquiry with Youth and Communities* (Thousand Oaks, CA: Sage, 2013).

3. Eve Tuck and K. Wayne Yang, "R-Words: Refusing Research," in *Humanizing Research: Decolonizing Research Methods with Youth and Communities*, ed. Django Paris and Maisha T. Winn (Thousand Oaks, CA: Sage, 2013), 223–248.

4. Eve Tuck, "Suspending Damage: A Letter to Communities," *Harvard Educational Review* 75, no. 3 (2009): 409–427.

5. Maisha T. Winn, "'Our Side of the Story': Moving Incarcerated Youth Voices from Margin to Center," *Race, Ethnicity, and Education* 13, no. 3 (September 2010): 313–326; Maisha T. Winn, "'Betwixt and Between': Literacy, Liminality, and the 'Celling' of Black Girls," *Race, Ethnicity, and Education* 13, no. 4 (December 2010): 425–447; Maisha T. Winn, *Girl Time: Literacy, Justice, and the School-to-Prison Pipeline* (New York: Teachers College Press, 2011); Maisha T. Winn and Chelsea A. Jackson, "Toward a Performance of Possibilities: Resisting Gendered (In)Justice," *International Journal of Qualitative Studies in Education* 24, no. 5 (September–October 2011): 615–620; Maisha T. Winn and Nadia Behizadeh, "The Right to Be Literate: Literacy, Education, and the School-to-Prison Pipeline," *Review of Research in Education* 35, no. 1 (2011): 147–173.

6. Maisha T. Winn, "The Politics of Desire and Possibility in Urban Playwriting," *Pedagogies: An International Journal* 7, no. 4 (2012): 317–332.

7. Erica R. Meiners and Maisha T. Winn, eds., *Education and Incarceration* (New York and London: Routledge, 2012).

8. Civil Rights Project/Proyecto Derechos Civiles, "An Open Letter to Honorable Arne Duncan, Secretary, U.S. Department of Education," http://tinyurl.com/cthucte.

9. David Domenici and James Forman Jr., "What it Takes to Transform a School Inside a Juvenile Justice Facility," in *Justice for Kids: Keeping Kids out of the Juvenile Justice System*, ed. Nancy E. Dowd (New York: New York University Press, 2011), 283–305.

10. Keisha Green, "Doing Double Dutch Methodology: Playing with the Practice of Participant Observer," in *Humanizing Research: Decolonizing Research Methods with Youth and Communities*, ed. Django Paris and Maisha T. Winn (Thousand Oaks, CA: Sage, 2013): 147–160.

11. RYDC Love is a pseudonym because the original title has the real name of the RYDC where it was written.

Chapter 4

1. Vivian Chávez and Elisabeth Soep, "Youth Radio and the Pedagogy of Collegiality," *Harvard Educational Review* 75, no. 4 (2005): 409–434; Fernando Naiditch, "Renewing Urban Education: Learning Cycles and the Pedagogy of Possibility," *Urban Learning, Teaching, and Research* 6 (2010): 45–60.

2. Rachelle Winkle-Wagner, *The Unchosen Me: Race, Gender, and Identity Among Black Women in College* (Baltimore: Johns Hopkins University Press, 2009).

3. Jeffrey Jensen Arnett, "Emerging Adulthood: Understanding the New Way of Coming of Age," in *Emerging Adults in American: Coming of Age in the 21st Century*, ed. Jeffrey Jensen Arnett and Jennifer L. Tanner (Washington, DC: American Psychological Association, 2006), 3–19.

4. James E. Côté and Charles G. Levine, "A Critical Examination of the Ego Identity Status Paradigm," *Developmental Review* 8, no. 2 (1988): 147–184.

5. Philip R. Newman and Barbara M. Newman, "Identity Formation and the College Experience," *Adolescence* 13, no. 50 (1978): 311–326.

6. Côté and Levine, "Ego Identity Status Paradigm," 162.

7. Michael W. Kirst and Kathy R. Bracco, "Bridging the Great Divide: How the K–12 and Postsecondary Split Hurts Students, and What Can Be Done About It," in *From High School to College: Improving Opportunities for Success in Postsecondary Education*, ed. Michael W. Kirst and Andrea Venezia (San Francisco: Jossey-Bass, 2004), 1–30.

8. Arnett, "Emerging Adulthood"; Winkle-Wagner, *Unchosen Me*.

9. Mary S. Hunter, "Lessons Learned: Achieving Institutional Change in Support of Students in Transition," *New Directions for Student Services* 114 (2006): 7–15.

10. Erica Rosenfeld Halverson, "Artistic Production Processes as Venues for Positive Youth Development," *Revista Interuniversitaria de Formacion del Profesorado* (Interuniversity journal of teacher education) 23, no. 3 (2009): 181–202.

11. Candance Doerr-Stevens, "Forging Space for New Identities and Literacy Practices Through Digital Media Composition of Radio Documentaries," *Proceedings for Annual Meeting of National Council Teachers of English Assembly on Research* (2011), http://conferences.library.wisc.edu/index.php/nctear2011;

Erica Rosenfeld Halverson, Rebecca Lowenhaupt, Damiana Gibbons, and Michelle Bass, "Conceptualizing Identity in Youth Media Arts Organizations: A Comparative Case Study," *E-Learning* 6, no. 1 (2009): 23–42.

12. Anne Burke and Roberta F. Hammett, *Assessing New Literacies: Perspectives from the Classroom* (New York: Peter Lang, 2009), 1.

13. Korina Jocson, "Steering Legacies: Pedagogy, Literacy, and Social Justice in Schools," *Urban Review* 41 (2009): 271.

14. Halverson, Lowenhaupt, Gibbons, and Bass, "Conceptualizing Identity"; Glynda Hull and Mira-Lisa Katz, "Crafting an Agentive Self: Case Studies of Digital Storytelling," *Research in the Teaching of English* 41, no. 1 (2006): 43–81; Elisabeth Soep, "Beyond Literacy and Voice in Youth Media Production," *McGill Journal of Education* 41, no. 3 (2006): 197–214.

15. Chávez and Soep, "Youth Radio"; Doerr-Stevens, "Forging Space"; Hervé Glevarec, "Youth Radio as 'Social Object': The Social Meaning of 'Free Radio' Shows for Young People in France," *Media, Culture, and Society* 27, no. 3 (2005): 333–351; Dana Walker and Deborah Romero, "When 'Literacy Is a Bennie': Researching Contested Literacies in Bilingual Youth Radio," *Ethnography and Education* 3, no. 3 (2008): 283–296.

16. Chávez and Soep, "Youth Radio."

17. Elisabeth Soep, "Beyond Literacy and Voice in Youth Media Production," *McGill Journal of Education* 41, no. 3 (2006): 197–214.

18. bell hooks, *Talking Back: Thinking Feminist, Thinking Black* (Boston: South End Press, 1989).

19. Ibid., 78.

20. Greg Smith, "First-Year Interest Groups Annual Report, 2011–2012 Academic Year," accessed May 1, 2013, http://figs.wisc.edu/documents/Annual_Report_FIGs_2011.pdf.

21. Ibid.

22. Colin Lankshear and Michele Knobel, *New Literacies: Changing Knowledge and Classroom Learning* (Berkshire, UK: Open University Press, 2003).

23. This American Life, "About Us," *This American Life*, Chicago Public Radio, www.thisamericanlife.org, accessed March 22, 2013.

24. Michelle Bass, "Exploring the Representations and Remixes of Underrepresented Students' Identities During Their Transition to College" (PhD dissertation, University of Wisconsin–Madison, 2012).

25. Robert E. Stake, "Case Study," in *Handbook of Qualitative Research*, 2nd ed., ed. Norma K. Denzin and Yvonne S. Lincoln (Thousand Oaks, CA: Sage, 2000), 435–454.

26. Andrew Burn and James Durran, "Digital Anatomies: Analysis as Production in Media Education," in *Digital Generations: Children, Young People, and New Media,* ed. David Buckingham and Rebekah Willett (Mahwah, NJ: Erlbaum Lawrence Associates, 2006), 273–293.

27. Nicole Fleetwood, "Authenticating Practices: Producing Realness, Performing Youth," in *Youthscapes: The Popular, the National, the Global,* ed. Sunaina Maira and Elisabeth Soep (Philadelphia: University of Pennsylvania Press, 2005), 155–172.

28. Unless otherwise noted, all the dialogue in this section is from the seminar Representing Self Through Media, University of Wisconsin–Madison, November 23, 2010.

29. Chris (RSTM student), interview with author (Michelle), October 2010.

30. Ibid.

31. Andrew Burn and David Parker, *Analysing Media Texts* (London, UK: Continuum, 2003); Burn and Durran, "Digital Anatomies: Analysis as Production in Media Education," in *Digital Generations: Children, Young People, and New Media,* ed. David Buckingham and Rebekah Willett (Mahwah, NJ: L. Erlbaum Associates, 2006), 273–294.

32. Burn and Parker, *Analysing Media Texts*, 13.

33. Jay Lemke, "Metamedia Literacy: Transforming Meanings and Media," in *Handbook of Literacy and Technology: Transformations in a Post-Typographic World,* ed. David Reinking (Mahwah, NJ: L. Erlbaum Associates, 1998), 283–301; Jay L. Lemke, "Travels in Hypermodality," *Visual Communication* 1, no. 3 (2002): 299–325.

34. Chris (RSTM student), interview with author (Michelle), December 2010.

35. Roz Ivanic, Richard Edwards, Candice Satchwell, and June Smith, "Possibilities for Pedagogy in Further Education: Harnessing the Abundance of Literacy," *British Educational Research Journal* 33, no. 5 (2007): 704.

36. Lalitha Vasudevan and Marc Lamont Hill, "Moving Beyond Dichotomies of Media Engagement in Education: An Introduction," in *Media, Learning, and Sites of Possibility*, ed. Lalitha Vasudevan and Marc Lamont Hill (New York: Peter Lang, 2009), 5.

37. Kevin Leander "Composing with Old and New Media: Toward a Parallel Pedagogy," in *Digital Literacies: Social Learning and Classroom Practices*, ed. Victoria Carrington and Muriel Robinson (Los Angeles: Sage, 2009), 147–164.

38. David T. Conley, "Rethinking College Readiness," *New Directions for Higher Education* 144 (2008): 3–13.

39. Bonita London, Geraldine Downey, Niall Bolger, and Elizabeth Velilla, "A Framework for Studying Social Identity and Coping with Daily Stress During the Transition to College," in *Navigating the Future: Social Identity, Coping, and Life Tasks*, ed. Geraldine Downey, Jacquelynne S. Eccles, and Celina M. Chatman (New York: Russell Sage Foundation, 2005), 45–63.

Chapter 5

1. American Academy for Child and Adolescent Psychiatry, "About Us," accessed May 20, 2012, www.aacap.org/cs/root/about_us/about_us.

2. Gloria Ladson-Billings, *The Dreamkeepers: Successful Teachers of African American Children* (San Francisco: Jossey-Bass, 1994).

3. Lisa Patel Stevens, "Maps to Interrupt a Pathology: Immigrant Populations and Education," *Critical Inquiry in Language Studies* 6, no. 1–2 (2009): 1–14.

4. Lisa Patel, *Youth Held at the Border: Immigration and Politics of Inclusion* (New York: Teachers College Press, 2013).

5. Richard Luecking and Meredith Gramlich, "Quality Work-Based Learning and Postschool Employment Success," *Examining Current Challenges in Secondary Education and Transition* 2, no. 3 (2004): 443–449; Peter F. Parilla and Garry W. Hesser, "Internships and the Sociological Perspective: Applying Principles of Experiential Learning," *Teaching Sociology* 26, no. 3 (1998): 310–329.

6. Internship Connections, "Internship Connections," accessed May 2, 2013, www.internshipconnection.com/.

7. Jeannie Oakes, *Keeping Track: How Schools Structure Inequity* (Binghamton, NY: Yale University Press, 1995).

8. Boston Private Industry Council, "Programs: Employment for BPS Students," accessed March 29, 2013, www.bostonpic.org/programs/employment-bps-students.

9. Mary Louise Pratt, "Arts of the Contact Zone," *Profession* 91, no. 33–40 (1991): 34.

10. R. C. Pintara, *Enhancing Relationships Between Children and Teachers* (Washington, DC: American Psychological Association 1999); Desiree B. Qin, "Gendered Expectations and Gendered Experiences: Immigrant Students' Adaptation in Schools," *New Directions for Youth Development* 100 (2003): 91–110.

11. Ramón Grosfoguel, "Colonial Difference, Geopolitics of Knowledge and Global Coloniality in the Modern/Colonial Capitalist World-System," *Research Foundation of SUNY* 25, no. 3 (2002): 203–224.

12. Cindi Katz, *Growing Up Global: Economic Restructuring and Children's Everyday Lives* (Minneapolis: University of Minnesota Press, 2004).

13. Pratt, "Arts of the Contact Zone."

14. Maria Elena Torre, "The Alchemy of Integrated Spaces: Youth Participation in Research Collectives of Difference," in *Beyond Silenced Voices*, ed. Lois Weis and Michelle Fine (Albany: State University of New York Press, 2005), 251–266.

15. Paulo Freire, *Pedagogy of the Oppressed* (New York: Continuum, 1970); Derrick Bell, *Faces at the Bottom of the Well: The Permanence of Racism* (New York: Basic Books, 1977); Richard Delgado and Jean Stefanic, *Critical Race Theory: An Introduction* (New York: New York University Press, 2001).

16. Pierre A. Bourdieu, *Outline of a Theory of Practice* (London: Cambridge University Press, 1989).

17. Lisa Patel, field notes, November 23, 2011.

18. Ibid.

19. Jennifer Vadeboncoeur and Lisa Patel Stevens, *Reconceptualizing the Adolescent: Sign, Symbol and Body* (New York: Peter Lang, 2004).

20. John Jackson, "Disrupting the Discourse" (paper presented at the Alumni of Color Conference, Harvard Graduate School of Education, Cambridge, MA, March 2, 2012).

Chapter 6

1. Amanda E. Lewis, *Race in the Schoolyard: Negotiating the Color Line in Classrooms and Communities* (Piscataway, NJ: Rutgers University Press, 2003); Jerome E. Morris, *Troubling the Waters: Fulfilling the Promise of Quality Public Schooling for Black Children* (New York: Teachers College Press, 2009); Na'ilah Suad Nasir, *Racialized Identities: Race and Achievement for African-American Youth* (Stanford, CA: Stanford University Press, 2011); Mica Pollock, *Colormute: Race Talk Dilemmas in an American School* (Princeton, NJ: Princeton University Press, 2005).

2. Zeus Leonardo, *Race, Whiteness, and Education* (New York: Routledge, 2009).

3. Lawrence D. Bobo, "Prejudice as Group Position: Microfoundations of a Sociological Approach to Racism and Race Relations," *Journal of Social Issues* 55, no. 3 (1999): 445–467; Eduardo Bonilla-Silva, *Racism Without Racists: Color-Blind Racism and the Persistence of Racial Inequality in the United States* (Lanham, MD: Rowman & Littlefield, 2003); Michael Omi and Howard Winant, *Racial Formation in the United States: From the 1960's to the 1990's* (New York: Routledge, 1994).

4. Linda Darling-Hammond, *The Flat World and Education: How America's Commitment to Equity Will Determine Our Future* (New York: Teachers College Press, 2010); Jonathan Kozol, *Savage Inequalities: Children in America's Schools* (New York: Crown Publications, 1991); Jeannie Oakes, *Keeping Track: How Schools Structure Inequality*, 2nd ed. (New Haven, CT: Yale University, 2005); Ann Arnett Ferguson, *Bad Boys: Public Schools in the Making of Black Masculinity* (Ann Arbor: University of Michigan Press, 2000); Lewis, *Race in the Schoolyard*; Prudence L. Carter, *Keeping It Real* (New York: Oxford University Press, 2005); Nasir, *Racialized Identities*; Pollock, *Colormute*; Rebecca Schaffer and Debra G. Skinner, "Performing Race in Four Culturally Diverse Fourth Grade Classrooms: Silence, Race Talk, and the Negotiation of Social Boundaries," *Anthropology and Education Quarterly* 40, no. 3 (2009): 277–296.

5. Carter, *Keeping It Real*; Ferguson, *Bad Boys*.

6. Ferguson, *Bad Boys*.

7. Diane Hughes et al., "Parents' Ethnic/Racial Socialization Practices: A Review of Research and Directions for Future Study," *Developmental Psychology* 42, no. 5 (2006): 747–770.

8. Carol D. Lee, "Profile of an Independent Black Institution African-Centered Education at Work," *Journal of Negro Education* 61, no. 2 (1992): 160–177; Kofi Lomotey, "Independent Black Institutions: African-Centered Education," *Journal of Negro Education* 61, no. 4 (1992): 455–462.

9. Alea Holman, "Gendered Racial Socialization in Black Families: Mothers' Beliefs, Approaches, and Advocacy" (doctoral dissertation, University of California, Berkeley, 2012).

10. Lewis, *Race in the Schoolyard*; Nasir, *Racialized Identities*; Pollock, *Colormute*.

11. Annika Rogell, *The Black Power Mixtape, 1967–1975*, directed by Göran Hugo Olsson (New York: Story AB, Louverture Films, 2011).

Chapter 7

1. Bahii's name and any other names of our participants are pseudonyms. We also use the term *Native Americans* and *Native* interchangeably to refer to Native people in the United States. The term *Indigenous* refers to international and global populations. We also capitalize the terms *Native* and *Indigenous* to coincide with the United Nations usage of the term, which recognizes Indigenous people's inherent rights to their lands and their political and cultural sovereignty.

2. George Jerry Sefa Dei and Gurpreet Singh Johal, eds., *Critical Issues in Anti-Racist Research Methodologies* (New York: Peter Lang, 2005); Michelle Fine and Lois Weis, *The Unknown City: The Lives of Poor and Working-Class Young Adults* (Boston: Beacon, 1998); Hava Rachel Gordon, *We Fight to Win: Inequality and the Politics of Youth Activism* (New Brunswick, NJ: Rutgers University Press, 2009).

3. Patricia Hill Collins, *Black Feminist Thought: Knowledge, Consciousness, and the Politics of Empowerment*, 3rd ed. (New York: Routledge, 2009); Linda Tuhiwai Smith, *Decolonizing Methodologies: Research and Indigenous Peoples* (London: Zed Books, 1999).

4. Ted Jojola et al., *Indian Education in New Mexico, 2025* (contracted by the New Mexico Public Education Department, Indian Education Division, 2010).

5. Smith, *Decolonizing Methodologies*; for more on antiracist methodologies, see Julio Cammarota and Michelle Fine, *Revolutionizing Education: Youth Participatory Action Research in Motion* (New York: Routledge, 2008). To protect the identity of individual participants, we changed the names of all participants and individual schools.

6. We also include a quote from one of the pilot focus groups we conducted with students who were not part of the study. There were a total of four Native American students who had formerly attended these schools located in these districts in the pilot focus group.

7. U.S. Census Bureau, "The American Indian and Alaska Native Population, 2010," *2010 Census Briefs* (Washington, DC: U.S. Department of Commerce: Economics and Statistics Division, 2012). According to the 2010 U.S. Census, about a tenth of the population in New Mexico is foreign-born.

8. New Mexico Public Education Department (PED), *New Mexico Tribal Education Status Report for 2009–2010* (Santa Fe, NM: New Mexico PED, Indian Education Division, 2012).

9. Ibid.

10. David Beaulieu, "Comprehensive Reform and American Indian Education," *Journal of American Indian Education* 39, no. 2 (2000): 29–38.

11. Jojola et al., *Indian Education in New Mexico, 2025*; Glenabah Martinez, *Native Pride: The Politics of Curriculum and Instruction in an Urban Public School* (New York: Hampton Press, 2010).

12. University of New Mexico, "2011 IPEDS Graduation Rate Component Data Summary," accessed March 29, 2013, http://tinyurl.com/d4t6s5q.

13. Glenabah Martinez, *Native Pride: The Politics of Curriculum and Instruction in an Urban Public School* (New York: Hampton Press, 2010).

14. Mary Eunice Romero, "Identifying Giftedness Among Keresan Pueblo Indians: The Keres Study," *Journal of American Indian Education* 34, no. 1 (1994), 35–58.

15. Greg Cajete, *Look to the Mountain: An Ecology of Indigenous Education* (Durango, CO: Kivaki Press, 1994); Angayuquq Oscar Kawagley, *A Yupiaq Worldview: A Pathway to Ecology and Spirit* (Prospect Heights, IL: Waveland Press, 1995).

16. Donna Deyhle, "From Break Dancing to Heavy Metal: Navajo Youth, Resistance, and Identity," *Youth and Society* 30, no.1 (1998): 3–31.

17. Martinez, *Native Pride*.

18. Tiffany S. Lee, "'If They Want Navajo to Be Learned, Then They Should Require It in All Schools': Navajo Teenagers' Experiences, Choices, and Demands

Regarding Navajo Language," Special Issue on Navajo Studies, *Wicazo Sa Review* 22, no. 1 (2007): 7–33.

19. Tiffany S. Lee, "Language, Identity, and Power: Navajo and Pueblo Young Adults' Perspectives and Experiences with Competing Language Ideologies," *Journal of Language, Identity and Education* (Special Issue: Indigenous Youth and Bilingualism) 8, no. 5 (2009): 307–320; Teresa McCarty et al., "Indigenous Youth as Language Policy Makers," *Journal of Language, Identity and Education* (Special Issue: Indigenous Youth and Bilingualism) 8, no. 5 (2009): 291–306.

20. McCarty et al., "Indigenous Youth as Language Policy Makers," 299.

21. Martinez, *Native Pride.*

22. Diné College, "Strategic Planning: Diné College's Vision, Mission, Philosophy, Values," www.dinecollege.edu/about/about.php, accessed March 29, 2013.

23. Collins, *Black Feminist Thought.*

24. Ibid., 319.

25. Ibid., 320.

26. Jojola et al., *Indian Education in New Mexico, 2025.*

27. Shawn Wilson, *Research Is Ceremony: Indigenous Research Methods* (Black Point, Nova Scotia: Fernwood Publishing, 2008).

28. Ibid.

29. Ibid.

30. Martinez, *Native Pride.*

31. McCarty et al., "Indigenous Youth as Language Policy Makers."

32. Cornel Pewewardy, "Ideology, Power, and the Miseducation of Indigenous Peoples in the United States," in *For Indigenous Eyes Only: A Decolonization Handbook*, ed. Waziyatawin Angela Wilson and Michael Yellow Bird (Santa Fe, NM: School for American Research Press, 2005), 139–156.

33. Martinez, *Native Pride.*

34. Paolo Freire, *The Politics of Education: Culture, Power and Liberation* (New York: Bergin & Garvel, 1985); Paolo Freire, *Pedagogy of the Oppressed* (New York: Continuum, 1993).

35. Hailey Heinz, "Skandera: School District Can't Split," *Albuquerque Journal*, June 9, 2012, www.abqjournal.com/main/2012/06/09/news/skandera-school-district-cant-split.html.

36. Karina Walters et al., "Bodies Don't Just Tell Stories, They Tell Histories: Embodiment of Historical Trauma Among American Indians and Alaska Natives," *Du Bois Review: Social Science Research on Race* 8, no.1 (2011): 179–189.

37. Cajete, *Look to the Mountain*; Kawagley, *A Yupiaq Worldview*.

38. A pseudonym.

39. Sovereignty Charter School, "SCS Announces First Graduation Ceremony After Six Years of Support," Press Release, May 15, 2012.

40. Sovereignty Charter School, "2010–11 Annual Yearly Progress (AYP) Scores: 11th Grade Students at Proficiency Level (SCS internal document).

Chapter 8

1. Pseudonyms are used throughout this chapter for the research site and study participants.

2. For a further discussion of the range of identities characterized as transgender, see Genny Beemyn and Susan Rankin, *The Lives of Transgender People* (New York: Columbia University Press, 2011).

3. For more on the social and historical contexts of transphobia in the United States, see Paisley Currah, Richard N. Juang, and Shannon Price Minter, eds., *Transgender Rights* (Minneapolis: University of Minnesota Press, 2006).

4. For more on trans youth's struggles to find parental acceptance, see Arnold H. Grossman and Anthony R. D'Augelli, "Transgender Youth and Life-Threatening Behaviors," *Suicide and Life-Threatening Behaviors* 37, no. 5 (2007): 527–537. For a critique of the pathologizing nature of "gender identity disorder," see Kelley Winters, *Gender Madness in American Psychiatry: Essays from the Struggle for Dignity* (Dillon, CO: GID Reform Advocates, 2008).

5. Maureen Carroll, "Transgender Youth, Adolescent Decisionmaking, and *Roper v. Simmons*," *UCLA Law Review* 56, no. 3 (2009): 725–753.

6. See Grossman and D'Augelli, "Transgender Youth," for statistics on trans youth suicidality. For more on the vulnerability of trans youth of color, see Kai Wright, "To Be Poor and Transgender," in *Reconstructing Gender: A Multicultural Anthology*, ed. Estelle Disch (New York: McGraw Hill, 2003), 64–69.

7. Examples include strategies for K–12 schools in John Peterman, "When Chris Becomes Courtney: Preparing a Pre-K–8 School Community for a Transgendering Student," *Independent School* 69, no. 4 (summer 2010): 60–65; strategies for K–12 principals in Micah Ludeke, "Transgender Youth," *Principal Leadership*

10, no. 3 (November 2009): 12–16; strategies for colleges and universities in Brett Beemyn et al., "Transgender Issues on College Campuses," *New Directions for Student Services* 111 (2005): 49–60; and strategies for teacher education programs in Kathleen E. Rands, "Considering Transgender People in Education: A Gender-Complex Approach," *Journal of Teacher Education* 60, no. 4 (September–October 2009): 419–431.

8. Emily A. Greytak, Joseph G. Kosciw, and Elizabeth M. Diaz, *Harsh Realities: The Experiences of Transgender Youth in Our Nation's Schools* (New York: Gay, Lesbian and Straight Education Network, 2009).

9. Ibid., ix.

10. Megan Davidson, "Rethinking the Movement: Trans Youth Activism in New York City and Beyond," in *Queer Youth Cultures*, ed. Susan Driver (Albany: State University of New York Press, 2008), 243–260.

11. Davidson, "Rethinking the Movement"; Shannon Price Minters, "Do Transsexuals Dream of Gay Rights? Getting Real About Transgender Inclusion," in *Transgender Rights*, ed. Paisley Currah, Richard N. Juang, and Shannon Price Minter (Minneapolis: University of Minnesota Press, 2006), 141–170.

12. "MSM" is frequently used in public health discourses to describe and appeal to men who engage in same-sex behaviors but may not self-identify as gay.

13. Currah, Jang, and Price Minter, *Transgender Rights*.

14. Lydia A. Sausa, JoAnne Keatley, and Don Operario, "Perceived Risks and Benefits of Sex Work Among Transgender Women of Color in San Francisco," *Archives of Sexual Behavior* 36, no. 6 (2007): 768–777.

15. Erin C. Wilson et al., "Transgender Female Youth and Sex Work: HIV Risk and a Comparison of Life Factors Related to Engagement in Sex Work," *AIDS and Behavior* 13, no. 5 (2009): 902–913.

16. For a fuller explanation of "butch queen," see Marlon M. Bailey, "Performance as Intravention: Ballroom Culture and the Politics of HIV/AIDS in Detroit," *Souls* 11, no. 3 (2009): 253–274.

17. More sexually explicit expressions included "Giving head in the alley," "gaping hole," and "Dick holders," all of which pejoratively referenced participation in sex acts by trans females who were involved in sex work.

18. Other descriptors included "Suckin' Dick in the Alley," "Suck dick for nothing," "yong [young] butt lovers!" and "**Do the same things that trannies do.**"

19. Ramona Faith Oswald, "Resilience Within the Family Networks of Lesbians and Gay Men: Intentionality and Redefinition," *Journal of Marriage and the Family* 64 (2002): 374–383.

20. See Bailey, "Performance as Intravention," for an explanation of the "gay mom" figure in black and Latino house/ball communities.

21. See Bailey, "Performance as Intravention," for an explanation of Black and Latino house/ball communities.

22. Erica R. Meiners and Therese Quinn, eds., *Sexualities in Education: A Reader* (New York: Peter Lang, 2012); Elizabeth L. Meyer, *Gender and Sexual Diversity in Schools* (New York: Springer, 2010).

23. Lance T. McCready, *Making Space for Diverse Masculinities: Difference, Intersectionality, and Engagement in an Urban High School* (New York: Peter Lang, 2010).

24. Davidson, "Rethinking the Movement"; Price Minter, "Do Transsexuals Dream?"

Chapter 9

1. Martin Carnoy, Amber K. Gove, and Jeffery H. Marshall, *Cuba's Academic Advantage: Why Students in Cuba Do Better in School* (Stanford, CA: Stanford University Press, 2007); Ezekiel Dixon-Román, "Products of the Revolution: The Social System of Comprehensively Conceived Education in Cuba," in *Thinking Comprehensively About Education*: *Spaces of Educative Possibility and Their Implications for Public Policy*, ed. Ezekiel J. Dixon-Román and Edmund W. Gordon (New York: Routledge/Taylor & Francis, 2012), 45–64; Antoni Kapcia, *Cuba in Revolution: A History Since the Fifties* (London: Reaktion, 2008); Jonathan Kozol, *Children of the Revolution: A History Since the Fifties* (New York: Dell Publishing, 1978); Marvin Leiner, *Children Are the Revolution*: *Day Care in Cuba* (New York: Penguin, 1974).

2. In our work, we use *hip-hop* to refer to the larger culture that encompasses the musical production of rap. Ezekiel Dixon-Román and Wilfredo Gomez, "Cuban Youth Culture and Receding Futures: Hip Hop, Reggaetón, and *Pedagogías Marginal*," *Pedagogies: An International Journal* 7, no. 4 (2012): 364–379.

3. Michel Foucault, *Discipline and Punish* (New York: Pantheon, 1977).

4. Kapcia, *Cuba in Revolution*.

5. Geoffrey Baker, *Buena Vista in the Club: Rap, Reggaetón, and Revolution in Havana* (Durham, NC: Duke University Press, 2011).

6. Michel Focault, "Of Other Spaces, Heterotopias," trans. Jay Miskowiec, *Diacritics* 16, no. 1 (1967, 1986): 22–27.

7. Baker, *Buena Vista in the Club.*

8. Jorge Dominguez, "Cuba Since 1959," in *Cuba: A Short History*, ed. Leslie Bethell (New York: Cambridge University Press, 1993), 95–148.

9. Maria Dolores Espino, "Cuban Tourism During the Special Period," *Association for the Study of the Cuban Economy* 10 (2000).

10. M. del Carmen Zabulla Argüelles, "Does a Certain Dimension of Poverty Exist in Cuba?" in *Cuba in the 1990s*, ed. J.B. Lara (La Habana, Cuba: Editorial Jose Marti, 1999); Michael Reid, "Revolution in Retreat (Special Report)," *The Economist*, March 24, 2012, 1–12.

11. Alejandro De La Fuente, *A Nation for All: Race, Inequality, and Politics in Twentieth-Century Cuba* (Chapel Hill: University of North Carolina Press, 2001).

12. Baker, *Buena Vista in the Club.*

13. Lourdes Suarez, e-mail message to authors, June 7, 2012.

14. De La Fuente, *A Nation for All.*

15. Baker, *Buena Vista in the Club.*

16. Ibid.

17. To maintain the anonymity of the artists we interviewed, we only refer to La Agencia Cubana de Rap, or the agency.

18. Baker, *Buena Vista in the Club.*

19. Ezekiel Dixon-Román, "Deviance as Pedagogy: A New Research Agenda On Indigenous Cultural Repertoires" (manuscript submitted for publication).

20. Ann Swindler, "Culture in Action: Symbols and Strategies," *American Sociological Review* 51, no. 2 (1986): 273–286.

21. Dixon-Román, "Deviance as Pedagogy."

22. Cathy J. Cohen, "Deviance as Resistance: A New Research Agenda for the Black Politics," *DuBois Review* 1, no. 1 (2004): 27–45.

23. Michel de Certeau, *The Practice of Everyday Life* (Berkeley: University of California Press, 1980, 1984).

24. For perspectives on media production, see chapters 1, 4, and 10 in this volume.

25. We acknowledge the tremendous assistance and support of Javier Martinez, Tomas Fernandez Robaina, Lourdes Suarez, and Nehanda Abodiun in doing this work as well as the very helpful feedback from Damon Freeman.

Chapter 10

1. Stanton Wortham, ed., "Youth Cultures, Language and Literacy. *Review of Research in Education* 35 (2011): vii–xi.

2. Kitty TeRiele, "Youth 'At Risk': Further Marginalizing the Marginalized," *Journal of Education Policy* 21, no. 2 (2006): 129–145.

3. Andy Brader, *Youth Identities: Time, Space and Social Exclusion* (Saarbrücken, Germany: Lambert Academic, 2010).

4. Edmund Rice Education Australia (EREA), *Including the Excluded* (Brisbane: Flexible Learning Centre Network Paper 2, 2009).

5. James Ladwig, "Beyond Academic Outcomes," *Review of Research in Education* 34, no. 1 (2010): 113–141.

6. David Buckingham and Julian Sefton-Green, *Cultural Studies Goes to School* (London: Taylor & Francis, 1994).

7. Shirley Brice Heath, Edward Boehncke, and Shelby Wolf, *Made for Each Other: Creative Sciences and Arts in the Secondary School* (London: Creative Partnerships, 2007).

8. Kimberley Austin and Nichole Pinkard, "The Organization and Management of Formal and Informal Learning," *Proceedings of the 8th International Conference on the Learning Sciences* 3 (2008), ACM Digital Library.

9. Digital Youth Network home page, accessed March 29, 2013, www.digitalyouthnetwork.org.

10. Pierre Bourdieu, "The Forms of Social Capital," in *Handbook of Theory and Research for the Sociology of Education*, ed. John Richardson (New York: Greenwood, 1986), 241–258.

11. Terence Lee, *The Media, Cultural Control and Government in Singapore* (New York: Routledge, 2010).

12. Gunther Kress, *Multimodality* (New York: Routledge, 2010).

13. Valentina Klenowski, *Developing Portfolios for Learning and Assessment* (London: Routledge, 2002).

14. Pierre Bourdieu, *Distinction: A Social Critique of the Judgement of Taste*, trans. Richard Nice (Cambridge, MA: Harvard University Press, 1984).

15. Heath, Boehncke, and Wolf, *Made for Each Other*.

16. Andy Brader, "Synchronous Learner Support for Music Sequencing Software," *Journal of Music, Technology and Education* 2, no. 2–3 (2009): 159–174.

17. Stephen Connolly, *Students' Cultural Capital: A Study of Assessment for Learning as a Field of Exchange* (PhD dissertation, Queensland University of Technology, Brisbane, Australia, 2012).

18. Maria Kaya, Paul Steffens, Greg Hearn, and Philip Graham, "How Can Entrepreneurial Musicians Use Electronic Social Networks to Diffuse Their Music," in *Proceedings of the 7th AGSE International Entrepreneurship Research Exchange*, ed. Janice Langan-Fox (Queensland: Swinburne University of Technology/ University of the Sunshine Coast, 2010), 679–691.

19. Richard Lanham, *The Economics of Attention: Style and Substance in the Age of Information* (Chicago: University of Chicago Press, 2006).

20. Julie Coiro, Michele Knobel, Colin Lankshear, and Donald Leu, eds., *Handbook of Research on New Literacies* (New York: Routledge, 2009).

21. Jerry Wellington, "Has ICT Education Come of Age? Recurring Debates on the Role of ICT in Education, 1982–2004," *Research in Science and Technological Education* 23, no. 1, (2005): 25–39.

Acknowledgments

Any major project is untenable without its parts. *Cultural Transformations* is no exception, and I wish to acknowledge various individuals and organizations for making this book possible. First, I am grateful to the authors who offered insightful contributions. It was a privilege to delve deeper into a number of educational projects that matter in youth's lives. The opportunity to learn from each of the authors, as well as the young people speaking or represented in their projects, was an opportunity to push an important educational agenda in a collective fashion. The authors were very generous with their time, and I am truly humbled by their commitment to education.

I extend my gratitude to the Center for the Humanities at Washington University in St. Louis for a multiyear seminar series grant, which first brought together several of the contributors in this book. Also to the Programs in African and African American Studies; American Culture Studies; Women, Gender, and Sexuality Studies; the Center on Urban Research and Public Policy; and Department of Education for endorsing the colloquia that ensued. Special thanks to Gerald Early for his initial encouragement to pull together scholars and artists whose work blends perspectives from the humanities and social sciences. Rising to the challenge meant drawing on synergies across multiple arenas, and I was fortunate to have had the support for this interdisciplinary endeavor.

I must recognize the editors of *Pedagogies: An International Journal* for engaging ideas in a focus issue that allowed me to see this book-in-the-making in a different light.

A heap of thanks to editor Nancy Walser of Harvard Education Press for her close reading of the manuscript. Her keen eye steered my own editorial pen into a sharper direction. I appreciate the HEP board and production team for seeing this project through. The artwork presented on the book cover is by Danièle Spellman (www.artselves.com) of Berkeley, California, who continues to inspire with worldly muses. The image titled *Can You Hear Me Now?* captures the essence behind this book.

It is an honor to have Shirley Brice Heath write the afterword. Her scholarship has been influential in my work. I value her critical insights as an extension of the perspectives in the chapters. I recall our "mentoring" moments near the Rodin Sculpture Garden at Stanford University as more than memorable; they were instructive. In this same vein, I must acknowledge all of my mentors and colleagues whose wise counsel has guided my professional path. The conversations often leave no room for mediocrity. I am indebted to my academic family for insisting on tenacity with human decency because "if we don't, who will" (several of them grace the pages of this book).

While on leave last fall, it was important to take time away so that I could focus on writing projects, including this one. I had the privilege to be a visiting scholar in the Department of Humanities, Social Sciences, and Social Justice in Education at the Ontario Institute for Studies in Education, which provided a distinct intellectual space for exchanging ideas. Many thanks to faculty, students, and staff for their enthusiastic reception.

Inspiration comes in many ways. It is through honesty that good ideas become better ones. A big nod goes to Jasiyah for keeping the line open despite the hour; to gRace for leading by example; and to Riqqs for embracing nature's gifts—all three remind me to write better for different audiences. Found moments of chatter and silence—regardless of terrain—have been priceless. To MF, DB, MC, and SM for being pillars in the Lou. To the

Ngeno/Conner, Carroll/Sawyers, and Jocson families for providing nurturing environments. Most especially, to my mother and father, thank you for sustaining me from the very beginning. I know no other way than to return the love. There is no other way.

—Korina M. Jocson

About the Editor

Korina M. Jocson is an assistant professor of education at Washington University in St. Louis. Her research and teaching interests include literacy, youth, and cultural studies in education. For over a decade, Jocson has collaborated with university programs, schools, and community-based organizations to promote literacy development among youth. She has published a number of journal articles and is the author of *Youth Poets: Empowering Literacies In and Out of Schools* (Peter Lang; 2008). Currently, she is completing a book tentatively titled *Youth Media Matters: Literacy and Education in a Participatory Culture.*

About the Contributors

Rocío Sánchez Ares is a doctoral student in education at Boston College. She is from the Celtic green countryside of Galicia, Spain. She is passionate about teaching and researching as a means to challenge social injustice and discrimination. She explores participatory creative methodologies such as theater, drawing, and photovoice in her collaborations with the poor. She actively works with immigrant youth and their parents as agents of change in their communities.

Michelle Bass is a recent PhD graduate of the educational psychology program at the University of Wisconsin–Madison, where she studied adolescent identity development, media literacy, and qualitative methodology. She has been a project assistant on multiple research projects studying digital media practices in and out of school environments and the key pedagogical moments associated with these practices in their respective structured learning environments. She is interested in identity development during the transition to college and first-year experience and how digital representations of self can foster the identity development of under-represented students.

Andy Brader specializes in music, education, and technology. For over two decades, he has assisted thousands of young people from disadvantaged locations to express themselves through the production of popular culture such as music, video, graffiti, and stop-frame animation. He is senior youth worker for Youth+ and adjunct research fellow for the Victorian Institute for Education, Diversity and Lifelong Learning. For more information, see www.andybrader.com.

Tomás Boatwright is a PhD candidate of teaching and curriculum at the University of Rochester's Warner Graduate School of Education. His dissertation explores the social and academic experiences of queer students of color and their identified educational support. His research interests include critical pedagogies, alternative educational space, intersectionality, youth cultures, and queer theories.

Ed Brockenbrough is an assistant professor of Teaching and Curriculum at the University of Rochester's Warner Graduate School of Education. His scholarly interests revolve around negotiations of identity, pedagogy, and power in urban educational spaces, with particular attention to black, masculinity, and queer issues in education. In addition to examining educational opportunities for LGBT youth of color, Brockenbrough directs the Urban Teaching and Leadership Program, a partnership with the Rochester City School District that prepares urban teachers with a commitment to social justice.

Brett Cook's work cohesively integrates the breadth and depth of his diverse experiences with art, education, science, and spirituality. For more than two decades, he has produced exhibitions, installations, curricula, and events widely across the United States and internationally. His use of participatory ethnographic strategies, progressive educational pedagogy, community organizing, and mindfulness connects his work to exceptionally wide audiences. He has received various prestigious awards, including the Lehman Brady Visiting Professorship at Duke University and University of North Carolina–Chapel Hill, the Richard C. Diebenkorn Fellowship at the San Francisco Art Institute, and residencies at the Skowhegan School of Painting and Sculpture (Maine), the Studio Museum (Harlem), Art Omi (New York), and the Headlands Center for the Arts (California). For more information, see www.brett-cook.com.

Maxine McKinney de Royston is an NAEd/Spencer Foundation postdoctoral fellow in the Graduate School of Education at the University of California, Berkeley. She uses sociocultural and sociopolitical perspectives on teaching and learning to examine how race, culture, and identity influence learning environments and pedagogies aimed at shifting racialized disparities in the educational outcomes, trajectories, and schooling experiences of nondominant youth, especially African Americans.

Ezekiel Dixon-Román is an assistant professor of social policy and education in the School of Social Policy & Practice at the University of Pennsylvania. His overall research interests are in the sociology of education, cultural studies, and quantitative methods. He is particularly concerned with the cumulative and residual effects of inheritance on social differences in human learning and development, how knowledge is constructed and produced regarding these differences, and identifying the potential resources, practices, and policies that may enable the mediation of these cumulative and residual effects. He edited, with Edmund W. Gordon, *Thinking Comprehensively About Education*, and is completing a single-authored volume, *Inheriting [Im]possibility*.

Melissa P. Dodd, chief information officer of the Boston Public Schools, leads educational technology solutions in a district with some fifty-six thousand students. She earned an EdM from Harvard Graduate School of Education before leaping into technology. She loves every moment with her daughter Lilia and dreams of traveling more to see friends in Spain and other far-off places.

Wilfredo Gomez's research interests focus on black cultural expressions throughout the African diaspora, with an emphasis on hip-hop, reggaetón, language, narrative, and performance in urban spaces in the United States, in addition to disability studies. More specifically, he is interested in cross-cultural communication and the formal and informal sites where cultural production, exchange, and learning take place. He is pursuing a PhD in anthropology and education at Teachers College, Columbia University.

Alex M. (Dodd) Gurn is working on his PhD at Boston College. He is from Buffalo and is married to another contributor—an amazing person—in this volume. His thesis is about troubling the blurred boundaries of public and private in education, through a critical, fragmented case study of corporate philanthropy in urban schools.

Erica Rosenfeld Halverson is an associate professor of digital media and literacy in the Department of Curriculum & Instruction at the University of Wisconsin–Madison. Erica's research focuses on how young people learn to make art about the stories of their lives and the role this art-making process plays in identity development and literacy learning. Erica has worked with young people across media, including theater, film, radio, and, most recently, makerspaces. Erica is a theater artist and the cofounder of Barrel of Monkeys, a Chicago-based arts education theater ensemble working to create an alternative learning environment in which children share their personal voices and celebrate the power of their imaginations.

Shirley Brice Heath is Margery Bailey Professor of English and Dramatic Literature and professor of linguistics and anthropology, emerita, at Stanford University. From 2003 to 2010, she was also Professor at Large in the Watson Institute for International Studies at Brown University. She has centered her research on learning tasks and environments that children and young people seek out on their own. From sports teams to laboratories of scientists and studios of artists, she has studied the language, personal interactions, and informational sources that young people voluntarily bring to their play and work.

Alea Holman is completing her doctoral studies at the University of California, Berkeley, in the Graduate School of Education's School Psychology Program. Her work is focused on racial socialization in families. Her doctoral work has resulted in an MA in education and a School Psychology credential. She completed her undergraduate studies at Stanford University with a major in human biology and a minor in African and African American studies, and she achieved the MPH in Health Promotion at Columbia

University. She works as a school psychologist in the California Bay Area. Additionally, she teaches in the University of California, Berkeley Psychology Department and assists with research projects examining school districts' initiatives for students and parents of color.

Eli Jacobs-Fantauzzi, a documentary filmmaker, has captured the voice of international hip-hop and documented the art of storytelling around the globe. He is a graduate of University of California, Berkeley, and Tisch School of the Arts at New York University. He completed his first acclaimed international documentary *Inventos: Hip Hop Cubano,* in 2003. His second film, *HomeGrown: Hip Life in Ghana,* is now on DVD. He is currently working on his third feature-length film, *Revolucion Sin Muertos* (Revolution without death), about youth in Medellin, Colombia, using hip-hop to expand a peace movement. Jacobs-Fantauzzi launched www.Fistup.tv, an online channel dedicated to documenting the global hip-hop movement. Follow the movement on Twitter and Instagram: @fistuptv.

Eun Jeong Yang (EdM) is currently working as a liaison and translator between Korean students' families and private schools in Massachusetts. Prior to this, she worked as a college counselor with Asian immigrant high school students in the Boston area. She has been volunteering for Critical Transitions Project since October 2011 and has strong passion for the project. Her future plans include pursuing a PhD in the immigrant youth development field.

Marc Bamuthi Joseph is one of America's vital voices in performance, arts education, and artistic curation. Joseph is an inaugural recipient of the Doris Duke Charitable Foundation Artist Award (2012) and a recipient of the Alpert Award in the Arts for Theater (2011). He is the Artistic Director of the seven-part HBO documentary *Russell Simmons Presents Brave New Voices* and an inaugural recipient of the United States Artists Rockefeller Fellowship (2006), which annually recognizes fifty of the country's "greatest living artists." Joseph has developed several poetically based works for the stage that have toured across the United States, Europe, and Africa;

these include *Word Becomes Flesh, Scourge*, and *the break/s*. As the Artistic Director of Youth Speaks, he mentored thirteen- to nineteen-year-old writers and curated the Living Word Festival and Left Coast Leaning. He is the cofounder of Life is Living, a national series of one-day festivals designed to activate under-resourced parks and affirm peaceful urban life through hip-hop arts and focused environmental action. For more information, see twitter.com/bamuthi.

Tiffany S. Lee (Diné/Lakota) is from Crystal, New Mexico, and Pine Ridge, South Dakota. She is an associate professor in Native American Studies at the University of New Mexico. Her research involves conceptualizing and investigating Native youth and young adults' language consciousness and language reclamation efforts. She also examines educational models known as Indigenous learning communities for promoting community-oriented goals, including contemporary practices of schools serving Native students.

Nancy López, associate professor of sociology, cofounded and codirects the Institute for the Study of "Race" and Social Justice, RWJF Center for Health Policy, at the University of New Mexico. She is the author of *Hopeful Girls, Troubled Boys: Race and Gender Disparity in Urban Education* (2003, second edition forthcoming), as well as several articles and book chapters. She also coedited two books, *Creating Alternative Discourses in the Education of Latinos and Latinas: A Reader* (2004), and *Mapping "Race": Critical Approaches to Health Disparities Research* (forthcoming in 2013).

Allan Luke teaches at Queensland University of Technology, Brisbane, Australia. His current work is on school reform in Aboriginal and Torres Strait Islander education.

Na'ilah Suad Nasir is an associate professor in the Graduate School of Education and the African American Studies Department at the University of California, Berkeley, where she has been on the faculty since 2008. Her program of research focuses on issues of race, culture, and schooling. For instance, one recent research project examines how children and adolescents think about race in relation to school. She is the author of *Racialized Identities: Race and Achievement for African-American Youth* (2011). She has also published numerous articles in scholarly journals.

Vanessa Norvilus is a high school graduate and an immigrant from Haiti who has been living, studying, and working in the United States since she was sixteen. Currently, she is working in administrative support in a large public school district, the same district of which she is a graduate.

Sung-Joon (Sunny) Pai began working in Boston Public Schools as a student teacher in 1998 at the Fenway High School. The following year, he became a founding faculty member at the Boston Arts Academy (BAA). Over seven years at BAA, Sunny was a science teacher, writing teacher, advisor, student government coordinator, department chair, interim curriculum coordinator, and principal intern. Sunny is currently the English Language Learner and Alternative Programs Director at Charlestown High School for Chinese and Spanish Sheltered English Instruction and Diploma Plus programs. Sunny holds degrees from the University of Pennsylvania (BA, Chemistry), Harvard Graduate School of Education (MEd, Teaching & Learning), and University of Massachusetts-Boston (Certificate of Advanced Graduate Study, Educational Leadership).

Lisa (Leigh) Patel is an educator, a writer, and a sociologist. She is an associate professor of race, language, and education at Boston College. Her ethnographic and participatory action research with youth focuses on the ways that society structures opportunities and obstacles to safety and status. Prior to working as a public intellectual, Patel was a journalist, policymaker, and high school teacher. She is the coauthor of *Critical Literacy: Context, Research, and Practice in the K–12 Classroom* (2007) and coeditor of *ReConsructing the Adolescent: Sign, Symbol and Body* (2004).

kihana miraya ross is a doctoral student in the Graduate School of Education at the University of California, Berkeley. Her work explores the intersections between language, literacy, identity, and culture within the classroom in urban schools. Her focus is on how school settings convey ideas about race in ways that create oppressive or liberatory conditions for African American students.

Maisha T. Winn is Susan J. Cellmer Chair of English Education in the Curriculum and Instruction Department in the School of Education at the University of Wisconsin–Madison. She is the author of several articles and books, including *Humanizing Research: Decolonizing Qualitative Inquiry with Youth and Communities* (2013, coedited with Django Paris), *Girl Time: Literacy, Justice, and the School-to-Prison Pipeline* (2011), *Writing Instruction in the Culturally Relevant Classroom* (2011, coauthored with Latrise P. Johnson), and *Education and Incarceration* (2011, coedited with Erica Meiners).

Index